The Irish Bridget

Irish Studies
James MacKillop, *Series Editor*

Annie Walsh, an Irish immigrant, worked as a domestic in Providence until her marriage in 1883. *Courtesy of Daureen Aulenbach, Annie's great-granddaughter.*

IRISH IMMIGRANT WOMEN IN DOMESTIC SERVICE IN AMERICA, 1840–1930

Margaret Lynch-Brennan

With a Foreword by Maureen O'Rourke Murphy

Syracuse University Press

Syracuse, New York 13244-5290

First Paperback Edition 2014
14 15 16 17 18 5 4 3 2 1

∞The paper used in this publication meets the minimum requirements of the American National Standard for Information Sciences—Permanence of Paper for Printed Library Materials, ANSI Z39.48-1992.

For a listing of books published and distributed by Syracuse University Press, visit www.SyracuseUniversityPress.syr.edu.

ISBN (paper) 978-0-8156-3354-9 (cloth) 978-0-8156-3201-6
(e-book) 978-0-8156-5267-0

Library of Congress Cataloging-in-Publication Data

The Library of Congress has cataloged the hard-cover edition as follows:
Lynch-Brennan, Margaret.
The Irish Bridget : Irish immigrant women in domestic service in America, 1840–1930 / Margaret Lynch-Brennan.—1st ed.
p. cm.—(Irish studies)
Includes bibliographical references and index.
ISBN 978-0-8156-3201-6 (hardcover : alk. paper)
1. Domestics—United States—History—19th century. 2. Domestics—United States—History—20th century. 3. Immigrants—United States—History—19th century. 4. Immigrants—United States—History—20th century. 5. Irish American women—United States—History—19th century. 6. Irish American women—United States—History—20th century.
I. Title.
HD6072.2.U5L96 2009
640'.46089162073—dc22
2008051731

Manufactured in the United States of America

For my loving husband,
John David Brennan

MARGARET LYNCH-BRENNAN began her career as a classroom teacher. Over time she taught at the middle school, high school, and graduate levels. For many years she served as an administrator with the New York State Education Department working on issues related to civil rights, high school reform, and professional development for teachers. Since completing her Ph.D. in American history at the State University of New York at Albany, she has published numerous essays and presented at conferences in the United States, Germany, Australia, and Ireland. She retired from the New York State Education Department in January 2008 and now works as an independent scholar; she is a member of the National Coalition of Independent Scholars.

Contents

Illustrations

Foreword

MAUREEN O'ROURKE MURPHY

The immigration of single women distinguishes nineteenth-century Irish immigration to North America from the pattern of other western European migration. More women than men emigrated, and they did so as single women who stayed in North America and sponsored other family members, not parents but siblings, to join them. Historians of Irish immigration from Arnold Schrier to Lawrence J. McCaffrey and Kerby Miller have commented on this phenomenon, and pioneering scholars of Irish women's immigration Hasia Diner and Janet Nolan have examined the history of those immigrant women in America. All have commented on the number of Irish immigrant women who worked as domestic servants, and some have included discussions of domestic servants' experiences, the way that their work in service supported their families in Ireland and affected the lives of their own families when they left their positions to marry. We have waited until now for a book devoted completely to their story. Margaret Lynch-Brennan's *The Irish Bridget: Irish Immigrant Women in Domestic Service in America, 1840–1930* examines the lives of the Irish women who worked in private homes in the urban Northeast. Nearly all of them were single Roman Catholics from rural Ireland. Since parents believed that education was the best investment they could make for emigrating girls, most young women had a national school education. Native speakers of Irish were literate in English.

A strength of this book is Lynch-Brennan's description of the worlds of the Irish Bridgets: their lives in Ireland and their lives as servants in American households. She begins by situating her Irish women in the culture of rural Ireland—rural cottages and their interiors, diet, dress, housework, education, social life, and religious beliefs—and she pays particular attention to the postfamine culture of emigration in rural Irish communities, a culture that encouraged and supported young women's decisions to leave their lives in Ireland for new opportunities in America. Lynch-Brennan enumerates the push-and-pull factors and the chain-migration phenomenon, the custom of immigrant women sending money or prepaid tickets to a younger sibling or niece or nephew who would in turn bring another family member, which accounted for periods of sustained migration from the Irish countryside.

Lynch-Brennan turns from rural Ireland to the American households where Irish domestic servants lived and worked. She analyzes American women's roles in their own homes, the difference in power between the Irish mothers the Bridgets knew and the American housewives who were their employers. She offers an anthropological survey of the American household: interiors, diet, housework including table service, and employers' interest in working for causes outside the house. A particular strength of this study is the attention to the relationship between the Irish domestic servant, her American employer, and the household where she worked and lived. She concludes that those relationships depended primarily on the amount of work required of the domestic servant, on her level of household skills, and on the personalities of servants and employers. An aspect of the personalities of Irish domestic servants was their well-known reputation for verbal assertiveness. Anecdotes of Bridget's repartee have become part of the folklore of households and of Irish domestic servant lore. Bridget's verbal assertiveness is part of a larger discussion of attitudes toward Irish domestic servants. Lynch-Brennan convincingly refutes Richard Jensen's arguments regarding "No Irish Need Apply," observing that the Biddy jokes and prejudices were part of the wider anti-Catholic bigotry associated with American nativism and the Know-Nothing Party.

Lynch-Brennan revisits Faye Dudden's *Serving Women: Household Service in Nineteenth-Century America* (1983) and other studies of American households to trace the history of Irish domestics, from finding work to experiencing the routine of the often ten-hour workday. She examines the amount and kind of housework required, the hazards of housework, and the improvement of servants' lives that came in the early decades of the twentieth century with the introduction of running water, screens, kerosene and gas lights, the carpet sweeper, wood and coal ranges, and electricity. Other aspects of servant life that she discusses include the fact that the path of upward mobility led from a one-maid household to one with a staff, and that living at the work site involved difficulties: lack of privacy, around-the-clock availability, and the possibility of abuse from members of the employer's family.

As much as possible, Lynch-Brennan uses interviews and letters to let the young women tell their own stories of the social world of the Irish Bridget. Their voices bring an authenticity and intimacy to this section. They reveal intense female friendships and yearnings for connections with home: letters, photographs, and local newspapers. They also maintained their connection with home by sending money, clothes, and prepaid tickets to others who wanted to emigrate. Like Bridget Moore, Derek Mahon's Irish servant-girl author of the letter in "To Mrs. Moore at Inishannon," who hears her mother's voice "calling me across the ocean," they dreamed of home.

Lynch-Brennan's sources provide some insight into the life of Irish domestic servants beyond their households. Mass and devotions were social as well as spiritual, as they were at home, and Irish immigrants tended to identify themselves by parish. They visited family and friends in other households, participated in parish activities, and attended Irish dances, particularly the county society dances that offered opportunities to meet people from home, including the single men whom many later married. They learned to ride bicycles. They went to weddings and baptisms, to amusement parks and picnics, to fairs and on boat rides. Domestic servants in big houses could look forward to an annual servants' ball, and they often summered with their families in summer homes at the shore or in the mountains. Their social life gave Irish domestics the excuse to indulge in their love of fashion. Out of her uniform, Bridget could pass for a middle-class American woman, so Bridget cartoons often portrayed the Irish domestic as a ridiculous figure with an over-the-top ensemble, sporting boas, boots, and bangles. Lynch-Brennan comments briefly about personal hygiene, including the accounts of bewildered young women who were unprepared for the onset of menses. Even a researcher as indefatigable as Lynch-Brennan found little information about sex.

In her thoughtful examination of the matters of service and status, Lynch-Brennan concludes that Irish domestics found their wages empowering, but when salaries lost ground in the early twentieth century, servant status dropped accordingly; however, Irish domestic servants generally did not accept that their work carried such a stigma. (Irish Americans did.) Their ability to adopt the mores of their middle-class employers and the promise of the opportunity to move their own families into the middle class mitigated their concerns about class and status. With robust opportunities for employment, many Irish domestics were able to negotiate their wages and working conditions through their own agency or with the help of family and friends.

In chapter 7, "Was Bridget's Experience Unique?" Lynch-Brennan investigates the question of the exceptionality of the Irish Bridget by comparing the Irish experience with the experiences of African American and Mexican American domestics. In light of such work as Noel Ignatiev's *How the Irish Became White* (1995), Lynch-Brennan considers the relationship between Irish domestics and African Americans for possible racism. Although Lynch-Brennan's title limits her study to the years 1840–1930, she updates the story of the Irish domestic servant with an examination of the Irish domestics who arrived in the 1980s. Like their earlier counterparts, these women live in their households, work long hours, and are "on call," but there is a crucial difference. Many of the late-twentieth-century immigrants are undocumented, that is, they arrived on visitors' visas that have lapsed and are not eligible for employment. Domestic servants and child- and elder-care givers thus work "off the books," and some domestics complain that they are threatened by their employers with exposure to the authorities and deportation. No domestic who arrived between 1840 and 1930 lived under such a sword of Damocles.

Lynch-Brennan's groundbreaking *Irish Bridget*—her survey of the scholarship of Irish women's emigration and women in service and valuable list of sources, including letters, interviews, contemporary documents, articles, and books—will inspire a new generation of scholars of the Irish diaspora to study the Irish domestic servant: her life and the influence of her experience in service on her people in Ireland, on her own people, and on the Irish in America.

Preface

A passing reference in a now long-forgotten work led me to write this book. It indicated that most Irish immigrant women in nineteenth-century America worked in some form of domestic service, that is, they worked as cooks, maids, waitresses, laundresses, and child nurses (nannies), and so on. This fact surprised me. I wondered why I, an American of Irish ancestry, was unaware of the association of Irish women with domestic service. Chuckling at the irony of the fact that I had done this kind of work myself, in 1994 I embarked on a quest to find out just who these women were.[1] I ended up becoming so driven to find out everything I could about Irish immigrant domestics that, at times, my research seemed to take over my life and has finally ended up as this book.[2]

The gestation of this book was so long that acknowledgments are due to the many diverse parties involved in its production. My late father, Daniel Joseph Lynch Jr. (1914–84), instilled in me his love of history, American and Irish (in that order), and thus started me on the path that led to this book. Although much revised and updated since, this book began life as my doctoral dissertation at the State University of New York at Albany. I will always be grateful to Professors G. J. Barker-Benfield, Ivan Steen, and Ann Withington who nurtured me and my work at that time. And without the assistance of the interlibrary loan staff at both the university and the New York State Library, I would not have had access to material that I needed to complete this work; thank you.

Professor Faye Dudden of Colgate University (then of Union College) was generous with help and advice when I first undertook the research that

1. In the summer of 1972, immediately upon earning my undergraduate degree, I cleaned houses on Cape Cod before beginning my first teaching job.

2. Some of my material appeared in an earlier book; see Lynch-Brennan 2007.

led to this book. Professor Emeritus Arnold Schrier of the University of Cincinnati kindly let me read the Irish emigrants' letters he had collected, and then referred me to Professor Kerby Miller of the University of Missouri–Columbia. Professor Miller generously let me read his collection of Irish emigrant letters and has been a kind and supportive adviser to me ever since. Dr. Patricia Trainor O'Malley shocked and delighted me when she shared with me her collection of unpublished letters written by Irish domestics. Dr. Patricia West, then of the State University of New York at Albany and now of the Martin Van Buren National Historic Site within the National Park Service, encouraged my initial research on Irish domestics and shared with me her knowledge of the Irish domestics Martin Van Buren employed at Lindenwald. And Professor Myra B. Young Armstead of Bard College alerted me to research one of her students had conducted on Irish domestics in the late twentieth century.

When they learned of my research interests, my extended family pitched in with pertinent material. My late cousin, Anne Shalvoy Graham, shared with me the letters of her Irish immigrant grandmother, Mary Malone McHenry, and my cousin Susan Lynch Gutman shared with me a photograph of her mother's very own Irish domestic. My cousin Karen Shalvoy Elias also shared with me her grandfather's correspondence and recollections of his Irish immigrant grandparents, Owen Shalvoy and Margaret Scollin Shalvoy. The one person most deserving of acknowledgment, however, is my husband, John David Brennan, who accompanied me on all my research trips, and put up with my absence during all the years I was sequestered in my study working on this book. Without him, I would not have finished this book.

Introduction

During the nineteenth century, having a live-in domestic servant, that is, a woman who worked as a cook, maid, waitress, child nurse (nanny), or laundress in a private home, was common among middle-class American families in urban areas.[1] Historian Faye Dudden claims that in 1850, up to as many as one-third of urban American households may have employed the live-in servants whose presence in a home served as a marker of a family's social status (1983, 1, 115). Domestic service was an important waged occupation for women, in general, in the United States throughout the period 1840 through 1930, and in the 1850s, in the urban East, Irish-born women constituted the largest single group among servants (McKinley 1969, 152). Overall, 54 percent of the women employed in America in 1900 who were Irish natives were domestic servants, and an additional 6.5 percent worked as laundresses (Katzman 1978, 67).

Irish dominance of this occupation continued into the twentieth century. An investigation into the social conditions of domestic service published in 1900 in the *Massachusetts Labor Bulletin* showed that the majority of the foreign-born servants involved in this study were born in Ireland, and 155 of the 231 study participants were Roman Catholics ("Social Conditions" 1900, 5, 6). And in 1920, Irish-born women constituted 43 percent of white, female, foreign-born domestic servants in America (Carpenter 1969, 288–90). The true number of Irish immigrant women who worked in domestic service between 1840 and 1930, however, will never be known precisely because it was not until 1870 that federal census takers tried to accurately record all female employment. Statistics collected subsequently on domestic service, however, are still specious. It is likely that census enumerators missed those

1. Throughout this book, the terms *servant, domestic, domestic servant, domestic worker*, and *household worker* will be used interchangeably.

females who worked in service on a sporadic basis, thus ensuring that some domestic workers were never factored into census counts.

Saint Brigid is second only to Saint Patrick in the litany of important saints in Ireland, and so Bridget (as the name usually was spelled between 1840 and 1930) has long been a popular girl's name there. In America, the name became directly connected with Irish immigrant girls working in domestic service. Authors of popular literature and the American public used the generic name "Bridget" or its diminutive "Biddy" to refer to female Irish servants; to a much lesser extent Kate, Katy, Maggie, and Peggy also served as nicknames for Irish domestics from 1840 through 1930. So strong was the association between the name Bridget and Irish servants that when Bridget McGeoghegan came to the Boston area from Donegal in 1923, her aunts insisted on calling her Bertha instead of Bridget because of the American Biddy jokes about Irish servant girls. Bertha/Bridget regretted the name change, saying, "I wish I never did have it changed, because I like Bridget" (1985, 33–34).[2] Yet despite the fact that nineteenth-century and early-twentieth-century popular American literature is replete with references to the Irish Bridget, when I began my research I discovered that no scholar had yet written a full-length work on female Irish servants; hence this book.

This book concerns Irish immigrant females who worked in domestic service in private homes in urban northeastern America between 1840 and 1930. The topic of Irish immigrant women in domestic service in the United States is so broad that it called for establishing parameters for the research, and so this study is restricted to Irish immigrant women who worked as servants in private homes and, for the most part, lived within the homes in which they worked. Those women who worked in service in hotels, boardinghouses, and so on, and those second-generation Irish American women who worked as domestic servants, as well as male Irish domestics, are excluded from this study.

This study begins in 1840 because, although Irish women worked in domestic service in the United States before 1840, truly large-scale Irish

2. In the United States, the family surname was also changed, to McGaffighan. Throughout this book, the Irish domestics known only by their maiden names while they worked in service will be referred to by their maiden names. The entries in the Works Cited note their married names in brackets.

immigration to America began about that time (U.S. Bureau of the Census 1975, 106). Female Irish immigration began to increase in the 1830s, and by 1840 the number of Irish women in domestic service was a remarked-upon factor of life in the urban American Northeast; by 1845 women constituted nearly 50 percent of all Irish immigrants to the United States (Adams 1980, 223, 224). The end point of this study is 1930 because, after that time, the United States was no longer the first-choice destination for Irish emigrant girls, as by then Irish girls made Britain their goal when emigrating (Rudd 1988, 307). Yet although they shifted their preferred destination, they continued in the line of employment in which they had historically been engaged both in America and in Britain, and "by the 1930s Irish servants were viewed as indispensable to the English economy" (Walter 2004, 479).[3]

Irish immigrants settled throughout the United States, yet their importance in changing the face of the urban Northeast is unquestionable. Large numbers of them concentrated there, and though some Irish men later moved beyond its confines, Irish women tended to remain in the Northeast (Foley and Guinnane 1999, 19, 26; Winsberg 1985, 8, 10, 12). Most of the correspondence and the oral interviews reviewed or conducted for this study related to Irish immigrants living in the urban Northeast. Therefore, with a few exceptions, this study is confined to Irish immigrant women domestic servants living in the urban Northeast. Irish domestics in Chicago, San Francisco, the rural Northeast, and other geographic locations in the United States are excluded from this study.

The employer's point of view predominates in the historical literature on domestic service in America.[4] Primary source information from servants themselves is scanty, yet scholars recognize that hearing the voices of our

3. Female Irish emigration to work in domestic service in Britain, of course, long predates the 1930s. As noted in chapter 4, many Irish girls worked in service in Britain in the nineteenth century. Discrimination against Irish Catholic servants in Britain can be deduced from the fact that employers, when seeking servants, sometimes specified that "No Irish Need Apply" or "Must be of the Church of England" (Horn 1975, 39).

4. Contemporary historical scholarship, as opposed to contemporary sociological scholarship, still tends to stress the employer point of view. For example, even though one chapter gives some voice to servants, Barbara Ryan, in her review of the literature of servitude, *Love, Wages, Slavery: The Literature of Servitude in the United States* (2006), still privileges the employer's perspective.

historical subjects is crucial to properly understanding their experiences.[5] So, as much as possible, this study concentrates on the Irish immigrant woman's point of view on domestic service. And to ensure the authenticity of the voices of the Irish women quoted in this book, their letters will be reproduced as they wrote them, without [*sic*] being used to indicate errors in spelling or grammar.

In researching this book, focus was placed on determining who the real human beings were behind the Bridget stereotype. Where in Ireland and from what kind of families had these Irish girls come? How old were they when they came to the United States? What were their lives like as domestic servants? Did most of them marry or stay in service all their lives? These and other questions guided the research and shaped this book. And though no one person's experience can serve as an archetype for all Irish domestics, certain patterns of experience emerged in the research. Ellen O'Loughlin, Nora McCarthy, Hannah Collins, Catherine (Katie) Murray Manley, Catherine (Kathleen) Mannion, Mary Anne (Mollie) Ryan, Sarah Byrne, and Catherine Larkin Vaughn, all shown in the illustrations, and all the other Irish women discussed in this book represent the real women behind the Bridget stereotype.

The story of the Irish Bridget is a transatlantic and transcultural one, beginning in Ireland and ending in the United States. To properly understand these Irish immigrant women, some understanding of the Irish world that formed them is required. Therefore, this book includes information on Ireland that is deemed relevant to the story of Irish domestics in America. In the chapters dealing with Ireland, the material culture from which the immigrant girls came is stressed, and in the chapters dealing with the United States, the material culture of the American world in which they lived and worked is stressed. Theirs was a material world, and so material culture is crucial to understanding the experience of the Irish Bridget in America.

Ireland was one country throughout most of this period. Until 1930 U.S. Census information did not distinguish between Irish immigrants from Northern Ireland and the South of Ireland. The reasons Irish girls

5. I recognize the possible problems inherent in the letters and oral interviews I use as primary sources for this book. Still, letters, in particular, constitute "the largest body of the writings of ordinary people of the past that historians . . . possess." Despite whatever problems they present, letters (and in my view oral interviews) "provide access to the immigrant's attitudes, values, aspirations, and fears" (Elliott, Gerber, and Sinke 2006, 3, 4).

emigrated remained fairly constant throughout the period 1840 to 1930, even after Irish independence. Therefore, this book includes information on Irish domestics from present-day Northern Ireland, as well as information on Irish domestics from what is now the Irish Republic.

Considering the lengthy time frame of 1840 through 1930 employed in this study, it was my initial expectation that research would show that technological improvements in the home radically changed the nature of domestic service over this period. To my surprise, my research convinced me instead that the experience of Irish domestics in 1930 was similar in many respects to the lives of Irish domestics in 1840. Although technological improvement occurred, it is the similarities in domestics' experiences in service over time that are striking.

Domestic service is an occupation that has frequently been in the news from the 1990s into the present. I wondered whether and how the experience of Irish immigrant women in domestic service from 1840 to 1930 was similar to or distinguished from the experience of other women who have worked in domestic service in the United States over time, and so the scholarly literature was reviewed, the results of which can be found in chapter 7. In many respects it appears that contemporary domestic service is remarkably similar to domestic service in the period 1840 to 1930; servants' reactions to domestic service in the late twentieth and early twenty-first centuries are very similar to servants' reactions in the 1840s and 1850s. According to those individuals who work in this occupation, domestic service remains physically taxing work and involves disadvantages that have remained fairly constant over time.

Irish emigration was unusual in the high number of women who participated in it. Although in recent years scholars have produced new work on Irish women, still much of the scholarly literature on the Irish in America continues to focus on Irish immigrant men. The underlying sentiment still seems to be that the experience of Irish men somehow serves as a proxy for the experience of Irish women. But it does not. Their gender and their domestic service, the form of labor in which they engaged, distinguished the experience of female Irish immigrant domestics from the experience of male Irish immigrants. Whereas there may have been Irish men who lived in some form of community with their fellow Irish, because most of the Irish Bridgets lived with their employers, female Irish domestics did not. Most native-born middle- and upper-class Americans likely had little interaction on a personal level with Irish men. If they had any direct experience with the Irish, it was probably through proximity to the Irish Bridget who lived and worked in the intimate sphere of the private American home. Through their personal interaction with the Irish Bridget, native-born Americans came to see the Irish less as "others," and more as fellow humans. Credit is due to the Irish Bridget for pioneering the way for the Irish to become accepted by native-born Americans and for helping the Irish, as a group, move into the American middle class.

The Irish Bridget

1

Home Life in Ireland

Who was the Irish Bridget? She was one of the girls who emigrated from Ireland to work as domestic servants in private homes in urban northeastern America between 1840 and 1930. For the most part, they were quite young girls—for example, Ellen O'Loughlin was only fourteen when she left Broadford, County Clare, Ireland, in 1893 for Hoosick Falls, New York, to work as a domestic servant (Unger 2006) (see ill. 1).[1] Overall, from the mid-nineteenth century until 1921 the median age of emigrant Irish females was about twenty-one (K. Miller 1985, 352). These girls were generally unmarried Roman Catholics[2] who hailed from rural Ireland,[3] and as the nineteenth century progressed into the twentieth, increasingly they came from the rural west of Ireland, where traditional Gaelic Irish culture persisted longer than it did elsewhere in Ireland. They were the daughters of people of limited means, rather than the children of either wealthy or extremely poor parents. They were raised in an Irish material and cultural world, yet later lived and worked in an American material and cultural world. How did their Irish

1. I obtained this and other information on Ellen O'Loughlin when I interviewed her daughter, Mary E. Unger, on April 21, 2006, at Mary's home in Loudonville, New York.

2. Whereas earlier Irish emigrants were primarily Protestants (often Presbyterians), from the 1830s on the number of Roman Catholic Irish emigrants increased, with Catholics dominating the Irish emigration to America from the Famine period (1845–52) onward (Akenson 1996, 223).

3. Patricia O'Hara indicates that even in the late 1990s, Irish people tended to identify with the rural tradition, and points out that aside from Dublin most people in late 1990s Ireland lived in what can be characterized as rural areas (1998, 1). Because the movement of Irish people was primarily from rural areas of Ireland to urban areas of America, some scholars have seen the Irish emigration to the United States as one version of the rural-urban migration, but in this case it was from the rural part of one country to urban areas in another country (R. Kennedy 1973, 66–67; Rhodes 1992, 252).

1. Ellen O'Loughlin, ca. 1897. *Courtesy of Jo-Ellen Unger, Ellen's granddaughter.*

world compare with their American one? In what kind of houses might they have been raised? What did they eat? What type of domestic work did Irish women typically perform in the home? What type of clothing did they wear? Did they drink alcohol? Was religion of importance to them? Did their Irish world prepare them for their American world? This chapter will focus on answering these questions.

Rural Irish Housing

The 1841 Irish census showed that the vast majority of the population lived in rural areas, and about 50 percent of rural families lived in the poorest type of housing, consisting of single-room cabins made of mud (Evans 1989, 46). Such housing was miserable, lacking, as it usually did, chimneys and windows and containing very little furniture. Data from the 1840s also show that housing of the one-story thatched-roof *ceann tuighe* variety prevailed in rural areas throughout Ireland (A. Campbell 1937, 226; Gailey 1987, 97). After 1845 the lowest type of one-room dwelling quickly vanished, and by 1851 most such dwellings were gone, their disappearance testimony to the effects of the Great Famine of September 1845 through 1852[4]—the disappearance, through death or emigration, of the poorest segment of the rural Irish population that had resided in them (Ó Danachair 1972, 91). Still, up until passage of the Labourers' Act of 1883, poor laborers in rural Ireland were said to have lived in "squalid housing conditions" that grew better only sluggishly after that date (Lane 2005, 118).

The linear country "house" of Irish tradition displays regional variations, and is distinguished from the lowest type of housing, from the housing of strong farmers (those with sizable farms), and from the housing of the gentry as well. Rectangular in shape, the linear house was one room deep, with a kitchen located between two bedrooms; if additions were made, they were in length rather than in depth or height. The roofs of such houses were usually made of straw or reed thatch, a lightweight roofing material that both kept the heat in the house during the winter and kept the house cooled off during the summer. By the end of the nineteenth century, however, slate came to be widely used for roofs. Irish domestic Mary Feely, who, in 1927, at age nineteen, left Tubbercurry, County Sligo, for Mount Vernon, New York, said, "When I was small, we only had a thatched house," but later the family "had a slated house" (1996).

From 1883 "cottages" were built for and rented out to laborers; the rural Irish, however, never confused such "cottages" with traditional thatched-roof "houses" because no matter how diminutive in size it might have been, a thatched-roof house was never a cottage (Ó Danachair 1962, 67). Residents of rural Ireland aspired to live in houses, not cottages, because the term *house* was associated with ownership (B. Kennedy 1993, 173).

Dirt floors were pervasive in rural Irish houses in 1840. Although wood floors became more widespread in Irish homes after that date, in those homes where dirt floors remained, the rural Irish used practical strategies to guard against the damp and rodents that might be lurking in the earth. For example, food, such as preserved fish and hams, as well as clothing, was

4. Following Kinealy 1995, 294, I use the time frame 1845–52 for the Great Famine. The blight was first reported in Ireland in September 1845.

often placed on straw ropes hanging from the rafters (Kinmonth 2006, 2, 22). Families living in such earthen-floored homes also kept cats to keep away unwanted creatures like rats.

The walls of such houses were periodically whitewashed inside and out both to decorate and to protect the house. According to tradition, it was women's responsibility to whitewash the house triannually, as well as to paint the doors red (Clear 2000, 165). Irish domestic Rose Kelly, who left County Derry for Philadelphia in 1925, remembered that her mother and grandmother used lime to whitewash their house. Whitewashing made a bold imprint on her mind because, as a child, she decided to help out and ended up splashing the whitewash in her eyes, at which point her grandmother "grabbed me up, took me into the couch, put me down, and licked it out of my eyes. That I could never forget. She licked it all out" (1995, 5).

Windows were not a prominent feature of rural Irish houses, partially because their absence served to increase the warmth of the house. The dearth of windows also reflected memory of the times when there was a window tax (windows were seen as signs of affluence), and their presence in a house could result in rapacious landlords raising the rent (Danaher 1964, 14). Natural light could be brought into the house through the front door, however, by opening its top half. Such doors were called *leath dhoras,* much like what is termed a Dutch door in America (A. Campbell 1937, 217). Besides increasing natural light, *leath dhoras* helped regulate the interior fire and, with the bottom half of the door closed while the top half was kept opened, helped to confine children indoors and animals outdoors, while still permitting conversation with those who might be passing by (Pfeiffer and Shaffrey 1990, 18). By the start of the twentieth century, in the rural West of Ireland, glossy paint was used to brighten the dim interiors of houses. This was accomplished by painting the bottom portions of walls (where wainscoting would normally be placed) a bright color, such as bright blue, and then leaving the walls above the brightly painted portion a more pallid color, thus enabling light to be reflected in the house (Kinmonth 2006, 73).

From 1840 to 1930 many rural Irish homes likely had minimal furniture, with the possible exception of the Irish dresser, the one important item of furniture generally found in the home. The open-shelved dresser, rather like what is termed a hutch in America, was associated with women, and can be seen as a sign of incipient domesticity, for it displayed the kitchen delph (crockery and dishes)[5] owned by the *bean a tighe*,[6] or the woman of the house.Located in the kitchen, probably opposite the front entrance, the dresser was usually made of pine or fir wood, or what the Irish term *deal.* The kitchen was the most important spot in rural homes—one woman remembered that the kitchen "was our dining-room and sitting-room as well" (Clear 2000, 152). In the kitchen there might have been a settle that provided seating during the day and bedding in the evening (Evans 1989, 87). Irish domestic Ann Kelly, who left County Offaly for New York City in 1925, recalled that her father made most of the furniture in the kitchen of her childhood home. It included "a dresser facing the . . . door with all our dishes and wares. . . . [T]hen there was a settle bed in the right hand corner. . . . [I]t opened up . . . like a cabinet, . . . but you could sit on it as a seat. . . . [We] called it a 'settleback'" (1991, 9–10).

Bedding varied in rural Irish homes. The poorest families might have strewn straw or rush in front of the fire, and lain down together before it in a specified order (Kinmonth 2006, 127, 130, 131). Some families would have had the settle bed mentioned above, or press beds (beds hidden in cupboards) that were stored away during the day (150). Other families would have had a bed, often curtained, partially to provide privacy, which was raised above the earthen floor and would likely have been placed near the fire (133, 138–39, 142, 144). Often, such beds were covered with a canopy of cloth or wood to protect inhabitants from rain and drafts and from dust and bugs falling from the thatched roof; such roofed beds were found even in the most impoverished homes in the nineteenth century (138, 141–43). Eventually,

5. The scholarship of Charles E. Orser Jr. regarding the recent excavation of two cabins in Ballykilcline, County Roscommon, whose occupants were evicted in 1847 or 1848, indicates a richer material culture than might have been expected in such housing. Orser mentions that "fine earthenware ceramic vessels—at least twelve dinner plates, . . . nineteen teacups (many with matching saucers)" were found in one of the cabins (2005, 54–55). It remains to be seen whether future excavations of other Irish cabins will uncover similar material culture and thus cause scholars to revise upward their estimation of the material culture of Irish cabins in the 1840s.

6. Caitriona Clear defines the term *bean a tighe* broadly to include any woman, single (for example, a woman in charge of a house for a single brother or widowed uncle), widowed, or married, who is in charge of the domestic responsibilities of a home. She contends that there is no real English equivalent, as the terms homemaker and housewife have narrower meanings (2000, 11, 12).

iron and brass beds, available for purchase from the 1890s, superseded covered beds (150–51).

Despite the fact that the material culture of rural Irish homes was primitive, artistic representations of them indicate that the Irish were interested in decorating their domestic interiors. Most of the Irish girls who worked in service in America in this period came from Roman Catholic families whose homes might have featured religious iconography that could have included a Saint Brigid's cross hung over the interior front door, a fount of holy water hung in the deep window well, and rosary beads either hung in the same place or hung from a shelf at the side of the door, or from the dresser (Kinmonth 2006, 14, 62, 67, 162). Prints of the Sacred Heart of Jesus (which became ubiquitous in Irish American homes) and images or prints of the Blessed Virgin Mary, particularly as the Madonna and Child, often adorned the walls of such homes. Clocks, especially the Connecticut clock, which was available from 1851, were prominently displayed in rural homes (65, 66). And some rural Irish families apparently enjoyed the music of a bird from the wild in their homes; such birds were kept in wicker cages hung from the rafters (105, 129, 139–41).

The common thread in traditional rural Irish housing was the centrality of the hearth. Home life in rural Ireland centered around the hearth, *teinteán,* with its floor-level turf (peat) fire that was never completely extinguished, a new fire being kindled every day from the embers of the old. Some such fires were known to burn continuously for more than three hundred years (Danaher 1964, 17). Meals were cooked over the open fire. The "bastible," an oven pot used mainly for roasting meat, was either hung over the turf fire or placed on a trivet, and located on the fire was the three-legged iron pot whose myriad uses have led to terming it the "countrywife's maid of all work." Tables around which a family ate meals originally were uncommon in Irish homes; instead, families ate their potatoes while sitting around the fire, holding on their knees a basket holding potatoes that was called a *skeehogue.* Low three-legged stools, often called "creepies," were placed around the hearth to help those sitting on them avoid smoke from the fire (Evans 1977, 67–77).

The floor-level fire in the hearth indicated the family's hospitality, and when the fire of an Irish home goes out, it is said that "the soul goes out of the people of the house" (Evans 1989, 59). Around the hearth, some rural Irish families whiled away the evenings with their visiting neighbors by listening to a *seanchaí,* or storyteller, who was usually a male—the famed

Irish storyteller Peig Sayers represents a major exception to this general rule. Because Irish men had more free time than women in which to socialize, it was generally men who tended to go "*miching* . . . *cuardáiocht* . . . *céilidhe-ing* . . . rambling, *scoruíocht,* walking or cabin-hunting," the various names by which visiting the neighbors was known in rural Ireland (Clear 2000, 182). Nonetheless, emigrant Irish females had fond memories of such social gatherings. Of them Irish domestic Margaret Convery, who left County Derry for Philadelphia in 1914, recalled, "We used to play the accordion and my brother Charlie played the violin, so on a Sunday there would be some of the neighbors would come in, you know, they'd have dancing, singing" (1991, 24). Such affectionate memories of their Irish homes notwithstanding, the houses in which Irish domestics grew up in rural Ireland bore no resemblance to the middle-class homes in which they would later work and live in urban northeastern America.

The Diet of the Rural Irish

Potatoes are so closely associated with Ireland that it is surprising to some Americans to learn that the potato is not native to Ireland but originated in South America and likely was brought to Ireland by the Spanish sometime between 1586 and 1600 (O'Riordan 2001, 31). Once introduced into Ireland, its cultivation spread; by the first quarter of the eighteenth century, potato culture was well established among the poor in the province of Munster (Whelan 1995, 19). In the pre-Famine period, before 1845, the Irish diet had traditionally included oats, commonly in the form of porridge (oatmeal), in addition to potatoes (Crawford 1995, 62). All classes of Irish people ate potatoes, but by the start of the nineteenth century, in the South and West of Ireland, the rural poor were no longer able to include oats in their daily diet, as they had in the past, but instead became completely dependent on the potato for their main food year-round (Austin Bourke 1993, 16–17, 20). It is estimated that by the 1840s, about 40 percent of the Irish were potato dependent (Kinealy 1995, 5). Just how many potatoes the Irish ate in a day is astounding. Data from the late 1830s indicate that men ate nearly thirteen and women close to ten pounds of potatoes per day (Clarkson and Crawford 2001, 73). While potatoes are very nourishing, a potato-based diet is a bland one, so the Irish offset the blandness with salt, water, or milk, or relishes of strong butter or salt herrings called "kitchen" (Evans 1989, 83; McHugh 1994, 392). Irish people also drank buttermilk (the liquid left after butter is churned) or skim milk in addition to the potatoes that were eaten "morning, noon and night"—it is reported that the adult laborer "drank about three pints of buttermilk" each day (Crawford 1995, 60; Clarkson and Crawford 1988, 190). Homely buttermilk has been called "the most refreshing drink in the world"; it was also used in baking bread and meal preparation, and the Irish believed it could remedy hangovers and that it was good for the skin to wash one's face in buttermilk (Mahon 1998, 87, 88).

Potatoes were easy to cook since they were usually boiled, although children sometimes roasted them in the ashes of turf fires,[7] and they required but a minimal amount of land for cultivation. Pigs, hens, and cows were also fed potatoes. Use of potatoes as pig feed was significant for those rural Irish families for whom the pig was their only consistent source of income. For such families it was the proceeds from the sale of a pig at a market fair that kept them going from one season until the next, so the pig was often called "him that pays the rint" (Carleton 1971, 3:173).[8]

Although they grew easily in Ireland, the major disadvantage of potatoes was that they did not store well and were difficult to ship. In addition, by about 1810, outside Ulster, cultivation of better-quality potatoes declined, and the poorer Irish instead grew and ate inferior varieties, such as the Lumper, because it was so productive, even on poor land. Potato dependence made the position of the rural poor precarious—they had no real safety margin to protect them from disaster—and unfortunately, their widely grown Lumper was susceptible to disease and "went down most heavily and fatally of all varieties in the first blight attacks of 1845–6" (Austin Bourke 1993, 13, 22, 24, 25, 36, 39).

Tea, a commodity in use in ordinary English and American homes by the mid-eighteenth century, came to Ireland in the early 1700s as a drink for the gentry. That it had cachet is indicated by its pronunciation in Ireland—"tay" as in the French, *thé* (Foster 1989, 220). Over the course of the nineteenth

7. The manner in which the Irish ate potatoes intrigued one observer. Asenath Nicholson, the American woman who visited Ireland just prior to the Famine, saw children eat potatoes out of their left hand while they held a cup of soup in their right hand and remarked that she had seen the Irish in America eat potatoes in a similar manner. According to Nicholson, the Irish preferred "eating the potatoe [*sic*] from the hand as bread, to using a knife and fork." When eating potatoes out of the hand, they peeled away the potato skin, using the fingers or thumbnail (1847, 169, 234, 247).

8. William Forbes Adams contends that this quote exaggerates the importance of the pig in the years 1815–45, when the pig, though important, could not alone pay the entire rent (1980, 18).

century tea moved from being a luxury item to becoming an item whose use was so widespread that by 1899 adults of all classes of Irish society throughout the country, including western Ireland, drank tea. The Irish were said to have a "mania" for tea, as indicated in the Irish expression *marbh le tae agus marbh gan é,* or "dead from tea and dead without it" (Nicholson 1847, 195; Mahon 1998, 40).

In rural Ireland tea was sold by traveling merchants known in the West as *Séainín á tae,* or "Sean of the tea" (Mahon 1998, 39). According to Ciara Breathnach, tea was also sold in the limited number of shops that were located in the rural West (2004, 83). There, with few competitors to worry about, mendacious shopkeepers were known to cheat their female customers by mixing cheaper tea in with better-quality tea and selling the mixture at high prices. Women tended not to complain about such fraudulent practices for several reasons: it was difficult to determine if the tea had been tampered with, they were loath to risk losing their credit with shopkeepers, and there were few alternative sources for tea. The spread of tea drinking to ordinary households in England and America is associated with increased leisure, domestic sociability, and women (Shammas 1980, 13–16). Ellie Driscoll Enright's recollections suggest that because tea was such a highly valued commodity, some Irish women were less than hospitable with it, and in fact were loath to share their tea. On July 3, 1900, reminiscing about their friends and relations back home in rural County Cork, Ireland, she wrote from Washington, D.C., to her friend Nora McCarthy in Massachusetts that "they certenley were a Cerciuse over there and Aunty and Peggie would hide the tea underneath their petticoats for fear any one would get a cup" (O'Malley Collection) (see ill. 2).

In Ireland women drank so much tea that in the early years of the twentieth century they were said to have suffered from stomach trouble as a result (Colum 1937, 39–40). On the other side, in America, tea continued to cause Irish women indigestion. So enamored of tea were Irish women that Americans complained that Irish domestics pilfered their employers' tea (D. Ryan 1983, 48; Bowker 1871, 497).

Whereas the advice literature in Ireland recommended that diets include Irish brown bread, fruit, and vegetables, by the later nineteenth century tea drinking and eating white bread became integral to, or at least a desirable part of, the Irish diet. Tea and white bread, symbols of ever important Irish hospitality, were served to visitors; in fact, because white bread was served to special guests such as the local priest, it was called "priest's bread" (Mahon 1998, 76). In 1906 G. W. Russell (Æ) criticized the Irish diet, complaining

2. Nora McCarthy, Haverhill, Massachusetts (Nora is on the right, Mary Hayes on the left). *Courtesy of Dr. Patricia Trainor O'Malley, Nora McCarthy's granddaughter.*

that in "household after household . . . white bread, tea, American bacon, potatoes, and cabbage seem to be the main food." In 1913 he argued that in contrast with the contemporary diet of white bread and tea, in the past the Irish had been well nourished by consuming dark bread, oatmeal, and milk. Russell lamented that the present diet, which was more costly than the older one, caused Irish people to look pallid (1978, 71, 375). Objections to the reliance of the Irish on a diet of tea, bread, and jam continued into the 1940s (Clear 1997, 197).

Thus, it seems clear that those Irish girls who became cooks in middle-class American homes probably did not learn the culinary arts in their family homes in Ireland. With the exception of tea, the food they ate, and the manner in which it was prepared, was nothing like what middle-class Americans expected in their meals. It is unsurprising then that Irish servants in America were not known for their good cooking. Instead, with lingering memories of "burnt steaks, . . . hard-boiled potatoes, . . . [and] smoked milk," one author declared that "as a cook, Bridget is an admitted failure" ("The Morals and Manners" 1873, 6).

Housework in Rural Ireland

In the pre-Famine period, before 1845, little housework of the kind that was expected in urban, middle-class homes in the American Northeast in the same period would have been required in rural Irish homes. Regarding the domestic responsibilities of the Irish woman of the house in rural Ireland in the pre-Famine period, Asenath Nicholson, a middle-class American woman who wrote about her visit to Ireland in 1844–45, said, "The cabin housewife has done her morning's toil, when the potato is eaten and the pigs and fowl have been fed; no making of bread, no scouring of brass and silver, no scrubbing of floors, or cleaning of paint makes her toil heavy" (1847, 186). In post-Famine nineteenth-century Ireland, rural women *did* face daunting domestic work, but its nature differed greatly from the housework performed in middle-class homes in the urban American Northeast. In the absence of running water, the daily domestic chores rural Irish women faced included hauling water to the house from its source—pumps, wells, or springs—a chore that had to done not once but several times a day. Hauling water added to the labor of doing laundry, which was hard, physical work anyway, yet, despite the hardships involved, a bright-white wash was desirable, as it was equated with respectability (Clear 2000, 143–44, 148). The lack of running water also meant that outhouses, rather than flush toilets, were the norm in rural Ireland.

Well into the 1930s, in the absence of gas and electricity, rural Irish women prepared meals by cooking them over an open-hearth fire. Open-fire cooking was not easy; it required deftness in dealing with pots over the fire and frequent back bending because the fire was at floor-level. Although by the 1920s gas and electricity were available for cooking in Irish cities and towns, in the 1950s cooking ranges were still somewhat of an anomaly in rural Ireland (Clear 2000, 153, 154, 159, 163). Testimony to this state of affairs comes from Eileen Murray, who left Cornafulla, County Roscommon, for Boston in 1953 at age twenty-five. She said that her mother cooked over an open fire in Ireland. Murray characterized this method of cooking as "hard," but said her mother "managed." She explained, "They had the pots. . . . They hang it. They had . . . a crane, and they had the hooks on the pot. And they'd hang the pot on there . . . boiling the potatoes, and they made bread" (1994, 35).

The modern conveniences associated with rising standards of housecleaning came slowly to rural Ireland. Irish nanny Helen Flatley, who was born in 1910, recalled of her family home in Kilkelly, County Mayo, that it "didn't have the electricity. . . . We only had the candles and the lamp" (1996a). She further reminisced that "there was no country lights or electricity in them days. And it was just an oil lamp that we had" (1996b). As late as 1956, only a little more than one-half of all rural Irish homes had electricity (Daly 1997a, 207). Running water lagged behind electricity in coming to rural Ireland, and according to Mary E. Daly this says something about the unequal relations between the sexes. She speculates that since running water was seen more as a boon to women than it was to men, with its promise of lessening women's daily domestic toil in obtaining the water necessary for washing dishes, doing laundry, and accomplishing even simple tasks such as making tea, it was not deemed urgent to bring running water to rural Ireland (207, 210–11, 213, 214, 218). In contrast, since electricity was connected more with relaxation that benefited men (for example, providing the ability to listen to the radio), its extension to rural Ireland was seen as an important governmental task (207, 208). In 1946 more than 60 percent of all Irish homes lacked running water and flush toilets (B. Kennedy 1993, 176). In that year, it was still pumps, wells, and so forth that served as the water sources for household use in more than 90 percent of rural homes. As late as 1956, municipal water was supplied to a mere 3 percent of rural Irish homes (Daly 1997a, 206–7). And despite the 1961 "Turn on the Tap" campaign extolling the advantages of running water, in 1971 it was still absent from more than 40 percent of rural Irish houses (215, 218).

The lack of running water in rural Ireland is more indicative of the differences between rural and urban life, however, than it is specifically of Irish life, for American farms (outside the Northeast) of the 1920s and 1930s also lacked running water, electricity, and indoor toilets (Hoy 1995a, 157–60). Changes in rural American conditions began only with the Rural Electrification Administration, a New Deal program begun in 1935. Not until the 1950s did 75 percent of American homes have indoor plumbing, including indoor toilets (172).

So although housework in rural Ireland was difficult, it hardly prepared Irish girls for doing housework in middle-class homes in urban northeastern America. Unsurprisingly, then, in America employers complained that the Irish Bridget was "ignorant . . . of the use of scrubbing brushes, since her floor at home was the hard earth" (Bridget 1871, 706) and that she did not know how to light a fire in a stove (Harrington 1855, 247).

Women and Dress in Rural Ireland

In the period just before the Famine, Mr. and Mrs. S. C. Hall described Irish girls as wearing the long blue hooded cloak traditional for Irish women (1860, 1:233, 2:55, 252, 272). A. T. Lucas claims that the hooded cloak served as "the standard woman's outer garment over the larger part, if not the whole, of Ireland," over most of the nineteenth century (1951, 104). It was blue, black, gray, or sometimes red, and its hood was lined with rich material such as satin. Whereas some cloaks were made of domestically produced frieze, others were purchased from shops. Irish women who could afford it preferred tailor-made cloaks of good-quality material such as fine broadcloth. Such cloaks could be costly items—in 1861 in Tralee, County Kerry, a cloak cost about three pounds; because of the cost, such cloaks were expected to provide lifelong wear. Underneath the hood of the cloak women often wore caps, frequently white ones; a cap often signified that the wearer was married. The traditional cloak had multiple uses—sometimes it even served as bedding (108, 110). Such cloaks were not washed, much to the dismay of observers like Mrs. Hall, who, in consequence, saw them as breeding grounds for infection. She also bemoaned the lack of attention Irish women paid to the clothing they wore beneath their cloaks (1860, 2:272). Beginning in the 1840s, some Irish women began replacing cloaks with shawls, which were washable and of lighter weight and less expensive than cloaks, yet, in Ireland, some women still continued to wear cloaks and shawls well into the twentieth century.

Although nineteenth-century observers decried the ragged attire of the Irish peasantry, it was common for Irish people to have a better set of clothing that was worn only on Sundays for attendance at mass. Secondhand clothing was a source of dress for the peasantry, and so stalls selling such clothing were fixtures of Irish fairs. Some Irish women managed to appear better off than they really were by wearing dresses of inexpensive cottons; observers could not see that beneath the dresses, they lacked sufficient underwear (Dunlevy 1999, 140, 142).

The move from using homemade to store-bought fabrics for women's clothing varied across Ireland, but by the 1880s middle-class women could shop in the ready-to-wear departments of stores like Switzer's in Dublin.

And by the 1890s, even working women earning paltry daily wages dressed according to the dictates of contemporary fashion (Dunlevy 1999, 167). With regard to her clothing, Irish domestic Margaret Convery, who was born in 1896, recalled that although her mother sewed some of her clothing, most of it was purchased in shops (1991, 30). Other rural Irish females, however, made do with clothing constructed of recycled domestic products such as flour bags. Irish domestic Ella Ahearn, who was born in 1902 and left County Kerry for Chicago when she was sixteen, recalled that in her youth, "we used to get flour in hundred and sixty-pound bags and cornmeal and they took it and they bleached it and they made dresses out of it and slips and underwear." Such attire, she said, was "very, very nice. . . . [T]hey weren't a bit coarse" (1989, 6, 8).

The Irish were said to be fond of brightly colored clothing, including red (a "lucky" color) clothing, allegedly worn to keep away the fairies, but they rarely wore green (an unlucky color), because it was the color of the "'people of the *sí*,'" or the fairies (Mahon 2000, 28). Over the course of the nineteenth century, observers remarked on the red clothing, especially petticoats, worn by Irish women (Nicholson 1847, 387; DeBovet 1891, 223; Synge 1980, 116, 123). In the West of Ireland girls were known to wear flowered bodices made of cotton paired with red skirts (Ó Danachair 1967, 10). According to artistic renderings from the second half of the nineteenth century, with such skirts rural Irish females also wore shawls drawn over their shoulders and crisscrossed, or drawn together, across their bodices (Kinmonth 2006, 13, 35, 61, 62). Observers also noted that Irish women went barefoot, but it was not unusual for people to own some type of footwear to wear to mass on Sundays. Irish domestic Ella Ahearn remembered that "we walked to school in our bare feet. . . . We had one pair of shoes for going to church on Sundays" (1989, 2). Often such footwear was carried to mass and put on only for the duration of the service itself, and Irish people who migrated to rural areas in America apparently continued this practice (Ó Cléirigh 2003, 185).[9] On October 8, 1899, Irish domestic Hannah Collins, who left Leap, Ballinlough, County Cork, for Elmira, New York, remarked on the change she made from going barefoot in Ireland to wearing shoes while she worked in America (see ill. 3). She wrote to a friend, "I had to laugh at Tim. So he

9. My late cousin Anne Shalvoy Graham, in correspondence to me in September 1995, cited family lore of the immigrant Malone-McHenry family in Middle Granville, New York, that holds they did so in the second half of the nineteenth century.

3. Hannah Collins, Elmira, New York, 1898.
Courtesy of Dr. Patricia Trainor O'Malley.

did not forget about my feet being so big but you tell him I wear shoes now every day which makes them smaller" (O'Malley Collection).

Sources indicate that Irish clothing was deemed inappropriate for America. On September 22, 1850, Margaret McCarthy wrote to family members in County Cork preparing to come to America, warning them to "bring enough of flannels and do not form it at home as the way they wear flannel at home and here is quite different" (Schrier Collection). A woman who returned from America to Ireland told an Irish mother whose daughter was leaving for America, "'Don't bother dressing her up, for her clothes will only be burned when she gets to the far side anyway'" (Neville 1995, 211).[10]

Clothing was costly in America. In 1884, Charlotte O'Brien estimated that it cost at least twenty-two dollars for an Irish girl to outfit herself

10. Grace Neville says the clothes would be burned "because the style and fashion were entirely wrong for America" (1995, 211).

decently enough to be able to secure employment in domestic service in America (1884, 534). Nevertheless, in the United States Irish girls were fond of fashion—Irish domestic Anastasia Dowling, for example, wrote home enthusiastically from Buffalo, New York, on January 20, 1870, "Thare is no end to fassions" in America (Schrier 1958, 30). So enamored of dressing well were Irish domestics that, in 1906, referring specifically to them, Mary Gove Smith observed that "the average domestic worker spends most of her week's wages on dress" (1906, 8). In America, employers criticized Irish domestics for their love of fashion. Even their fellow Irish criticized them. Irish-born author Mary Sadlier made disapproving references to Irish domestics' expenditures on fashionable clothing in America (1863, 135, 162, 163), and their countrymen in the United States criticized them for dressing too well for their station in life (Ernst 1994, 67).

Drink

Hospitality was an obligatory and integral part of social life in rural Ireland. Social life involved, and hospitality required, sharing strong drink such as whiskey, a drink that helped imbibers counterbalance the wet Irish climate. The word *whiskey* itself comes from the Irish *uisce beatha,* meaning "water of life," and Irish whiskey was renowned by the reign of Queen Elizabeth I. Because they could not afford to purchase legal taxed whiskey, in the pre-Famine period Irish people produced *póitín* (poteen), home-distilled illicit whiskey that they believed was a better product than licensed whiskey, and the making of which served to augment the family income. Until about the third quarter of the nineteenth century, *póitín* making was common in the western and northwestern seaboard areas of Ireland; thereafter it declined, and in the second half of the nineteenth century beer superseded *póitín* in Irish tastes (Connell 1996, 24–48).

Although in America the Irish have the reputation for loving strong drink, in reality they have a high rate of abstinence from alcohol (Malcolm 1986, 331–32; Cassidy 1997, 448). Temperance in Ireland has a long history: Father Theobald Mathew conducted a very popular temperance crusade in pre-Famine Ireland, beginning in 1838, in which many Irish decided "to take the pledge" to totally abstain from alcohol, and in 1849 he brought this crusade to the Irish in America (O Muirithe 1972, 97; Rosenzweig 1983, 104). In Ireland in 1898 a priest and female nondrinkers founded the Total Abstinence League of the Sacred Heart for Females Exclusively, which, as the name implies, initially was for women only. By 1899, however, Father James Cullen, the power behind this movement, welcomed men into the ranks of the organization, which came to be known as the Pioneer League (Malcolm 1982, 14, 15).

Their philosophical orientation may have separated many Irish temperance enthusiasts from their American counterparts. Elizabeth Malcolm argues that, unlike some Protestant Americans, many Irish, including members of the Roman Catholic clergy, did not see alcohol, per se, as inherently wicked; they pointed out that, after all, alcohol was a legal beverage, and wine consumption is mentioned without censure in the Bible (Malcolm 1982, 2, 10). They advocated temperance, that is, moderation in drinking alcohol, rather than total abstinence. Most Irish people, therefore, probably did *not* agree with Father Mathew's view that drunkenness was "the root cause of most of Ireland's problems" and that therefore the eradication of drink would solve Ireland's problems (Malcolm 1986, 146).[11]

Irish women as well as men drank, both before and after the Great Famine. In the pre-Famine era, much drinking in rural Ireland was done outside, at special events like fairs, in which women mingled easily with men, drinking and dancing. According to Irish scholars, the best and most accurate account of rural Irish life before the Great Famine, in the 1820s and 1830s, can be found in Irish author William Carleton's *Traits and Stories of the Irish Peasantry,* and the female characters in the stories contained in this work drank alcohol (Colum 1937, 82; Kiberd 2001, 265–86).[12] In

11. Elizabeth Malcolm believes that the Catholic Church in America, concerned with ensuring that its immigrant members be seen as respectable, and that they move forward socially in an essentially Protestant society, was more supportive of temperance than was the church in Ireland (1982, 9). Although Malcolm may be correct with regard to the church hierarchy in the United States, it is likely that the average American Catholic held the more traditional, and more moderate, view of alcohol reflective of Catholics in Ireland.

12. Padraic Colum calls Carleton "that acknowledged master of Irish life and manners" (1937, 82). Declan Kiberd contends that Carleton "was himself a countryman and could write about the peasantry from within. And he would write about them with utter accuracy, so that the young people in the cottages, on taking up his books, would confirm their truth" (2001, 266). Kiberd addresses Carleton's place in the national literature of Ireland as well (265–86). Carleton's work was also popular with the Irish in America, judging by advertisements that appeared in the *Boston Pilot* in the 1850s and 1870s. The issue for November 24, 1855, for example, contains an advertisement for Carleton's *Willy Reilly and His Dear Coleen Bawn* that, quoting the *Irish American*, declares, "This is the latest production of the celebrated Irish novelist, Carleton, and will be read with pleasure, we have no doubt, by thousands of our country people on this Continent" (5). The issue for January 8, 1870, also contains an advertisement for Carleton's novels (7).

"Phelim O'Toole's Courtship," for example, Peggy drinks whiskey from an eggshell with Phelim (1971, 2:282–83). With the imposition, beginning in the 1830s, of government regulation of the sale of alcohol outdoors, opportunities for outdoor social drinking decreased, but did not completely disappear, and pubs became the major site of drinking in Ireland from 1850 on (Malcolm 1999, 70–72). In Ireland, as in England and America, where they evolved earlier, pubs were gathering spots for males seeking escape from the women in their lives. Irish women did not drink in pubs, but it was deemed acceptable for them to drink at weddings and other special community affairs (51). In urban northeastern America, however, their acceptance of drinking alcohol would place Irish domestics at odds with their middle-class female employers. In the United States, over the nineteenth century, *not* drinking alcohol became intimately associated with middle-class notions of "propriety" (Rorabaugh 1987, 40–42, 45).

From the complaints of American employers we know that some Irish domestics drank to excess at the wakes and funerals they attended or when the employer left temptation out in the form of "Bourbon and Cogniac." On the whole, though, Irish servants in America were known for moderate drinking of alcohol; of them it was said, "Sobriety, though not the strong point of the Irish character, is rarely transgressed by our female servants" ("Your Humble Servant" 1864, 57). And some Irish Bridgets did not drink alcohol at all. Certainly, those Irish girls who came to America to work as domestic servants in the 1920s, during America's unsuccessful experiment with Prohibition, distinctly remembered that they did not drink. When asked if the Irish girls drank at the Irish dances in New York, one former domestic who came to America in 1928 exclaimed, "Oh, my goodness, no. . . . [Y]ou would only have a soda" (Flatley 1996b).

Religion

As noted, the majority of the Irish girls who worked in domestic service in the United States between 1840 and 1930 probably were Catholics.[13]

13. The religious situation in Ireland from the seventeenth century to the first part of the nineteenth century was, in a word, peculiar. Through the Penal Laws, first enacted in 1695, members of the Anglican Church of Ireland, who formed a small portion of the Irish population, established stringent legal sanctions against Roman Catholics, who constituted the bulk of the Irish. The result, according to Maureen Wall, was a situation that had no parallel in western Europe (1995, 218). Although the late 1700s saw the rescinding of most of the

Catholicism was an integral part of the experience of the rural Irish, as the Irish expression, *Is giorra cabhair Dé ná an doras*, or "God's help is nearer than the door," illustrates (Lysaght 1999, 29). The standard Irish language (as the Irish term their Gaelic language) greeting for "Good day" is *Dia duit*, or "God to you," which is a contraction of a longer phrase that means roughly "The blessings of God to you." The standard reply is *Dia's Muire duit*, or "God and Mary to you," which is a contraction of the longer phrase "The blessings of God and Mary to you" (Ní Ghráda n.d., 42).[14] These expressions indicate the religious feeling that permeated the lives of the Irish. They were very attached to Catholicism—to die without receiving the last rites of the church was deemed an awful fate (Carleton 1971, 4:220–23, 226). Priests were held in high esteem, and it was said that the ultimate aspiration of an Irish peasant was to have a son become a priest (2:5, 78).

From the Reformation on, church buildings in Ireland became the property of the established Protestant Church of Ireland, rather than the property of the Catholic Church. Consequently, in the pre-Famine era, especially in rural areas, there was a dearth of buildings to serve Catholics. Mass was celebrated in various ways—in people's homes or at "mass rocks" out in the open, or under a protective *scáthlán*, or shelter (Wall 1995, 226). Otherwise, in the country, mass would have been celebrated in plain thatched buildings that were called chapels, the established Church of Ireland reserving to itself use of the word *church* for buildings in which religious services were held (224). Some religious affairs doubled as social affairs, and Irish women participated in those aspects of rural Irish social life that entwined with religion. They gathered for "stations"—that is, neighbors gathered at a particular local house where a priest would say mass for them (these stations are distinct from the Catholic devotion known as the Stations of the Cross)—and "patterns," which were pilgrimages or fetes connected with patron saints—*patron* was pronounced "pattern" (Ó Giolláin 1999, 201).

Penal Laws, in 1800, according to J. H. Whyte, Catholics were still ineligible to become members of Parliament and judges and to hold ministerial-level government positions, certain posts in the army and navy, and high-level civil service jobs (1995, 249). Through the efforts of Daniel O'Connell, who roused the Catholic masses to political action in the Catholic Association, Catholic Emancipation was finally effected in 1829, but not until 1869 was the Church of Ireland actually disestablished.

14. I thank my Irish language instructor, Thomas Hedderman of Delmar, New York, for his mention to me of the longer forms of the greetings and their English translations.

Because drinking and unruly behavior often followed the religious portion of such events, the Catholic Church tried to suppress them; in consequence, patterns declined in the second half of the nineteenth century (211, 214–15). Irish people, however, continued to visit holy places and to make pilgrimages. Mary Costello, who was born in 1906 and left County Mayo for New York City in 1922, just before she turned sixteen, remembered visiting the Shrine of Our Lady of Knock in County Mayo during her childhood. She also recalled that her mother made the pilgrimage to the summit of Croagh Patrick, also in County Mayo, a pilgrimage that remains popular in Ireland today (1994, 10–11).

Before the Famine, people from rural areas often incorporated earlier Irish folk beliefs into their religious practice. Folk religion waned, but did not entirely disappear, in the post-Famine period. Its decline was in tandem with Paul Cardinal Cullen's post-Famine campaign, which consolidated what has been termed the Devotional Revolution, to reform the Irish Catholic Church by tightening religious discipline and building up the physical plant of the church (Larkin 1999, 57–89; Hynes 1978; D. Miller 2005a).[15] Not only did attendance at mass increase, but the number of Catholic church buildings increased, too, as did the number of priests to service people in these churches; in addition, the number of Irish women who chose to become nuns also increased. Wearing a scapular became more common, and people made use of religious medals and holy pictures; they also became involved in such devotions as "novenas . . . benediction, vespers, . . . jubilees, triduums, pilgrimages, . . . processions and retreats" (Larkin 1999, 78).

Using rosary beads to say the rosary was very popular with the Irish. In December 1893, Julia Lough, writing from Winstead, Connecticut, to

15. David W. Miller acknowledges the controversy surrounding the term *Devotional Revolution*, but points out that it is now generally accepted that "Catholic devotional practice underwent remarkable changes between the pre-Famine decades and the end of the [nineteenth] century" (2005b, 67). Emmet Larkin (1999), Eugene Hynes (1978), and David Miller (2005a) differ with one another regarding various aspects of the Devotional Revolution, such as its causes and why mass attendance increased. After reviewing the work of other scholars, including Larkin and Hynes, Miller finds that the various reasons proffered for the increase in mass attendance all have some merit (95). He concludes, however, that there was a direct link between "shopping" and increased attendance at mass held in chapels: "The emergence of a well-articulated hierarchy of retail service-centers in nineteenth-century Ireland seems to be the most robust factor for explaining the triumph of chapel-based practice over its rivals based on the natural landscape and the household" (104, 106).

her mother in Ireland, recalled her mother's devotion to the rosary, saying, "I am sure you make those [rosary] beads of yours rattle in fine time every night. I remember them well the size of them" (Schrier Collection). Having family members kneel down together every evening to say the rosary, led by the father or the mother, became very common in Irish families. Irish nanny Helen Flatley remembered the importance of this family devotion: "There was one thing—God forbid if you were out with your friends and you were visiting somebody, if you weren't in at ten o'clock for the rosary, it was God help you. You wouldn't be out the next night" (1996a).

Thus, the material culture of rural Irish life between 1840 and 1930 did not prepare Irish girls for the work of domestic service in middle-class homes in urban northeastern America. Nor did their beloved Catholicism prepare them for life in Protestant America, where anti-Catholicism was rampant, as will be discussed in chapter 4. If their Irish life failed to prepare them for domestic service in the United States, why, then, did Irish girls go to America? Some aspects of Irish life can be seen as, in effect, helping to "push" them away from Ireland, whereas others can be viewed as helping to "pull" them to America. In chapter 2, those factors of Irish life that can be seen as having helped to push Irish girls away from Ireland will be examined.

2

From Ireland

The Irish Bridgets emigrated from Ireland primarily for economic and social reasons that remained fairly consistent over the period 1840 through 1930. Some of their Irish life circumstances can be seen as in some way impelling their emigration, while others can be viewed as pulling them to America. In this chapter those aspects of Irish life that in some fashion helped "push" the Irish Bridgets away from Ireland will be examined. These reasons include the effects of the Great Famine of 1845–52, the changes in land inheritance patterns and family life that followed the Famine, and the employment situation for women, all of which, in some way, factored into the emigration of women from Ireland between 1840 and 1930.

An Gorta Mór: The Great Hunger

From the late eighteenth century on, the population of Ireland increased, rising from about five million people in 1800 to its 1845 size of about eight and one-half million people, although, as Cormac Ó Gráda points out, the rate of population increase slowed after 1821, and at that time was not totally out of line with European norms (1995, 69). The cause of this rapid population rise is not entirely clear, but the survival of more people in the absence of warfare, Irish potato culture, and the reduction in deaths owing to disease may have been factors (E. Green 1994, 265; Guinnane 1997, 81).

Before the Famine, economic and social conditions in Ireland varied by geographic locale. That is, circumstances were better in the East than in the West, and more specifically they were better in the Southeast than in the Northwest (Stout 2005, 83). But much of the population growth mentioned above was centered in areas of poor land where increased population translated into increased competition for land; as a result, subdivision of land followed. Families subdivided their land to accommodate their children's need for it, in a system that resulted in layers of ever smaller farms. Land was sometimes let out in bits as small as an acre or less, at a time when it was believed that a farm needed to be in the range of five to eight acres in order to satisfactorily support a family (K. Miller 1985, 50). The difficulties of their circumstances caused the poor of rural Ireland to cleave resolutely to their holdings, no matter how small. Potato dependence, as previously noted, made the position of the rural poor precarious, so when the potato blight struck in September 1845, they had no real safety margin to protect them from disaster.

There is no question that the Great Famine of 1845–52 devastated Ireland. This famine, in which a blight, caused by the fungus technically known as *phytophthora infestans,* destroyed potatoes, was not, however, the first famine to affect Ireland. There had been earlier famines, such as the famine of 1740–41, and later food scarcities, such as the potato crop failures of 1879–86, 1890, 1897, and 1904 in the West, that adversely affected the country, but not to the same extent as the Great Famine (Dickson 1995; K. Miller 1985, 399, 402). The Great Famine precipitated a flood of emigration throughout the English-speaking world, and thereby, more so than earlier and later famines, it profoundly affected not only Ireland but also the countries to which its people emigrated, in particular the United States. Before the Famine, the peasantry, consisting of "cottiers, landless laborers and the poorest smallholders," constituted about 75 percent of the rural Irish population (K. Miller 1985, 53). Although the Famine affected all classes of society in Ireland, it basically destroyed the cottier class at the base of Irish society and brought about the depopulation of Ireland: approximately two million people disappeared, one million left Ireland, and one million died, mainly from diseases that included typhus, relapsing fever, and dysentery rather than from starvation (E. Green 1994, 270–71, 274).

Some of the Irish Bridgets came to the United States during the Famine, for reasons most likely related to it. For example, records of the Emigrant Industrial Savings Bank in New York City for the period September 30, 1850, to July 24, 1852, show that most of the Irish-born female depositors working in some form of private domestic service came to America between September 1845 and July 1852, that is, during the Famine period (Rich 2000). Similarly, bank records for the period July 24, 1852, through July 29, 1854, also indicate that most of the Irish-born female depositors working in some form of private domestic service, for whom an arrival date in America is noted, came to the United States during the Famine (Rich

2005).[1] Irish domestic Ann McNabb said it was the Famine-related death of her sister Maria that prompted the eventual emigration to America of most of her family. McNabb, who hailed from Ulster and worked as a cook in the United States, remembered that her sister Maria "died the famine year of the typhus and—well, she sickened of the herbs and roots we eat—we had no potatoes" (Holt 1906, 144–45).

Post-Famine Changes in Irish Life

Following the Great Famine, changes in land inheritance patterns and family life among the Irish peasantry accelerated emigration. Impartible

1. In 2000, Kevin J. Rich published volume 1 containing information from the bank's first test book, dealing with the bank's first 2,500 depositors, most, but not all, of whom were Irish immigrants. In 2005, he published volume 2, covering accounts 2,501 through 7,500. In the future he expects to publish a third volume, at which point the complete contents of the first test book will have been published. The complete records (fifty-nine volumes) of the Emigrant Industrial Savings Bank collection are housed in the New York Public Library. For most, but not all, depositors, the information in volumes 1 and 2 includes the depositor's occupation and address in America, as well as remarks on the depositor's place of birth, family, the name of the ship he or she took to America, and the date and place of the depositor's arrival in North America. These bank records show that for volume 1, approximately sixteen different categories were used, without definition, to indicate what appears to be some form of domestic service. These categories are Domestic; General Housework or Housework; House Cleaner; Chamber Maid; Servant, Serving, or Service; House Servant; House Keeper; Lives Out; Works Out; Cook; Cook and Washing; Laundress; Washer-Ironer; Washer and Washer Woman; Governess; and Nurse. I included in my count all the Irish immigrant females who worked in these categories. Laundry work was done both in the homes of private employers and in the homes of the laundresses themselves, but because there was no means of distinguishing between the two, I included all those women employed in some form of laundry work in my count of domestics. I excluded from the count those women who worked in public domestic service, that is, in hotels. *Nurse* is a term that could mean either nanny or nurse in its contemporary meaning. I excluded from my count those women who appeared to be the latter and counted only nannies. By my count, then, volume 1 indicates that 191 Irish immigrant women bank depositors worked in some form of private domestic service, and 123 of the 191 for whom an arrival date is indicated came during the Famine period, that is, between September 1845 and July 24, 1852, the date of the last entry in volume 1. In my analysis of volume 2's records, I used the same methodology outlined above. In volume 2, however, eleven categories of what could constitute domestic service were used: Chambermaid, Cook, Domestic, Housekeeper, Servant, Nurse, Laundress, Washer, Washer and Ironer, Washer and Sewer, and Washer Woman. My analysis indicates that 306 of the 391 female depositors who were Irish born, whose arrival date is known, and who were working in some form of domestic service came in the immediate Famine period of September 1845–52.

inheritance, associated with strong farmers before the Famine, became more widespread among small farmers after it. That is, it became the norm for only one son to inherit the family farm, instead of continuing with the previous practice of subdividing farmland to accommodate all of a family's children. After the Famine, the need for a woman to have a dowry, or a "fortune," as it was called in Ireland, in order to marry also became more widespread. Marriages became affairs arranged by parents, who made matches for their daughters predicated on economic motives. They wanted to match the girl with a man whose economic circumstances were similar to hers, or offered her improvement. Occasionally, the couple getting married did not know one another before marrying. So it was for Martin Flanagan and Mary Murphy of County Galway when they married. According to their daughter Cecelia Flanagan, who left the family farm in County Galway for Brooklyn in 1925 at age eighteen, "My father didn't know my mother when he got married to her. . . . It was a match" (1994, 3). This is not to say that such arranged marriages failed completely to take into account the wishes of the bride and groom. As Irishman Robert Lynd contends, even if a girl did not choose her husband, she was "generally at liberty to refuse a husband she does not want." Most fathers took into account their daughters' wishes when arranging a match. Lynd maintains that the match system worked comparatively well in Ireland, arguing that if it did not, "Irish homes would not be so full of a pleasant atmosphere of affectionateness as they usually are" (1910, 43).

In the post-Famine period many Irish had long families (that is, many children) and could afford to provide a dowry for only one daughter. Generally, without a dowry an Irish girl could not marry. The absence of a dowry, combined with the dearth of employment opportunities, meant that a daughter could be left in the unenviable position of living as a dependent on the family farm. Thus, some Irish girls for whom a match could not be made left Ireland to find husbands in America. As one Irish girl wrote home, "Over in Ireland people marry for riches, but here in America we marry for love and work for riches" (Schrier 1958, 26).[2]

2. Kerby A. Miller, David N. Doyle, and Patricia Kelleher hypothesize that some Irish girls sought work in America in an effort to earn money to make them more attractive in America to potential marital partners of high quality (1995, 54). I agree that this hypothesis is a likely one, but none of the primary source material that I consulted specifically supports this conjecture.

4. Catherine (Katie) Murray Manley. *Courtesy of Catherine Hassey, Katie's granddaughter.*

On the other hand, some Irish women for whom a match *could* be made in Ireland rebelled against the matches intended for them and emigrated instead, as did Catherine (Katie) Murray Manley from Tullyegan, Ballina, County Mayo (see ill. 4). According to family lore, Katie's father made a match for her, which she rejected. Instead, in Ireland in 1891 she married a man of her own choice, Martin Manley.[3] Martin then went to the United States and later sent

3. Katie and Martin Manley's wedding certificate from Cathedral Church, Ballina, County Mayo, indicates that in Ireland the family name was spelled "Monnelly."

for Katie. She joined him in New Bedford, Massachusetts, where she worked in domestic service in private homes on a live-out basis.[4]

Still other Irish girls for whom a match could have been made in Ireland ostensibly spurned the idea in favor of taking their chances on a different life in the New World. As Irish domestic Lillian Doran, who left Ballymore, County Westmeath, for New Haven, Connecticut, in 1912 at age fifteen, said when asked what her life would have been like had she remained in Ireland, "Oh, I'd be a farmer's wife digging in a little garden," where she would have had to work "outside, and every kind of hard work in the country, digging and everything." This prospect was apparently very unappealing to Doran, who said, "I never could do that" (1993, 41).

Female Employment

Irish females emigrated not only in search of marriage but in search of employment as well. Other than farmwork, employment opportunities were scarce, especially in rural Ireland. During the nineteenth century the industrialization that had begun earlier in Ireland actually declined. For example, in 1841, 27 percent of the Irish workforce was employed in the manufacturing industry, but by 1891, only 17 percent of the workforce was so employed (Daly 1981, 74). The industrialization that existed was limited mainly to cities in the Northeast of Ireland, although some industrial activity was located in the cities of Dublin, Waterford, Cork, and Limerick. The fact remains, however, that few Irish women were employed in factory and millwork (Daly 1997b, 28). Nonetheless, some women *did* earn wages in nineteenth- and twentieth-century Ireland. In addition to domestic service work, Irish women's paid work ran the gamut from work in "millinery, drapery and retail services" to clerical work, taking in lodgers, and working in pubs and as wet nurses and charwomen; then, too, some Irish women were beggars and some were prostitutes (Luddy 2005a, 50). Although scholarship on Irish women's employment is not extensive, some information does exist on Irish women's involvement in agricultural work, home industries, and domestic work, all of which will be discussed below.[5]

4. I obtained this and other information on Katie Murray Manley when I interviewed her granddaughter, Catherine Foy Hassey, by telephone on September 24, 1995, and in person in New Bedford, Massachusetts, on November 12, 1995.

5. Maria Luddy points out that quantification of women's employment from 1840 to 1930 is hampered by how the Irish census defined "productive labour." She indicates that

Agricultural work, especially dairy work, remained a major source of paid and unpaid work for Irish women on the family farm. Women constituted more than 40 percent of all the workers in the broad category of jobs making up the dairy industry in 1881. Traditionally, Irish women milked cows and made butter for their own use, selling the extra and putting the money to such uses as paying off shopkeeper bills; changes in the dairy industry, however, led to a decline in female participation in it at the end of the nineteenth century (J. Bourke 1993, 82, 80).[6] Raising poultry was also a traditional way for Irish women to earn money, and the money earned was central to the family economy. With their egg money, women could pay the rent on the farm and purchase food (170, 171). They could barter eggs for food purchases, as some rural women did up to the second half of the twentieth century (Clear 2000, 91).[7]

Home industries, like lace making, crocheting, and embroidery, waxed and waned over the nineteenth century and eventually declined in the twentieth. Irish domestic Rose Kelly recalled that at home in Ireland she and her widowed mother embroidered to earn money. Rose remembered that "we had to take out so much [material to be embroidered] for the week, you know, of

---

from 1871 forward, unless a woman indicated that she was engaged in a specific occupation other than her husband's, she was listed "as being in an unpaid domestic occupation." This practice, Luddy argues, "led to a gross under-representation of the numbers of women who were actually productively engaged in farm work, or other labour within the context of the family business or farm" (2000, 45).

6. Joanna Bourke argues that the increased involvement of men in dairying, and the rise of sizable, often cooperative, creameries that took butter products out of women's control in the home, led to the diminished importance of dairying as a means for women to earn money (1993, 83, 85, 87).

7. Joanna Bourke argues that the rise of creameries had a negative impact on this source of income, too, because it became an established practice to bring eggs to creameries. Instead of the wife directly receiving the proceeds of the sale of eggs, it was creamery practice to give all of a family's money, milk as well as egg money, in one sum to the husband. Bourke argues that, no longer in direct receipt of the proceeds of their egg sales, women faced a decrease in their limited financial independence. To keep control of the proceeds, some women opted to sell their eggs on their own, even if they got a lower price than they would have gotten at the creamery (1993, 188). Ciara Breathnach, however, citing scholarship that the poultry industry remained important to the family economy and remained dominated by women in the twentieth century, disputes Bourke's contention that men usurped women's dominance of the poultry industry, arguing instead that "women were traditionally the [poultry] producers and remained so" (2005, 55).

seven days, and finish it up and take it back in on, in our town it was Tuesday you went down to the market. So, . . . you took it down, and you took out some more. And that kept the house going. . . . [W]e used to take out dozens and dozens and dozens of handkerchiefs" (1995, 12–13). Although making lace was a social experience in rural Ireland—females gathered of an evening to, as Mary Coleman says, "chat, exchange news and 'be at the sewing'" (1985, 85)—this home industry failed to flourish for many reasons, including marketing problems, administrative ineffectiveness, the inadequate work habits of home workers, the mechanizing of such industries, and the absence of a home market for their products (J. Bourke 1993, 120–21, 130, 132–35, 138). It also failed because of what Coleman calls the "'stigma of poverty'" that the Irish associated with making lace (1985, 92).

Two growth areas of employment for Irish women in this period were in teaching and the religious life, and these positions overlapped in the sense that many nuns worked as teachers. The number of women teachers in Ireland rose from 32 percent in 1841 to 63 percent in 1911 (J. Bourke 1993, 33). The number of nuns increased, too, from a little more than one hundred at the start of the nineteenth century to more than eight thousand by the first year of the twentieth century, and nuns continued to be an important factor in Irish society through the middle of the twentieth century (Fahey 1987, 7). Many Irish women saw a religious vocation as a very positive life choice, believing that religious life offered them "an arena in which to use their education, develop their talents, and assert a measure of their independence" (Hoy 1995b, 70).

Still, domestic service was the most usual waged occupation for females in Ireland, as it was for females in America, from the nineteenth century well into the twentieth, and it was the sole form of paid employment for women that actually grew after the Famine (Luddy 2000, 52). Irish domestic service differed from American service in that in Ireland service was a factor in rural as well as urban life. In rural Ireland, the line between servants and farmworkers often was ambiguous, so that rural service for females often involved outdoor farmwork (including responsibility for poultry and cows) as well as indoor (domestic) work. In consequence, to an Irish girl, domestic service in private homes in urban America, which generally involved solely indoor work, might have appeared more attractive than domestic service in Ireland. It is also telling about the nature of domestic service in rural Ireland that, into the twentieth century, servants often obtained their positions through hiring fairs at which they were taken on for a given time period, usually six months (Hill and Pollock 1993, 41). The nature of these hiring fairs was such that they were likened to "cattle fairs and slave markets" (Hearn 1993, 27). In return for her service, the servant received room, board, and a monetary amount that was paid at the conclusion of the service period.

For those servants who were married and had children, domestic service in Ireland also involved the hardship of separation from their families. On December 24, 1850, Bessie McManus Masterson, a domestic servant in County Kilkenny, wrote to her cousin in America that "I am a 100 Miles from my husband and Children . . . in the County Meath. . . . [T]he Situation I have I Cannot leave one day to Go See him or the Children but the Come to see me and he Writes to me Every week we never Can live together in Ireland because the Gentry are Comeing down and Keeps So few Servants and low wages" (K. Miller Collection).

Domestic service in Ireland also evidences some similarities with service in the United States, as later discussion will show. In both countries it was considered a low-status occupation, and employers looked longingly backward to an alleged golden age of service. In addition, in both Ireland and America, servants often differed from their employers in both class and religion, for employers in Dublin, as in the United States, tended to be Protestant, while their servants were generally Catholic (Hearn 1993, 8, 12, 13). Female servants in Ireland, like their Irish counterparts in America, were usually single, were joked about, changed positions frequently, and had little training for their work (14, 20, 22, 44). Elizabeth Smith, the mistress of Baltiboys in County Wicklow, Ireland, vented her complaints about her Irish domestic servant in her September 10, 1846, diary entry. Sounding rather like a complaining American employer, she wrote, "I discovered that Biddy had cut up a bedroom carpet into long strips to cover the back stairs, and burned the handsome rug in the drawing-room in five or six places that very morning. . . . [I]n short the less I used my eyes in her department the better" (1980, 100).

To some, female emigration was connected to the decreased employment opportunities for females associated with the spread of creameries. The home industries, too, became associated with emigration, for the complaint was made that Irish girls who became expert in lace making tended to emigrate. The alleged dearth of domestic service employment opportunities available to them in Ireland is also cited as a cause (J. Bourke 1993,

98, 136, 66).[8] Thus, the absence of employment options clearly pushed some Irish girls to emigrate. Irish nanny Helen Flatley, for example, said of her emigration from County Mayo to New York City in 1928, "I came out here because there was really nothing to do" in Ireland, where "at that time there was no such thing as factories or nothing, just absolutely nothing to do" (1996a). And Bridget Lacknee, who left Ballinasloe, County Galway, for New York City in 1923 and worked as a saleslady, said she decided to go to America because she believed she would "have opportunities" there (1974, 4, 10–11).[9]

Social Life

For both men and women in rural Ireland, social life was sparked by market fairs, weddings and wakes, and dancing at crossroads. Fairs were convivial and welcomed breaks in the routine of rural life. J. M. Synge tells us that regular fairgoers at the fair at Aughrim, County Wicklow, included mountain people, shepherds, successful farmers, children, mendicants, and "tinkers," the itinerant, Gypsy-like Irish people that today are called Travellers. Entertainment from ballad singers was an attraction at such fairs. Sometimes, after fairgoers imbibed alcohol, the events became raucous at night (1980, 51, 53–55, 92). Affirming the often unruly nature of Irish fairs, on June 24, 1896, Katie McCarthy wrote from County Cork to her brother Tim in Massachusetts, "They had great sport Leap fair day in Tom Kingstown's loft. They broke it down almost" (O'Malley Collection). Aside from entertainment, the function of fairs was to provide for the exchange of goods. Margaret Convery recalled her parents going to a fair, held monthly at Maghera, County Derry, to sell cattle (1991, 19–20).

For Irish women, social life also entwined with work, and singing was a form of recreation that provided an outlet for them while they worked. For

8. It is possible that the dearth of servant jobs was more apparent than real. Joanna Bourke suggests that at least part of the problem might have been that those girls available for service jobs were from rural Ireland, whereas the opportunities were in urban areas where employers were not anxious to hire untrained girls from the country (1993, 66).

9. In the transcription of the interview, her name is spelled "Lacknee," but the transcriber does not appear to have verified the spelling. Consequently, because of other spelling errors I found in the transcription of this interview (for example, I assume the *"Comic" Tribune* mentioned is in fact the *Connacht Tribune*), "Lacknee" is probably meant to be "Loughney," "Laughnane," or "Loughnane," all of which are listed in MacLysaght 1999, 199.

example, women sang while herding cattle, which was a peculiarly female job in Ireland. Some work songs, designed to be sung in group situations, perhaps while women weaved or spun, mirrored the beat of the work being done. Since Irish women were accustomed to associate singing with working, it is unsurprising that in America, Irish domestics were known to sing on the job.

Single women in rural post-Famine Ireland are said to have had more limited lives than single men, causing them to "get tired of it [their home town] sooner than the young men" (Colum 1937, 43). Post-Famine rural Irish society has been portrayed as a society in which sex segregation was pervasive and hostility between the sexes prevalent (Diner 1983, 4). It has also been characterized as a joyless society dominated by a puritanical Roman Catholic Church that discouraged "normal" male-female relations (Colum 1937, 28). An Irish woman's lot was a hard one, and so it has been said that, in search of adventure in a bigger world, Irish girls emigrated. According to the conventional wisdom, those girls who "went away" were the lucky ones, rather than the ones who secured a match and married in Ireland (Neville 1995, 206). Yet most of the evidence for church promotion of "a more puritanical lifestyle" dates to post-1920 rather than to the late nineteenth century (Daly 2006, 16). Women who spent their youth in Ireland during the second half of the nineteenth century and the first part of the twentieth century, and their adult life in America, remember their social life in rural Ireland differently. For example, the correspondence that Irish domestic Nora McCarthy, who lived and worked in Bradford and Haverhill, Massachusetts, kept up in America with her childhood friends from County Cork, who also emigrated to work in service in the United States, speaks of youthful good times rather than consistent dreary repression in rural Ireland. Even though allowance must be made for nostalgia in the recollections of their youth in Ireland for the elderly women cited below, Nora McCarthy's friends wrote their letters shortly after they left Ireland, ostensibly before nostalgia might taint the veracity of their memories.

Nora's correspondents had happy memories of their social life in rural Ireland that included recollections of "normal" male-female social interaction. On June 1, 1900, Hannah Collins wrote that her boyfriend had taken her for a buggy ride in the countryside outside Elmira, New York. She described the countryside, saying that "it was a lovely place the hills looked so nice and green it reminded me of sweet Ballinlough hill over the Lake where you & I spent many a happy sunday. I am lonesome for them happy days many a time." Convivial male-female interactions featured in Mary Anne Donovan's recollection of her social life in rural Ireland, too. On January 17, 1897, writing from a town near Boston, she asked Nora to check with her brother Tim on whether he remembered a mutual acquaintance named Catherine: "Ask him if he Thinks of the dancing He used to have With her before he Came out hear." Ellie Driscoll Enright, too, remembered the boys and girls having fun together in Ireland. In a letter she wrote to Nora from Washington, D.C., on March 14, 1900, she mentioned a mutual friend named Denis, saying, "I remember him very well he used to be Hugging the girls just like Tim the great big roague" (O'Malley Collection).

Katie McCarthy's correspondence from County Cork with her sister Nora in Massachusetts also mentions fun times in rural County Cork. On May 24, 1895, she wrote from Ireland, "Yesterday was a holiday. I went to ten o'clock Mass, it was a lovely day. . . . It was a great day in Leap, I never had seen so many shapers from all parishes. . . . The Slippers [a nickname for Nora's friends] and all the fellows around as usual. . . . They had a merry day singing and drinking until night." She also wrote that "the fellow do be bowling every sunday" (O'Malley Collection).

Those Irish women who emigrated in the 1920s had similar recollections of their social life during their youth in Ireland. Rose Kelly remembered that in County Derry, Northern Ireland, there was "singing at parties and that kind of thing, and we loved to dance, and we had a cousin that used to come down . . . and he was a great violin player, so we used to love to dance" (1995, 3). Helen Flatley also remembered having fun during her youth in County Mayo. "We always and always visited. . . . And then on Saturday nights, as we got a little older, maybe fourteen and fifteen, somebody in the village would give a dance. . . . [W]e had the Victrolas because . . . we had the Yanks coming over, and that was the one thing they brought over—dozens and dozens of records" (1996b).

I am by no means arguing that post-Famine rural Ireland was an exciting place for young girls, but it appears that for at least some of them the country was not necessarily as dull and repressive a place as it has been portrayed. Rather, it was the emigration of spirited young people that decimated the social life of those individuals left behind in Ireland, and in turn probably prompted further emigration of the young. Katie McCarthy, for example, bemoaned the decline of her social life that came with her sister Nora's emigration to America. She wrote to Nora on November 24, 1895, "As lone some as ye are this winter we are more lonesome. The slippers or any one dont come to visit us any night now" (O'Malley Collection).

The Status of Irish Women

Scholars have generally concluded that Catholic Irish women in the post-Famine period had low status and existed in a position subordinate to men. In reaching this conclusion, however, they rarely compare the status of Irish women to the position of women from other peasant societies in Catholic European countries (for example, Spain or Portugal) in the same period.[10] Was the Irish situation exceptional, or was it similar to the experience of other comparable European countries? The definitive answer to this question is dependent on future scholarship. There is no doubt that although Irish women's status was low by twenty-first-century standards, it may have been no lower than the position of women in other comparable societies, and it might actually have been slightly higher.

Certain factors of Irish life mitigated the low status allegedly accorded Irish women. First, in both pre- and post-Famine Irish society women (and men) acquired adult status through marriage rather than through the amount of money they earned; unmarried people had lower status than married people. Traditionally, married Irish women, who continued to be called by their maiden names after marriage, acquired authority through motherhood, as the heart of the family. Children were seen as positive additions to the family, and, in fact, a childless marriage was deemed a deficient one. Following her visit to Ireland at the end of the nineteenth century, French tourist Anne Marie DeBovet commented, "In the lower Irish classes the mother is looked upon as the most useful member of the family. She works harder than the man, earns more, and drinks less" (1891, 52). In 1910, G. W. Russell (Æ) attested to the importance of the Irish mother, saying, "The mother moulds the character of the generations as they pass. She gives the child its heart. . . . [I]n these great matters of character moulding and education in its true sense women have much more to do with in life than men have, and the whole realm of society or social intercourse is theirs to rule and govern" (1978, 235–36). Further testimony to the importance of the mother comes from Nora Tynan O'Mahony, who in 1913 referred to the "old-time honour and reverence due and hitherto

10. There are two notable exceptions. First, David Fitzpatrick compares post-Famine Irish marriage customs to the conventions of peasants in Europe in general and concludes that they were similar (1985, 125). Second, Maryann Valiulis contends that the vision of the ideal Irish woman in the interwar period was very similar to the vision of the ideal woman in fascist Italy because both were based on the Roman Catholic ideal woman (1995, 177–78).

accorded to motherhood" in Ireland. According to O'Mahony, "A mother's influence, a mother's dignity, is very sacred and holy; hardly less so, . . . than that of the priesthood itself" (Luddy 1995, 17, 19). The maternal role was also central to Irish labor feminism in the early part of the twentieth century, as such feminism was said to be "grounded in an ideal of separate spheres, domesticity and motherhood" (Buckley 2004, 113).

Emphasis on the mother's role continued to imbue rural Irish society over time. Married Irish women often had considerable prerogatives. Well into the twentieth century, especially in the West, it was often Irish mothers, rather than fathers, who controlled the family purse, commanded the children, and made decisions regarding the children's education. Indicative of the power and prerogatives of at least some Irish mothers is Irish domestic Cecelia Flanagan's recollection that in her family life in Ireland, all the hard domestic work was done by the children, rather than by their mother. Her mother, she said, "didn't do any work at all. . . . You did the work, not my mother. She wouldn't dirty her hands" (1994, 7). James T. Gleeson's recollection also supports the power of Irish mothers. He said that in 1927 it was his mother who prevailed in the selection of the country to which the family emigrated. His father thought the family would be better off in Australia or New Zealand. According to Gleeson, however, "My mother, who had sisters and brothers in the United States, felt otherwise and I say they compromised and did it her way" (1993, 5).

Second, Americans characterized the Irish women who came to work in domestic service in the United States as impertinent and assertive (Bridget 1871; Dickens 1874, 584). It seems that despite the patriarchal nature of Irish society, a certain broader latitude, in terms of acceptable female behavior, was allowed Irish girls (and married women) than was allowed middle-class women in urban America of the same period, who, according to the tenets of the American cult of domesticity or true womanhood, were expected to be submissive (Welter 1976, 21).

Assertive Irish women, married as well as unmarried, abound in Irish author William Carleton's stories; he is reputed to have accurately portrayed the Irish peasantry, so these women must reflect the peasant Irish women he knew. Carleton reports that on occasion, in refusing a suitor, a feisty Irish girl was known to smack him (1971, 1:120). Then there is Nancy, who rules her husband, Ned, in Carleton's "Ned M'Keown." When angry with him, she lectures him. "Ned's conduct on these critical occasions was very prudent and commendable; he still gave Nancy her own way; never "jawed back to her" (1:13). In "The Three Tasks," Carleton tells us, "The lady would not be put off; like a ra-al woman, she'd have her way" (1:69). His Peggy in "Phelim O'Toole's Courtship" gets fed up with Phelim after all his shenanigans (he gets himself engaged to three women simultaneously, one of whom is Peggy). She ends up defying her father by refusing to marry Phelim, saying, "I'll never join myself to the likes of him. If I do, may I be a corpse the next minute!" Her assertiveness leaves her father outraged at her "contempt of his authority" (2:329). These examples illustrate that it was accepted in rural Irish society for women to use their keen verbal skills to assert themselves. As Larry says to his wife, Sheelah, in "Phelim O'Toole's Courtship," "The edge of your tongue's well known" (2:206).

Irish storyteller Peig Sayers quotes an Irish expression, "A woman's tongue is a thing that doesn't rust," which indicates the verbal assertiveness of Irish women (1962, 81). Peig's tales of her own behavior show that she was not one to be intimidated by any man. Irish-speaking Peig held her own with an English-speaking man in an argument over a seat on a train, telling him, "I have bought this seat as well as you. There was no bad penny in my money when I paid for it." Faced with her assertiveness the man backed off, leaving a male observer to ask him, "'Didn't you always hear, . . . that nobody ever got the better of women?'" The defeated man replied, "'I did, . . . and it's true'" (78).

A long tradition of strong, activist, assertive women exists in Irish history and culture. In the ranks of these women can be placed Saint Brigid; Queen Medb, or Maeve; the female pirate Gráinne Mhaol, or Grace O'Malley;[11] and Eibhlin Dhubh Ní Chonaill, or Eileen O'Connell, author of the famous poem "Caoineadh Airt Uí Laoghair" (Lament for Art O'Leary).[12] Their ranks also include Mary Ann McCracken, who was involved in the 1798 Rebellion (during which common Irish women also supported rebel troops), and Anne Devlin, who worked for Robert Emmet

11. Mary O'Dowd argues that representations of Irish women such as Gráinne Mhaol as assertive and autonomous "are a later folk tradition," because Mhaol's exploits are "ignored in contemporary Gaelic literature" (2005, 253). The fact that O'Dowd acknowledges that strong Irish women are part of Irish tradition supports my thesis that peasant Irish society accepted assertive Irish women. But the fact that Gaelic sources ignore Mhaol's exploits is more indicative of the misogyny of the male writers than it is that such exploits were not recognized as notable events.

12. For more detail on these women, see MacCurtain 1985, 37–49; Ó Corráin 1979, 10; Simms 1979, 18; Ní Chuilleanáin 1985, 115–20; and Angela Bourke 1988.

and was subsequently tortured and imprisoned for refusing to betray the leaders of the 1803 Rebellion (Ó Céirín and Ó Céirín 1996, 63–64, 134–35). Strong Irish women of all classes continued to make themselves known in Irish society from the 1800s through 1930. For example, Irish court records from the late 1830s provide evidence of assertive women, including domestic servants, using the "law" to achieve their desired ends. In East Galway in the late 1830s a domestic servant named Catherine Burke lodged a successful civil complaint against her former employer, a Mrs. Mick Lyons, for firing her without justification. The court awarded Catherine both compensation and payment of court costs (R. McMahon 2000, 159). Assertive Irish women also were involved in the tithe wars of the 1830s; an 1833 news report indicates that they took part in stoning two tithe proctors in County Cork (Luddy 1995, 246).

Irish women participated in food riots during the Great Famine, engaged in voter intimidation to help "Tenant Right" candidates in 1852, and were involved in election rioting in 1868 (Luddy 1995, 245, 247–48; 2005b, 47). Some women aided the Fenian movement by rallying for the release of Fenian prisoners, and at least one woman appears to have assisted in the covert importation of rifles to support the cause (Luddy 1995, 250). Peasant women were involved in the boycott movement during the Land War, protested against evictions, participated in the return of the evicted to their homes, were subjected to violence, and were arrested and imprisoned by the authorities for their activities, as well (TeBrake 1992). During the Land War, some women in King's County (now County Offaly) attacked and struck a process server (Luddy 1995, 250).

Women were involved in the labor union movement in Ireland in the early twentieth century. Cissy Cahalan, Mary Galway, Catherine Mahon, Delia Larkin, Helena Molony, Louie Bennett, and Helen Chenevix numbered in the ranks of these women (Luddy 2005b, 49–52). Women were active in Irish revolutionary activities, too. In 1914, as an adjunct to the Irish Volunteers, the Cumann na mBhan (Women's Council) was formed, and women were arrested and interned during the 1916 Easter Rising (Luddy 1995, 243, 317–18).[13] There were also women hunger strikers during the Irish Civil War (Ó Céirín 1996, 132–33, 141–42). And labor leader Louie

13. Maria Luddy notes that because the records of the Cumann na mBhan have not been analyzed, not much is known about the class and educational background of the women who belonged to it (2005b, 54).

Bennett and Hanna Sheehy Skeffington were involved in the women's suffrage movement in Ireland (19–20, 201). In the United States, this female assertiveness that was accepted in Irish culture would serve the Irish Bridgets very well, for they found the United States to be a country where, as Irish domestic Hannah Collins put it in July 1899, "every-body [is] for themselves" (O'Malley Collection).

The unquestionably powerful and patriarchal Roman Catholic Church in post-Famine Ireland has been seen as complicit in the alleged low status accorded Irish women, for it has been assumed that Irish women conformed to the church's narrow orthodox vision of their appropriate role and how they should behave, a vision that involved the submission of women to men, including male clerics. Undoubtedly, the church's vision for women was a rigid one in which they were to be confined to hearth and home and subservient to men. Whether all Irish women completely internalized and accepted this vision is another matter. Cara Delay's work (2005) shows that, in contrast to the official passive role envisioned for them, after the Famine Irish women frequently crossed swords with priests, suggesting that at least some Irish women were unbowed by the clergy. For example, in 1876, a Clare woman, upset that her parish priest declined to call on her when she was ill, went so far as to take her grievance straight to the pope. The Vatican ordered her bishop to look into and resolve the matter himself, which he did. The case of Mary Neylon indicates that even uneducated Irish women felt free to challenge the Catholic clergy. In 1913, Neylon, an elderly Galway widow, was perturbed when the seat in church that her family had held for nearly a half century was appropriated by another family. When she complained to the parish priest, rather than give her satisfaction, he told her she was free to find a seat in the local Protestant church. She then enlisted the aid of her relations to pen correspondence to her bishop asking for his intervention in the matter—and threatening to convert to Protestantism if the matter was not resolved.

Despite church teachings, women's self-assertion continued in the early years of Irish independence. In the 1920s and 1930s, in contrast to church rhetoric on women's proper role, Irish women worked for a living, remained single, emigrated, and were involved in "exploring their sexuality . . . going to dances, wearing imported fashions and going to films . . . agitating for political rights, [and] demanding a public identity" (Valiulis 1995, 176).

Two factors, therefore, served to mitigate the alleged low status accorded women in post-Famine Ireland. The first factor was that Irish women acquired status through marriage and motherhood, and the second was that a certain broad latitude, in terms of acceptable female behavior, particularly in terms of verbal assertiveness, was permitted females in Irish culture. The status of Irish women was probably higher than scholars have acknowledged, although, of course, it was low by twenty-first-century standards. If the status of any Irish females *did* decline in the post-Famine era, it may have been that of unmarried girls, for they are said to have had little individual independence and to have held a servile position within the family (Rhodes 1992, 194–95). And if they remained unmarried on the family farm after the inheriting brother married and brought in his wife, their position was subordinate to that of the new woman of the house, and they were subject to her bidding.

Factors related to the Famine itself impelled the departure from Ireland of some of the Irish Bridgets. Others left in search of husbands, spurred to emigrate by post-Famine changes in Irish land inheritance patterns and family life, including marital practices. Still others were propelled away from Ireland by the dearth of opportunities, including paid employment, available to them there. Given their limited options, the Irish Bridgets chose the one they believed offered them the best chance of an improved, but not necessarily an easy, life—emigration from Ireland to work in domestic service in private homes in urban northeastern America.

3

To America

The emigration from Ireland of the Irish Bridgets involved "pull" factors as well as the "push" factors discussed in chapter 2. The development of a culture of emigration in Ireland, improved educational opportunities, acquisition of English-language skills, chain migration, the American letters and the American money that they received from expatriate relations and friends, and the influence of returned Yanks all served, in some manner, to "pull" or attract them to the United States between 1840 and 1930. In addition, some of these "pull" factors simultaneously served to "push" girls away from Ireland.

A Culture of Emigration

Although the Great Famine accelerated emigration, large-scale Irish emigration to America actually preceded the Famine. In 1816 and again in 1817, between six and nine thousand Irish people left for America. Irish emigration was heavy in 1831 and 1832, and, with the exception of 1838, between 1835 and 1839 at least thirty thousand Irish came to the United States each year (Adams 1980, 71, 159–60). In 1840, almost forty thousand Irish people immigrated to America (U.S. Bureau of the Census 1975, 106). The number of women in the Irish emigrant stream increased from the 1830s on. And during the nineteenth century, the religious affiliation of the Irish who came to the United States shifted; earlier Irish emigrants had been primarily Protestants (often Presbyterians), but from the 1830s on, the number of Roman Catholic Irish emigrants increased, with Catholics dominating the Irish emigration to America from the Famine period onward (Adams 1980, 223, 396–97; Akenson 1996, 223).

Years before the Famine, women were leaving Ireland to work in domestic service in middle-class homes in urban northeastern America. In 1825, applications from Irish women accounted for almost 60 percent of the more than two thousand employment applications received by New York's Society for the Encouragement of Faithful Domestic Servants' employment registry (Strasser 1982, 164–65). In 1840, one Irishman reported that it seemed to him that he had met at least a thousand female Irish domestics in Boston (Adams 1980, 224). American writer Asenath Nicholson indicated that not only had she employed Irish women as servants when she lived in New York City, but she also intended to meet their parents during her stay in Ireland (1847, 86). And Irish-born author Mary Sadlier set *Bessy Conway; or, The Irish Girl in America* (1861), her American novel concerning an ideal Irish domestic servant in New York City, in the period immediately preceding the Famine.[1] In addition, volume 1 of the records of New York City's Emigrant Industrial Savings Bank shows that around 19 percent (37 of 191) of the depositors who were Irish-born females working in some form of private domestic service came to the United States between 1816 and May 1845—in other words, before the Famine (Rich 2000).

Over time, a culture of emigration took root in Ireland in which "the more commonplace it became, the more firmly the expectation of emigrating was built into the economic and social system" (Fitzpatrick 1980, 126). This culture of emigration began first in the East and then spread over time into the West, where a Gaelic Irish culture and point of view resistant to permanent emigration persisted longer than elsewhere in Ireland. According to David Fitzpatrick, the number of women who emigrated from Ireland in the nineteenth century has been put at more than three million, a number greater than the number of women resident in Ireland in 1901. Further, Fitzpatrick indicates that more Irish men than women emigrated during the twenty-five-year period preceding and following the Famine,

1. Mary Anne Madden Sadlier was born in County Cavan, Ireland, in 1820 and emigrated to America after her father's death. She later married James Sadlier of the Catholic Sadlier publishing concern (McDannell 1986b, 53–54). Sadlier said she wrote *Bessy Conway* for the large population of Irish women who worked in domestic service in America (1863, 3, 4). Charles Fanning indicates that Sadlier was an important literary figure among nineteenth-century Irish immigrants. Her works were serialized in the *Boston Pilot*, the most important newspaper for Irish Americans of the time. He contends that Famine-era Irish American literature embraced "sentimental rhetoric, stereotyped characters, simplistic conflicts and moralizing themes" and that Sadlier's writing was typical of this literature (1997, 97–98, 15, 100). Further, Colleen McDannell notes that Sadlier sought to instruct her readers in living a proper life in America—the middle-class mores Sadlier deemed suitable for life in America (1986b, 54).

whereas during the Famine the number of female emigrants was comparable to the number of emigrant males. By comparison with other European countries, however, the number of women in the Irish emigrant flow was extremely high, and by the end of the nineteenth century, more Irish daughters than sons left Ireland (1990, 173). The pattern continued with more Irish women than men emigrating during the period 1901 through 1911; female Irish emigrants also exceeded male Irish emigrants between 1926 and 1936 (Travers 1995, 188). And, as previously remarked, up to about 1930, most of the Irish females who emigrated went to the United States, where many of them became domestic servants. In 1912 and 1913 alone, some 87 percent of the Irish emigrant women who went to America worked in some form of private or public domestic service (Akenson 1996, 129). As Fitzpatrick points out, "Ireland's abnormally heavy female emigration ensured that American domestic service would become very much an Irish domain" (1984, 32).

Emigration was not endorsed by all sectors of Irish society. For example, the Catholic Church, which constituted an extremely important element in Irish society, did not necessarily support emigration. Instead, the church warned young Irish girls against the danger of immorality that faced them in the United States (K. Miller 1985, 456). The church also cautioned that through emigration, Irish girls chose the "kitchens, factories and dancehalls of other lands" and left "the green fields of Ireland to [go to] the grey streets of an alien underworld" (Travers 1995, 190). An informant to the Irish Folklore Commission said that the church particularly warned those Irish girls leaving to work in domestic service abroad that "they'd have to work down in a kitchen underground, where they'd never see daylight" (Neville 1995, 205).

Education

The Irish greatly valued education. Irish author William Carleton claimed that Irish peasants in the pre-Famine period so loved and valued learning that even illiterate Irish families might have owned books in readiness for the family member who could one day read them (1971, 2:159). Mr. and Mrs. S. C. Hall, who traveled extensively in Ireland in the pre-Famine period, believed that the Irish greatly valued knowledge "as a means of acquiring moral power and dignity." They reported on Irish peasants who could converse in Latin and had some Greek, both of which they learned in hedge schools, the education-for-a-fee schools run by schoolmasters that predated a national educational system (1860, 1:258–59).[2]

A system of national schools, first established in 1831, facilitated the spread of English-language literacy in Ireland.[3] Instruction in these primary schools, many of which were of the one-room-schoolhouse variety, was provided to students of both sexes aged four to eighteen, with fourteen being the usual age at which students left school. Not until 1967 was free secondary education provided in Ireland. Irish domestic Ella Ahearn, who was born in County Kerry in 1902 and emigrated at age sixteen, remembered walking barefoot to the national school she attended (1989, 2). James Gleeson recalled the national school he attended in County Cork before he emigrated in 1927 as "a one-room schoolhouse. One side was the boys and one side of the room was girls" (1993, 15). And Mary Feely, who worked in service in America, said of schooling during her childhood in Tubbercurry, County Sligo, that "you only went to the . . . eighth grade [age thirteen] in country schools at that time" (1996).

National schools used a standardized state-set curriculum that focused on reading and writing. Attendance was voluntary until the imposition of compulsory attendance laws, but the first such law, passed in 1892, applied only to towns. These state-funded national schools were also sectarian—instruction was provided in the child's religion. As most Irish children were Catholics, instruction in Catholicism was an important component of the education provided in the national schools.

As Irish parents became aware of the link between education and success in America, they began to show "a desire to have their children properly taught, as they learn from their friends in America how difficult it is to get on there if their education has been neglected" (Fitzpatrick 1990,

2. Antonia McManus indicates that hedge schools came to the fore in the early 1800s when the Penal Laws forbade Catholics from publicly teaching and so "forced Catholic teachers to work underground" (2004, 15). According to Maria Luddy (1995, 89) and Sean McMahon (1997, 93), such schools provided one of the few ways in which the Roman Catholic peasantry could acquire an education.

3. With regard to education, Paddy Lyons points out that when British government efforts to educate all in mainland Britain began in the mid-nineteenth century, the elementary schools established used material based on *The Irish Readers*, which were developed earlier in Ireland for Irish use (2006, 89). That is, "colonial" reading materials formed the basis of material used to foster literacy in the colonizer's population.

183). Thus, education entwined with emigration: education was seen as necessary for the Irish to flourish in America, and therefore Irish girls likely felt more "pulled" to America, and possibly simultaneously more "pushed" from Ireland, after they had acquired some education. It is known that Irish girls made good use of the educational opportunities available to them, especially the classes in domestic economy supported by the Congested District Board at the end of the nineteenth century, which they used to prepare themselves for domestic service both in Ireland and in the United States (D. Smith 1996, 222–24). With education, over time, the Irish grew ever more literate in English. In the period 1851 to 1860, approximately 29 percent of female Irish emigrants and 40 percent of male Irish emigrants were literate (K. Miller, Doyle, and Kelleher 1995, 63n41). By the end of the nineteenth century, however, English-language literacy was almost universal among all Irish likely to emigrate. In fact, such basic literacy was actually more commonplace among females by the end of the nineteenth century (Fitzpatrick 1987, 164).

Language

Many Americans think of Ireland as an exclusively English-speaking country. Yet the historic language of Ireland was Gaelic, or "Irish," as it is called in Ireland. The Irish language is said to carry "the dialogue of mind and spirit which occurred over two thousand years of the development of the human psyche in its Gaelic dimension" in Ireland (Denvir 1995, 127). The Irish words interspersed with the English of the common Irish, as recorded by William Carleton, are highly expressive, and many are terms of endearment. For example, the Irish, described by Carleton as "a deeply feeling people," were wont, he claims, to use phrases replete with "beauty and tenderness," such as *a-suilish mahuil agus machree* (light of my eyes and of my heart) and *acushla agus asthore machree* (the very pulse and delight of my heart) in their everyday speech (1971, 3:355, 354, 4:290, 2:182). According to Carleton, "The Irish language" is one that "actually flows with the milk and honey of love and friendship" (3:353–54).

In Ireland, the number of people who spoke Irish was probably at its height in the late 1700s, and it was the primary language of nearly three million Irish people in 1800 (Dickson 1990, n.p.; Denvir 1995, 105). By that date, however, English was already the language of the public domain, while Irish was relegated to the language of the private domain of home and hearth.[4] By the end of the nineteenth century the number of primarily Irish-speaking people in Ireland had fallen to fewer than thirty-nine thousand people (Denvir 1995, 105). The Irish Bridgets, therefore, came from a country that abandoned its native language, Irish, very rapidly during the nineteenth century.

Economic factors have been cited as a major reason for the precipitous decline of the Irish language (Ó Cíosáin 2005, 141). Its decline has also been connected to the late and limited efforts to publish in Irish, owing to peculiarly Irish circumstances. Another reason given for the decline is that increased literacy was connected with the spread of English because English, not Irish, was the language of instruction in the national schools, even in those areas where the students' first language was Irish. Not until 1904 was Irish-English bilingual education provided to students whose first language was Irish. English became a necessity for those individuals seeking upward mobility in Ireland. In fact, English became "necessary not only to get on in the world, but to deal with the humdrum formalities of the world around one" (Cullen 1990, 31, 38–40). Ireland's nineteenth-century Great Liberator, Daniel O'Connell, a native Irish speaker, favored Irish adoption of the English language because he saw it as a mode of "modern communication" (Crowley 2005, 103).[5]

After the Famine, Irish also declined because its use became associated with the destitution of its speakers, as "Irish speakers gradually accepted

4. Nevertheless, the Irish language played a role in both Roman Catholic religious practice and court proceedings in the nineteenth century. Ostensibly, the church was not kindly disposed toward preservation of the Irish language, but nevertheless Catholic religious materials, including sermons, a catechism, and elegies, were produced in Irish during this time. Especially from 1820 forward, although English was the language of the Petty Sessions, testimony could be given in Irish through an English-language translator, and the state paid the cost of translators (Ó Cíosáin 2005, 148–51). The use of English in Irish courts, in a country where in the first part of the nineteenth century so many people spoke Irish, could be used to one's advantage in certain instances. Witness William Carleton's character Phelim O'Toole, who when called to give evidence against Ribbonmen conveniently forgets his English and requires an interpreter (1971, 2:244).

5. According to Tony Crowley, one of the great ironies of the monster meetings held in the early 1840s during O'Connell's repeal movement (that is, the movement he led to repeal the 1800 Act of Union through which Ireland was joined directly with Great Britain) is that he addressed the crowds in English, which was likely not well understood by the majority of his Irish audience (2005, 102).

colonial theories about the inferiority of Irish culture" (Doherty 2004, 135, 149). Some Irish came to view their language as "a cause of shame, an impediment to progress, a sign of utter poverty and deprivation and, above all, the language of a defeated race and class which was better abandoned" (Denvir 1995, 105). In consequence, some Irish Bridgets remembered parental pressure to *not* speak Irish. Irish domestic Cecelia Flanagan, for example, who emigrated from County Galway in 1925 at the age of eighteen, recalled that while at school she "learned Latin," but her mother "wouldn't let us learn Gaelic, because when she went to school, they hit her because she spoke nothing but Gaelic" (1994, 5). Kathleen Magennis, who worked as a waitress in a private club when she first arrived in New York City from Belfast, Northern Ireland, in 1921 at the age of twenty-two, when asked if she spoke Irish, responded, "You weren't allowed. I learned to say the 'Our Father' and the 'Hail Mary' and to bless myself. But you were not allowed to speak the Gaelic." Ironically, she thought the Irish-speaking Aran Islanders on her ship over to America were strange, remembering that on board "there were a lot of Irish there that we thought really they were not Irish because they never spoke English. They spoke Gaelic. . . . But they were Irish" (1994, 43, 57–58).

The decline of the Irish language and the spread of the English language in Ireland also bore relation to emigration, for "knowledge of English was an essential requirement for those who aspired to emigrate" (Daly 1990, 155). Acquisition of English-language fluency, therefore, can be viewed as a factor "pulling" Irish girls to America. It is possible, too, that simultaneously, acquisition of English-language skills also served to "push" them from Ireland. Still, many of the Irish who came to America *were* Irish speakers. In fact, up to about 33 percent of Famine-era emigrants were Irish speakers (K. Miller 1999, 183). And no fewer than five hundred thousand Irish speakers (mainly bilingual Irish-English speakers) left Ireland for America between 1856 and 1880 (Doyle 1996, 737). An Irish-speaking world existed in English-speaking America. For example, between 1850 and 1900, between seventy and eighty thousand Irish speakers are said to have lived in the New York City region. Testimony to the reality of this Irish-speaking world can be found in the *Irish-American* newspaper, which in 1857 noted that possibly thousands of Irish speakers lived in New York. The *Irish-American* intermittently ran an Irish-language column for these Irish speakers from 1857 until the paper went out of business in 1915. Further evidence of this Irish-speaking world can be found in the mention that was made in the *Irish World* in 1872 of an unsuccessful effort that had been undertaken in one section of New York City to include the Irish language as a course in public schools. Detailed evidence of the Irish-speaking world in America, however, is scanty, because most Irish speakers—working-class people who were probably illiterate in Irish—left little behind to mark their world's existence (Nilsen 1996, 253–74).

Scholars tend to see the Irish Bridget as privileged over other non-English-speaking immigrant domestics, like Swedish and German immigrant domestics, because English is presumed to have been the native language of the Irish. Yet although most Irish domestics probably *did* speak English, the information previously noted on Irish speakers in the United States would seem to indicate that some Irish Bridgets were Irish speakers. And some evidence exists that Irish-speaking domestics, like their Swedish and German counterparts, may have dealt with language problems as household workers in America (Nilsen 2004, 322, 324). How many of them were primarily Irish speaking or bilingual, however, remains one of the great unknowns because not until 1910 did the U.S. Census begin to inquire into people's first language.

From the work of Kenneth E. Nilsen we know that many of the Irish girls who emigrated from Irish-speaking areas of West Galway between 1880 and 1920 and went to work as domestic servants in Portland, Maine, were Irish speakers (2004, 297). Their ranks included Catherine ("Ceata") Foley Concannon, who was born in Teach Mór, Cois Fharraige, in 1894 and came to the United States in 1913; she worked as a domestic for a decade, until she left service to marry. In Portland the Irish-speaking servant girls were known to spend their limited time off strolling on the Western Promenade with other young Irish people; in fact, the Western Promenade was known as the Irish servant girl's "happy hunting ground" (329). Irish was also the native language of Annie O'Donnell, who emigrated from Galway in 1898 and ended up working as a nanny for children of the famous Mellon family in Pittsburgh (Murphy 2005, 6, 10, 11). The first language of Nora Joyce, who was originally from one of the Aran Islands and came to the United States in the early 1920s, was also Irish. She said, "I couldn't say a word of much English. I had some 'cause I learned it in Dublin, but if I didn't leave the island, I wouldn't even have a yes and no" (O'Carroll 1990, 37). And a former Irish maid who was bilingual reported in 1975 that she "remembered that her employers spoke French so that the servants would not know what was being said. When she and her friends 'below stairs' then spoke 'Irish,' however, her mistress became furious and told her to cease or face dismissal" (D. Clark 1982, 172–73).

Chain Migration

The Irish who came to America from 1840 through 1930 tended to come as individuals rather than in family groups.[6] They came in a chain migration, in which a relative already established in the United States paid for their passage. Once settled in America, it was expected that one would do the same for another family member. Through chain migration, the Irish Bridgets were "pulled" to America by expatriate relations. Sometimes chain migration simultaneously served to push them away from Ireland. For example, Rose McGurk, who left Draperstown, County Derry, for New York City in 1928 at age sixteen, said, "I didn't want to come," but since her aunt had sent her a ticket to America, she "had to come" (Aisling 2006, 7–8). Similarly, Catherine Mannion, always called Kathleen, from Dunmore, County Galway, had a sister working in domestic service in Boston who was lonely and wanted someone from home to join her, so Kathleen's mother ordered her to "pack her bags and go to Boston" in 1929 (McDonagh 2002) (see ill. 5).[7] The key to Irish chain migration was family rather than gender, for in this family-based movement, siblings and relatives of either gender brought brothers, sisters, nieces, nephews, or other relations. Irish domestic Margaret Convery said that it was her brother Dan who "sent me my ticket to come." He did so because "he got lonely so he wanted somebody [of the family] out so he sent for me" (1991, 26, 27).

Once on the other side, in America, Irish women were interested in reconstituting their families. They did this via a two-step process, in which they first gathered together siblings and cousins to, according to their view, make their "family" in the United States. Later, through marriage and children, they added their own nuclear family unit, and perhaps their husbands' relations in America, to the "sibling-cousin" family. Even after marriage and the formation of their own nuclear family unit, Irish women often continued to be involved in reconstitution of the "sibling-cousin" family. Married Irish women often maintained a "home" where friends

6. David Fitzpatrick asserts that the tendency of the Irish to move as individuals, rather than in family groups, distinguishes the Irish emigration from other European emigrations. He notes, however, that the period when Irish emigration in family groups was probably at its height was in the late 1840s, which, of course, was during the Famine (1984, 7).

7. The information on Kathleen Mannion was obtained through an interview, by telephone, with her daughter Maryellen McDonagh on May 29, 2002.

5. Catherine (Kathleen) Mannion. *Courtesy of Maryellen McDonagh, Kathleen's daughter.*

and relatives, male and female, could get together on their days off. Irish domestic Hannah Collins's correspondence with her fellow domestic Nora McCarthy indicates that in the late 1890s, in the Elmira, New York, area, Hannah's cousin Mrs. Dempsey provided her with just such a "home" away from where she lived in service. Writing to Nora on September 21, 1898, Hannah remarked that Mrs. Dempsey "is kind to us we make our home with her and they do be a big crowd there Sundays." Likewise, Nora's sister Mary Donovan provided a "home" for Nora in Haverhill, Massachusetts. In the same letter to Nora, Hannah wrote, "Its so nice for you to have your sisters home to go to Sundays and when you are tired or out of work" (O'Malley Collection).

Parental Reaction to Emigration

How did Irish parents feel about the removal of their children to foreign parts? Irish immigrant saleslady Bridget Lacknee said her parents "felt good" about her emigration. According to Lacknee, "Most of the Irish people, they had so many children, that they figured out that the children, when they were old enough, that they would be all so mature enough to make their own living. They couldn't feel sorry for them, or anything else, because there was no means of making a living in Ireland" (1974, 7).

According to some scholars, gender considerations influenced parental reaction to emigration. Some Irish families deliberately sought to have their daughters, rather than their sons, emigrate; they "pushed" their daughters to emigrate. These families reasoned that daughters would be more likely to send home money, and would be less tempted to waste their earnings, than would sons. Such parents feared that their sons might spend their earnings on themselves rather than send their money home to the family in Ireland. These parental fears may have rested on fact, for Irishman John Francis Maguire contends that Irish girls living in American cities sent home more money than did city-dwelling Irish men (1969, 321).[8] But whether they had positive or negative feelings about their children's emigration, parents missed them when they were gone. Irish writer J. M. Synge mentions a balladeer in County Kerry who sang the laments of Irish mothers whose children all go to America (1980, 106). Irish fathers, too, mourned the loss of their children through emigration. In the early 1920s, one Irishman said, "Every man has his rearing, except the poor Irishman. This is the way with him. When his children grow up, they scatter from him like the little birds" (Colum 1937, 174).

Some parents actively opposed their daughters' emigration. Irish domestic Bridget McGeoghegan's mother so strongly opposed her daughter's leaving that when Bridget's brother sent her the passage she said, "My mother hid it on me" because "she didn't want me to leave, naturally." Bridget's sister, however, told her where the passage ticket was hidden, and Bridget

8. Maguire notes, however, that Irish men living in the country or in small towns, which offered fewer opportunities to spend their wages, were faithful in sending remittances home to Ireland (1969, 321–22).

took action: "So I took the ticket with me, and I just went right to the American consul [in Derry] and I entered the ticket. So there was nothing she [her mother] could do about it then," and thus Bridget went to the Boston area in 1923 (1985, 9, 10). Some emigrants felt sorry for the parents left behind in Ireland, as Hannah Collins's correspondence shows. Regarding Nora McCarthy's parents in Ballinlough, Leap, County Cork, she wrote on May 12, 1898, "I suppose they feels quiet lonesome. they aint got anybody home with them" (O'Malley Collection).

The American Wake

For much of the nineteenth century, when young people left Ireland, it was "for good." In recognition of this fact, paralleling the wake for the dead, the "American Wake" was held in Ireland for both male and female emigrants because "people made very little difference between going to America and going to the grave." Combining laughter and sadness, the American Wake was held the night before the emigrant's departure, and often stretched into the wee hours of the morning. These affairs tried the emotions of emigrants. According to one woman, speaking of her own American Wake held in the 1890s, "It would not have been so bad," she said, "only in the morning everyone said so-long to you and you would know by them that they never expected to see you again. It was as if you were going out to be buried" (Schrier 1958, 85, 89).

Over time, as transportation improvements increased the safety and comfort of an emigrant's voyage to America, and consequently increased the possibility that the emigrant might someday return to Ireland for a visit, the American Wake was sometimes transformed into a party that emphasized merriment over mourning. Irish domestic Margaret Convery said that when she left for America in 1914, they "had a big dance that night, the night before we left . . . and all the neighbors came" (1991, 32). Irish nanny Ann Sexton, who left County Cavan for Brooklyn in 1922, said that the night before she emigrated, "they give me a big party, and I loved to dance then. . . . [T]here was two violins, and it was a really nice party" (1986, 8). And Irish nanny Helen Flatley, who emigrated in 1928, said, "When I left, they had a party. They used to call it the farewell do. . . . [A]ll the neighbors came and they danced and they danced and they sang and, oh, everything like that. It was a great thing. And all the families, you know, when somebody left for America, . . . oh, it was celebrated, but at the same time it was very lonely" (1996a).

The American Letter

Although other emigrants—for example, English, Scottish, and Swedish emigrants—also wrote letters home, the "American letters," those letters sent home to friends and relations in Ireland by the Irish who went to America, are seen as especially important in having encouraged Irish people to come to America (Schrier 1958, 40–42). It appears that they "pulled" the Irish Bridgets to America, for it was reputed that girls from rural Ireland more often heard about employment opportunities for domestic servants through American letters than they did through Dublin newspapers (J. Bourke 1993, 66). American letters convinced the parents of Josephine Keenan, who worked for the telephone company, to emigrate from County Sligo to Sheepshead Bay, Brooklyn, in 1930. In their American letters, her emigrant relatives insisted, "'You have to come to America, it's wonderful.' You know, 'The land of opportunity, you'll be so happy, we'll all be together'" (1994, 10, 13).

The arrival of the American letter, penned by the literate themselves or their literate friends or acquaintances, occasioned excitement in rural Ireland, where friends and relations shared its contents.[9] On May 24, 1895, from Ballinlough, Leap, County Cork, Katie McCarthy wrote to her sister Nora in Massachusetts that upon the receipt of Nora's first letter home, "all the neighbours around come to the house to hear it read, they speaks about you every hour" (O'Malley Collection). Illiterate recipients brought their letters to the parish priest, a schoolmaster, or another literate person to be read. Sissy O'Brien remembered that during her youth in the post-Famine period, no matter how busy her mother might have been, she took the time to read American letters brought to her by illiterate parents eager for news from their emigrant children. Sissy said that never would her mother "keep the 'caller at the door' waiting, especially when this was an old father or mother bringing a letter from America to be read." Such letters, Sissy said, reminded Irish parents "that they were loved as of old and not forgotten" by their far-away children (Carbery 1973, 64).

9. The *Boston Pilot*, which was widely read by the Irish throughout America, contains advertisements for women looking for someone to write their American letters. The May 29, 1852, issue contains the following advertisement: "The subscriber begs leave to acquaint those of her female friends wishing to communicate with their friends in Ireland, that she will be happy to write letters for them, at her residence, No 3 Province street, Boston, from 10 a.m. to 8 p.m. Anne Brady" (7).

American Money

Even during the Famine period, female Irish domestics were opening savings accounts in American banks. Approximately 31 percent (191 out of 621) of the female depositors listed in volume 1 of the records of New York City's Emigrant Industrial Savings Bank were Irish immigrants employed in some form of private domestic service (Rich 2000). In addition, about 8 percent of the *total* depositors (415 out of 5,000) listed in volume 2 were Irish Bridgets (Rich 2005). At least some of the money they saved probably ended up in remittances sent home to Ireland; in fact, a nineteenth-century Irish economist credited female Irish domestics in America as the original source of almost 33 percent of all the money in circulation in Ireland in the 1870s (Diner 2007, 141). By 1880 the Irish Bridgets in Boston remitted close to two hundred thousand dollars annually through one Boston money exchange alone. So great were the remittances Irish emigrants sent via their American letters that they prompted the 1871 establishment of a postal money-order system between the United States and the United Kingdom. Prepaid passage tickets, cash, money orders, and bank drafts numbered among the various methods used to send remittances to Ireland. Indicative of the pull of American money is that "prepaid passage tickets . . . paid for more than 75 per cent of all Irish emigration in the fifty years following the famine" (Schrier 1958, 106–7, 111).[10]

Irish people, however, distinguished between passage money or prepaid passage tickets and money for the family's use at home, the latter being what they considered true "American money" (Schrier 1958, 110). Usually small in amount, American money frequently was sent at Christmas or Easter. Mary Malone McHenry, for example, wrote from Middle Granville, New York, to her parents in County Kilkenny, Ireland, on December 1, 1891, that, "as now Chrismas is coming I taught I would send ye two pounds for a preasant so ye would have a good Christmas of it" (Lynch-Brennan Collection) (see ill. 6). An American letter that came without any money enclosed was called "an empty one" (Carbery 1973, 64).

American money greatly improved the material life of the Irish at home. It was used mainly to pay the rent on the family farm, but it had other uses, including funding the building of farmhouses. An 1847 account tells

10. Cormac Ó Gráda indicates that Schrier's estimation of the remittance money sent to Ireland by emigrants is probably conservative (1995, 228).

6. Mary Malone McHenry. *Courtesy of Anne Shalvoy Graham, Mary's granddaughter.*

of American money (equivalent to ten pounds) that was sent at Christmas being used to pay obligations and purchase food and fuel (E. Smith 1980, 122). According to the Irish Folklore Commission Collection, the mother of an emigrant Irish girl boasted, "'We're getting a pound a month: we can put on the kettle now.' Another girl emigrated: the monthly amount increased to two pounds. Others went. The family house was slated and general improvements made" (Neville 1995, 207).

American money also provided the "fortune" necessary for some Irish girls to marry at home. So important was American money to the family at home in Ireland that the money sent home by Irish Bridgets in New York reputedly kept some families in turn-of-the-century Connemara from destitution (Synge 1980, 142). Members of the McCarthy family of Ballinlough, Leap, County Cork, certainly appreciated the American money they received. On December 30, 1895, Katie McCarthy wrote to her sister Nora, an Irish domestic in Massachusetts, that "we never can return ye thanks enough for your Christmas present. . . . Father is twice the man since he got the letter. He is very thankful to ye for sending the money. Mother is going to leap now changing it" (O'Malley Collection). That is not to say that all Irish people lauded the remittances sent home from America. Some, like Ellen Mahony, who in the 1860s was a New York City–based proponent of Irish freedom, saw emigrant remittances as propping up the British colonial system in Ireland (M. Kelly 2005, 58).

The Irish Bridgets sent home American money throughout the period 1840 to 1930. Betty Fitzgerald Arnold said of her late mother, Mary Anne (Mollie) Ryan, who emigrated from Castletownroche, County Cork, Ireland, in 1925, "She came to this country, she worked as a domestic and she used to get ninety dollars a month. And she would send it all back home" (1996) (see ill. 7). In sending home American money, Irish domestics made the girls at home aware of the money to be made in the United States, and thus American money can be seen as "pulling" other Irish girls to America.

Family members left behind in Ireland may never have understood how their emigrant girls suffered to save the money they remitted to Ireland. Testimony to their privations comes from a remittance agent in West Troy (now Watervliet), New York. He said that to ensure that they sent home the maximum amount possible, some Irish Bridgets walked the fifty to sixty miles from where they worked in Vermont to West Troy (Potter 1960, 121). Irish people at home apparently knew little of the loneliness attendant on emigration and the difficulties life abroad entailed. Irish author Alice Taylor rightly asks, "When the dollars came back across the Atlantic to help those at home, was it ever realized what a price in human suffering was paid for them?" (Pfeiffer and Shaffrey 1990, 11). Apparently not, because some parents have been criticized for using their emigrant children, especially their daughters, as money machines—extracting from them as much American money as possible (Neville 1992, 280). Because of the American money that they sent home in their American letters, such emigrant children served as a kind of old-age insurance for their parents (Fitzpatrick 1989, 606). Other Irish parents, however, felt differently about the money their emigrant children sent them, "knowing the bitterness of having to send their young boys and girls to work abroad for a few pounds return" (Colum 1937, 194).

Nonetheless, American money may have looked like easy money to the Irish at home. An expression used in Donegal illustrates this point—there

Photograph of bearer

Mary Anne Ryan

JAN 25 1932

This passport is good for travel in all countries unless otherwise limited.

This passport is valid for two years from the date of issue unless limited to a shorter period.

4

5

I, the undersigned, Secretary of State of the United States of America, hereby request all whom it may concern to permit safely and freely to pass, and in case of need to give all lawful aid and protection to Mary Anne Ryan a citizen of the United States.

The bearer is accompanied by his

Wife,

Minor children,

Given under my hand and the seal of the Department of State at Washington Oct. 21st 1930

Henry L Stimson

2

Description of bearer

Height 5 feet 2 inches.

Hair Brown

Eyes Blue

Distinguishing marks or features:

Place of birth Castletownroche, Ireland

Date of birth Jan 26, 1904

Occupation Maid

Mary Anne Ryan

Signature of bearer

3

7. Mary Anne (Mollie) Ryan's passport. *Courtesy of Donald F. Arnold, Jr., Mollie's grandson.*

something acquired without much trouble was likened to "money from America" (Schrier 1958, 93). The American letters and the American money they received gave rise to an Irish view of America as an "El Dorado"; this view of America held sway in many Irish minds through the twentieth century. As Irish domestic Margaret Convery, said, "I always felt America, you didn't have to work. You just got the money for nothing. So I found out different" (1991, 15).

Returned Yanks

Between 1858 and 1867, Irish emigrants returning to Ireland, "returned Yanks," as the Irish called them, were more likely to have been males than females, according to David Fitzpatrick's analysis of the lists of passengers arriving in Ireland from America at that time (1989, 567). Later, however, the situation was different, for from 1895 until 1913 more women than men returned to Ireland, and many of the returning women were Irish Bridgets, having worked in domestic service in America (Fitzpatrick 1996, 634–35). Some of these women went back to Ireland temporarily, for a visit, whereas others, such as Irish domestic Margaret Hegarty, who returned from New York to County Kerry early in the twentieth century, made their stay permanent by marrying in Ireland (R. White 1998, 78, 87, 90).[11]

The female returned Yanks who went to back to America and the ones who remained in Ireland both affected the material culture of Ireland. Asenath Nicholson reported that during her travels in Ireland just before the Great Famine, she spoke with one Irishman, who had himself returned from America, who observed, "This goin' to America, makes the Irish, when they

11. Kerby A. Miller suggests that some servants earned money in America that they hoped to use as dowries upon return to Ireland (1985, 408). J. M. Synge cites Irish informants who claimed that girls did return with money to marry in Ireland. An Irishman in Mayo told Synge that so many female returned Yanks had come home to marry that "there is hardly a marriage made in the place that the women hasn't been in America" (1980, 146). Arnold Schrier's work also supports Miller's thesis—he cites Irish informants who recalled women who returned to Ireland from America with money sufficient to secure husbands, despite the fact that they might have been old and unattractive at that point in their lives (1958, 131). Nonetheless, as David Fitzpatrick points out, good statistical records were not kept on the Irish returning from America, so it is difficult to speculate accurately about them (1989, 567). With regard to returned Irish domestics who married in Ireland, I feel compelled to note that Margaret Hegarty's return to Ireland brought her a hard life and unhappiness; she told her daughter Sara Walsh White that she was sorry she came back to Ireland (R. White 1998, 80, 89).

come home, quite altered entirely." Nicholson's comments on her visits to the Irish homes of families whose daughters she had employed as domestic servants in America support this contention. She noted that she spoke with the mother of one of these girls who mentioned that her daughter, on a return visit to Ireland, turned the family's cabin upside down, making them clean it. Nicholson also noticed that the cabins of Irish females who had worked in service in America were much cleaner than their neighbors' homes (1847, 172, 88, 334–35). At the turn of the twentieth century Irish writer J. M. Synge likewise noticed the difference between cabins of female returned Yanks and their neighbors' cabins. He saw a returned Yank's cabin that he said "was perfectly clean" (1980, 150).

Their clothing identified returned Yanks, for Synge referred to one as wearing "a new American blouse" (1980, 150). Female returned Yanks were the objects of intense scrutiny in Ireland because of their fashionable clothing. An informant told the Irish Folklore Commission: "A woman of course would have more 'style' on coming home than a man and all the other women would manoeuvre into a good position at the chapel gate to insure that they would get a look at the Yankee. Then when they went home they would discuss her clothes from shoes to hat" (Neville 1995, 212). Irish author Padraic Colum commented that although new American-influenced clothing was worn in Ireland, simultaneously older forms of female Irish dress persisted. Of the women he observed at an Irish funeral in the first quarter of the twentieth century, he commented that the returned females in attendance brought with them "dresses and fashions that were incongruous here," while other Irish women at the funeral "still wore the peasant shawl" (1937, 180).

Both Synge and Colum also noted American influences on Irish homes. Synge commented that the Mayo home of a female returned Yank displayed "a large photograph of . . . the Sistine Madonna," whereas Irish cabins, he contended, tended to display "the hideous German oleographs on religious subjects" sold by traveling salesmen (1980, 150). Colum, noting that in the bedroom of one home the bed was draped with American dresses, said such items were "expressive of the influences that are changing rural Irish life" (1937, 174).

Returned Yanks, notable for their fastidiousness and fashionable dress, as well as their diligence and self-assuredness, brought to Ireland new standards of material culture, and new standards of personal comportment. They not only broadcast the attractions of America, thereby stimulating further emigration, but also showed a different mode of living to those

Irish who would never emigrate (Schrier 1958, 133–34). The result, as David Fitzpatrick puts it, was that "the cumulative impact of emigration was to Americanise the mentality of the Irish female whether or not she left Ireland" (1987, 163).

The emigration of the Irish Bridgets between 1840 and 1930 involved the "pull" factors discussed in this chapter, as well as the "push" factors delineated in chapter 2. Chain migration pulled them to America, whose attractions were made known to them through the American letter, American money, and returned Yanks. So they left, in search of husbands, employment, and more adventure than they thought was available to them in rural Ireland. In the United States, as will be shown in the chapters that follow, they found employment in a familiar category, domestic service.

The World of the American Mistress

The Irish Bridget migrated to live and work as a domestic servant in an American world that was very different from Ireland. Most of the Irish Bridgets were Roman Catholics, while the America to which they came was a very Protestant country. In fact, prior to the mass immigration of the Irish in the nineteenth century, being American was seen as equivalent to being Protestant. These Irish girls came from people of limited means, but generally lived and worked in the homes of middle- and upper-middle-class Americans. In the urban Northeast, in the homes of (generally) Protestant Americans, Bridget and her American mistress (as the female employer was known) faced each other across a gulf of class, cultural, ethnic, and religious differences. It was the American home, rather than urban politics or industry, that constituted the most familiar frontier of contact between Irish immigrants and middle-class Americans. Americans' view of the Irish, and the Irish view of Americans, was strongly influenced by the close personal interaction of Americans with the Irish servants who both lived and worked in the private American home.

Separate Spheres

Urbanization and industrialization transformed the American Northeast in the nineteenth century. Americans began moving to cities in large numbers between 1820 and 1860. Men's work, but not women's domestic work, moved away from the home. And with this shift came the increased differentiation between women's and men's roles and work that constituted the separation of the sexes that Alexis de Tocqueville thought helped democracy to function in America (1990, 214). Historians have used several terms to describe this nineteenth-century cultural schema of separate spheres: *woman's sphere,* that is, the ideology of the *cult of domesticity,* and the *cult of true womanhood,* and I shall use these terms interchangeably (Cott 1977; Welter 1976).

It was not a nineteenth-century innovation to assign women responsibility for the domestic sphere (Kerber 1988, 18). The idea of separate spheres, the view that the public sphere, wherein men worked outside the home, was a specifically male sphere, whereas women's sphere was restricted to the private sphere of the home, however, involved a new and strong emphasis on women's roles as wives and mothers. In the private physical space of the home they were to wield a positive "female influence" over their families, and hence society at large; in the home they had a "social mission" (Sklar 1973, 237; 1991, 174).

Domesticity was both a positive and a negative force for middle-class women in urban America. On the one hand, it restricted them, circumscribing their behavior and limiting their world to the domestic one. In the cult of true womanhood, the expectation was that women would demonstrate certain attributes—"piety, purity, submissiveness and domesticity"—adherence to which would bring them "happiness and power" and without which "all was ashes" (Welter 1976, 21). On the other hand, it joined them together—for example, in supportive friendships with other women that provided them with deep, meaningful, emotional connections to each other (Cott 1977, 193). It was also seen as a source of power. Catharine Beecher, for example, believed that it was women who made democracy work, for it was women, in bearing children, who issued the most precious product of a democracy—future citizens. Beecher saw women "as an elite who had special access to moral resources because they themselves were engaged in the production of a valuable resource . . . the 'character of the mass of the people.'" She espoused "domestic feminism," that is, she promoted female autonomy in, and female control of, the domestic sphere (Sklar 1991, 173, 174, 169). In the home, she believed, women could control their own lives. While Beecher's home-based feminism rested on the "self-sacrifice" of women, through which she believed women would find fulfillment, she still urged women to fight to obtain the same esteem for their work in the home that males accrued for their work in the public sphere. Her ideas provided "an ideology that gave women a central place in national life. The home and family, she believed, could be redefined as the social unit that harmonized various national interests and synchronized different individual psyches. She used this ideology to promote both cultural homogeneity and female hegemony" (Sklar 1973, xiv, 267, xiii).

With domesticity, focusing on family, women ostensibly found a sphere of influence over which they could exercise control. Such was the attention paid to their role in the home as mothers that Harvey Green has found "a cult of motherhood" embedded in domesticity (1983, 29–58). Unlike the mothers in rural Ireland discussed previously, however, middle-class American women had little actual power as wives and mothers; they had only their "influence" to deal with the duties and obligations with which they were charged (57–58). Or, as Sarah A. Leavitt puts it, "the true [American] domestic fantasy was that women held the power to reform their society through first reforming their homes" (2002, 5).

The terms *separate spheres, woman's sphere, cult of domesticity,* and *cult of true womanhood* have been both widely used and widely criticized by historians (Nicolosi 2005, 373; M. Roberts 2002, 150; Hewitt 2002, 159). But it was never so simple—the separate spheres were never completely distinct from one another, and some women used the ideology of domesticity to expand their territory and their authority (Hewitt 2002, 157). The notion of separate spheres has also been deemed inadequate "to explain the history of gender constructions, and their interactions with class, ethnicity and race" (Lasser 2001, 116). Still, the cult of true womanhood continues to be valued for suggesting "the competing forces that shaped northern white women's lives throughout the nineteenth century and the myriad responses available to them" and for providing the "groundwork for the later development of feminism by crediting women with a moral authority which implicitly empowered them to extend their moral influence outside the home" (Hewitt 2002, 161; Cruea 2005, 190).

The Material Culture of the American Home

In the world of middle-class urban American women, refinement was emphasized, good taste was associated with Christian morality, and the parlor, books, and piano were seen as indications of a family's respectability. The seat of women's domestic influence was the parlor, and having a parlor signified membership in the middle class. At mid-nineteenth-century, the parlor, featuring a center table, was the ultimate symbol of domesticity, and in this room, as the nineteenth century progressed, the presence of a piano signified refinement. In fact, "by the turn of the century, . . . anyone with serious social and musical pretensions had a piano" (Schlereth 1991, 211).

In the parlor women found a place of their own from which they could extend their "influence" outward to the world. Here, intellectual improvement took place through reading the books that, like magazines and newspapers, were more widely available at lower prices after 1830. With more materials available, reading, which was intended to improve minds, increasingly also provided entertainment.

From about 1850 until at least the 1890s, the parlor, the seat of women's power, was furnished with suites emphasizing gender distinctions—certain larger pieces such as chairs with arms were designed for men, whereas others, such as smaller armless chairs, were specifically intended for women. In the parlor straight-backed furniture encouraged the proper posture that women were supposed to display. And from around the middle until the end of the nineteenth century, parlor walls were graced with framed embroidered mottoes, copies of Italian Renaissance Madonnas, and chromolithographs, like those of Currier and Ives. Only at the end of the nineteenth century did negative reaction to the stiff propriety of the parlor lead to its replacement by the homier living room, which by the second decade of the 1900s replaced the parlor as the "true heart of the house" (Schlereth 1991, 123, 124). But parlors did not completely disappear—they live on in the modern American propensity for having a formal living room as well as an informal family room in the private home.

New foods became more widely available to middle-class Americans in this period—oranges by the 1870s and bananas by the 1880s. Irish immigrant domestic Ellen O'Loughlin's first experience with a banana was less than tasty: the priest who met her when she landed in New York from Ireland in 1893 gave her a banana to eat on the train north to her intended destination of Hoosick Falls, New York, but neglected to tell her to peel it before she ate it. Poor Ellen ate the banana, skin and all (Unger 2006)!

Sardines, newly available in cans, and celery were prestigious foods in the late nineteenth century. Two developments factored into making salad, with its aura of French glamour, a key component of middle-class American dinners: improved transportation methods involving refrigeration and the early-twentieth-century development of iceberg lettuce, which was suited for long-distance dispatch; previously, only rich Americans were able to enjoy salads. By the close of the nineteenth century, granulated white sugar became increasingly more affordable, replacing loaf sugar, and French desserts, like charlotte russe, made an impressive appearance at American dinner parties (Williams 1996, 110–25).

While coffee remained the drink of Americans, tea, a symbol of refinement whose use was formerly restricted to the elite, came into widespread use throughout America from the late 1770s on. By the mid-1830s, one result of the British East India Company's loss of control over the manufacturing and importing of tea was that more Americans drank tea (Williams 1987, 7). Tea was drunk for breakfast and at afternoon and evening teas. In the nineteenth century tea became increasingly popular not only as a special drink but also as a social event, sometimes specifically for women. It has been claimed that afternoon tea, which was generally an exclusively female affair, "helped counteract the isolation of the strictly defined confines of the 'woman's sphere' in nineteenth-century America" (10). Tea parties in the evening also became fashionable as the nineteenth century ended, and social events invoking the word *tea*, such as the "tea dance" and the "'High' or 'Sit-Down' Tea," took place into the 1930s (Williams 1996, 148; Chambers 1936, 42, 49).

With tea came use of its accoutrements, elaborate silver teapots and china serving pieces. Silver, in particular, became more widely available after the mid-nineteenth-century discovery of the Comstock Lode in the United States, and the subsequent discovery of other silver deposits elsewhere in the world led both to its increased availability and to its decreased price. Instead of laborious hand manufacture, new machine processes such as electroplating and the application, by 1870, of machine technology to its manufacture led to the mass production of elaborately designed silver-plated pieces, and new types of silver serving pieces came on the market in the late nineteenth century (Williams 1987, 5, 6; Rainwater 1987, 177, 179, 181). Aside from flatware, it was understood that a tea service was a must for the genteel middle-class home. By the second decade of the twentieth century, however, the taste for the formal entertaining signified by use of elaborate sliver and china waned as more informal entertaining became popular among middle-class Americans.

In the American home, service of food became more elaborate after the mid-nineteenth century as Americans shifted from Old English service, where all dishes were placed on the table at the same time at the start of each course, to, by the late 1870s, service à la Russe, where the courses of a meal followed a set progression in which food was placed on a sideboard and from there served to diners by servants. In service à la Russe, diners were sharply distinguished from servants.

With an increase in the elaboration of meals in middle-class homes by the 1880s came elaboration in the space and furnishing of the room in which meals were served—the dining room. Dining room furniture generally was the most costly furniture that a family owned. Sideboards, with elaborate types particularly notable at midcentury, were prominent furnishings in dining rooms. Dining rooms provided a venue in which, through their decoration of it, women could demonstrate their artistry and taste. By the end of the nineteenth century the presence of a dining room in one's home came to signify one's membership in the middle class (C. Clark 1987, 147–71).

Manners

Manners as a code of conduct for the middle class became increasingly important over the nineteenth century, with etiquette books serving as the "social bible" of the American middle class. The proper behavior detailed in etiquette books provided "a means of maintaining social order," and etiquette, or adherence to proper social forms, served to distinguish refined, genteel middle-class people from those individuals lower on the social scale, like the Catholic Irish (Williams 1996, 17, xv, 21–22). The middle-class stress on manners insinuated that "'bad' manners made people poor or kept them poor," so it is unsurprising that etiquette books did not even mention new immigrants (Ames 1992, 211; Kasson 1995, 54). In the etiquette-conscious American world, demonstrating proper manners at table was of crucial importance. The late-nineteenth-century formal dinner party has been described as "an excruciating ordeal by fork, 'the great trial' on which one's social reputation depended" (Kasson 1987, 132). It was a trial that, some, like Silas Lapham, who got drunk at the Coreys' dinner party in William Dean Howells's 1885 novel, *The Rise of Silas Lapham,* failed, to their chagrin.[1]

The Middle Class

As noted, the concept of domesticity, which became prominent around 1830, has been used by historians as a notion for understanding American women's experience in the nineteenth and early twentieth centuries. The terms *domesticity, cult of true womanhood,* and *separate spheres,* however, all really refer to the experience of the few—white middle- to upper-middle-class women in urban America—rather than to the experience of all American women in the nineteenth century. There never was an all-inclusive unity of American women during this period. Class, cultural, ethnic, racial, and religious differences among women militated against it.

1. Richard L. Bushman discusses the contradictions and tension inherent in the adoption by middle-class people in the American Republic of gentility originating in aristocracy. He concludes that to assert their new power, the American middle class had no other model to emulate but aristocracy: "In the very moment when they were attempting to eradicate aristocratic rule from government, they were compelled to cover themselves with an aristocratic veneer—to ratify their new authority" (1993, 409–13).

The separate sphere of women rested on the economic prosperity that resulted from the interplay of urbanization, industrialization, and democratic capitalism that led to the rise of the American middle class. But this new middle class was anxious about its position in a fluid society. It felt threatened by immigrants, first the Irish, with their alien (to Americans) Roman Catholic religion and peasant non-Anglo-Saxon culture, and later, after 1880, by the new immigrants from southern and eastern Europe, including Jews, Italians, and Greeks. The Know-Nothing movement of the 1850s stands as testimony to the public anti-Irish and anti-Catholic feeling then extant in America (Levine 1966, 62–63). An incident from the history of the Irish in Danbury, Connecticut, serves to illustrate how anti-Catholicism worked out in everyday life. The Know-Nothing Party was powerful enough in Danbury to ensure that when Catholics of the newly formed St. Peter's parish requested permission to use the courthouse as a space in which to hold mass until they could build a church, their request was denied. From then on, the priests of St. Peter's served as the Irish community spokespersons in opposition to the nativist *Danbury Times* (Devlin 1984, 36). The rise of the American Protective Association, an organization at its zenith in the mid-1890s, indicates that such anti-Catholic nativism endured over the nineteenth century. Anti-Catholic nativism and Anglo-Saxon nativism have been identified as two of the three themes running through the history of American nativism, with anti-Catholic nativism said to have "completely overshadowed every other nativist tradition" (Higham 1994, 80–87, 6, 9, 11). It is further argued that anti-Catholicism persists in modern American life (Jenkins 2003).

Employers and Domestic Service

Standards of cleanliness rose with industrialization, urbanization, and the rise of the urban middle class and the spread of gentility in America. With a newfound affluence attributable to the economic benefits of industrialization, middle-class women had the means to free themselves from the daunting tasks of housework by hiring servants.[2] Of course, the Irish Bridget was employed in the households of the famous and the wealthy, as well as the households of middle-class Americans. Had it not been for her County

2. How many American households employed at least one servant at any given time between 1840 and 1930 is difficult to ascertain. Servants were more a factor in urban that rural American life. Mary Pattison estimated that about 8 percent of *all* American families employed servants in 1918 (1918, 52).

Tipperary–born maid-of-all-work Margaret Maher, whose employment in the Dickinson house commenced in 1869, Emily Dickinson's poems might never have been published (A. Murray 1999).[3] In addition, from the late 1830s through the mid–nineteenth century, female Irish servants were employed at Sunnyside, the Tarrytown, New York, home of Washington Irving; at Lindenwald, the Kinderhook, New York, home of President Martin Van Buren from the 1840s to the 1860s; and at Sagamore Hill, President Theodore Roosevelt's Long Island home, in the late nineteenth and early twentieth centuries (Haley 1994; P. West 1992; Hagedorn and Roth n.d., 52, 58, 59).

Hiring servants provided mistresses with free time for such pursuits as writing letters, reading, and taking morning naps. It also provided women with the leisure to make formal social calls. If those whom they visited were not at home, proper etiquette required the visitor to leave her engraved calling card in the card receiver proffered by the servant who greeted her. Such formal social-call etiquette was practiced from the mid–nineteenth century until the twentieth. By the middle 1920s, however, among young people in general, the formal social call was replaced by less formal social visiting that did not involve use of calling cards, although young women were admonished to make calls to "older ones who have invited them to their parties," and men were advised "to pay visits to their hostesses or to leave cards at the houses where they have dined and danced continuously and casually during the season" (*Vogue's Book* 1925, 233–34). An etiquette writer of the 1930s made reference to the "visiting card" having replaced the calling card (Chambers 1936, 40–41).

Employing servants also provided women with the time to "do good" through volunteer work for "temperance, moral reform, Sabbatarianism, domestic and foreign missions, and aid to the poor" (Dudden 1983, 241). American women worked to establish the principle that middle-class

3. Aife Murray (1999) argues that employment of a domestic in the Dickinson household freed Emily from household chores and thus provided her with the time she needed to write poetry. According to Murray, Maher's trunk served as the repository for Dickinson's manuscript books. Maher promised Dickinson that she would burn the poems upon Emily's death. It is lucky for posterity that, despite her conflicted feelings on the matter, Maher broke her promise. According to Murray, Maher was born in 1841 and, with her siblings, left Ireland for America at age fourteen; she returned to Ireland just once thereafter, to bring her parents to the United States.

propriety dictated that genteel Americans did not drink alcohol. When her husband, Rutherford B. Hayes, became president of the United States in 1877, Lucy Hayes prohibited serving alcohol in the White House, earning her the nickname "Lemonade Lucy" (Rorabaugh 1987, 36–37). Root beer was ensconced as the "National Temperance Drink" in America (Williams 1996, 137).

Many middle-class Protestant Americans saw alcohol and the saloon as social evils. Unsurprisingly, their female Irish servants' acceptance of drink as a part of social life was repugnant to middle-class American mistresses holding such views. Middle-class Americans were also threatened by the independence represented by laboring men in saloons. Probably the most important venue for the American temperance campaign was through the Women's Christian Temperance Union (WCTU), led by Frances Willard; it became "the most powerful middle-class woman's organization in the United States." Adherents of the WCTU blamed alcohol for such social evils as "crime, poverty, wife beating, child abandonment, and political corruption" (Rorabaugh 1987, 41). Middle-class American women thought that if alcohol was outlawed and the saloon eradicated, they could bring about broad social reform. Instead, however, America's experiment with Prohibition, which began with ratification of the Eighteenth Amendment to the United States Constitution in 1919 (it was implemented in 1920) and ended with its 1933 repeal by the Twenty-first Amendment, showed that Prohibition fostered crime and corruption.

Securing women the right to vote was the second of the WCTU's two major goals. Because temperance advocates believed that in some respects women were the superiors of men, they did not trust men to protect women's welfare, and instead fought for suffrage for themselves. As historian Faye Dudden points out, however, women's quest for suffrage was facilitated by their reliance on other females, as middle-class American women used the leisure that the employment of servants afforded them to fight to secure themselves the vote. Famous feminists such as Elizabeth Cady Stanton employed Irish domestics. Apparently, she shared the then prevalent negative view of Irish servants, for she revealed in her correspondence that "she feared being hung for 'breaking the pate of some stupid Hibernian for burning my meat or pudding on some company occasion'" (Dudden 1983, 241, 121).

For middle-class American women, as for middle-class British women, hiring servants also advertised class standing; servants were status symbols for the family. In the second half of the nineteenth century, the demand for servants increased; in 1860 it was said that even "families who have barely income enough to pay their rent and food and clothing are driven to keep at least one servant," so there were plenty of domestic service jobs available ("Household Service" 1860, 408). Few native-born Protestant American women would take up low-status domestic service work, whereas Irish immigrant women provided a pool of eager, if generally untrained, workers willing to be employed as domestics. Their gender was deemed sufficient to make them eligible for this type of work. The fact that most of them spoke English was seen as an additional advantage. And so their "service, in the want of better," was deemed "indispensable" ("Your Humble Servant" 1864, 54). By the mid-nineteenth century, the Irish Bridget became a recognized factor in middle-class American domestic life in urban northeastern America.

Middle-class American women enthusiastically embraced the idea of turning over the most onerous of their domestic chores to others, namely, their Irish servants. But since most of these young Irish girls came from material circumstances that, as described in chapter 1, were primitive in comparison with the material culture of the middle-class home in the urban Northeast, they were generally unprepared for the work that constituted American domestic service. Mary Theresa Meehan McGowan, who emigrated from County Mayo, Ireland, in 1921 when she was almost fifteen, said that in her first post as a live-in domestic in the home of some well-off people in St. Louis, Missouri, she experienced "culture shock," so different was this house, which she termed a "mansion," from the "thatched roof" house, lacking indoor conveniences, in which she had grown up in Ireland (Janet Nolan 2004, 81, 82).

Because the American mistress found training servants to be hard work, she wanted to employ servants who were already trained. She did not wish to spend the time that was supposed to constitute her leisure training servants, and so she resented the inexperience of Irish servants (DeForest 1855, 329; Herrick 1904, 31). The fact that some middle-class American women did not themselves know much about proper methods of executing housework just compounded the problem (Neal 1857a, 520–22; Barker 1915, 5). In addition, it irked American mistresses that, despite their lack of training, Irish servants felt justified in demanding high wages. Then, too, mistresses found the claims of Irish serving girls to be descended from Irish heroes and royalty irrelevant to their domestic duties, noting that their allegedly prestigious background did not improve their ability to do housework (Spofford 1977, 62–64).

Thus, the groundwork was laid for complaints about Irish servants, and ridicule of them. Foreign travelers visiting the United States, such as Harriet Martineau, viewed with sympathy the plight of the American mistress, forced to rely on "low Irish" for her domestics (Wittke 1956, 44). With the post-Famine improvement in the material life of the rural Irish, and with Irish girls' use of the domestic training available in Ireland to prepare them for service in America, criticism of the ignorance of Irish servant girls waned somewhat, but it did not disappear. Comment on the deficiencies of Irish servants continued in popular American literature and the advice literature from the nineteenth century into the twentieth. Ridiculing the Irish domestic servant was not an exclusively American phenomenon, however, as disparaging the female Irish domestic servant in Australia was known as "Biddyism" (Hearn 1993, 103).

In America, the Irish servant was said to be guilty of "ignorance, rawness, . . . stupidity" (Bridget 1871). "Bridget's ignorance and awkwardness" were such that employers complained that "'these Irish servants are the plague of our lives'" ("Your Humble Servant" 1864, 53–54). Biddy was unfamiliar with the concept of drinking glasses, "ignorant of the names of utensils," and, in general, "ignorant of the manners of the country" (Harrington 1855; Bridget 1871). Bridget was also wont to take her duties less than seriously—the mistress was likely to "find cuffs and collars tucked away in odd holes and corners, instead of being washed and ironed." The mistress might also find other mementos of Bridget's questionable work habits such as "precious glass and china broken, and no word told of it till the moment of its imperative need for use," prompting some to call for making maids pay for any china that, through carelessness, they might break (Bridget 1871; Springsteed 1894, 126; Herrick 1904, 18). Clarence Cook blamed the "carelessness" and "slovenliness" of "the invasion of the Biddy tribe from the bogs of Ireland" for the loss of "certain ways of living that were pleasant" in America (1995, 271).

Although it is likely that many Irish servants would have been raised on the bland and limited diet discussed in chapter 1, the complaint was made that once presented with the rich foods available in her employer's home, the Irish Bridget learned to love them, and sometimes indulged in "savory dishes to the point of sickness" ("Your Humble Servant" 1864, 56; Bridget 1871). Bridget was known to complain if the food presented to her was not up to her new standards (Barker 1915, 36). She was said to insist on having for her own use "coffee, tea, sugars, butter . . . cost what they may." As previously noted, to her employer's chagrin, the Irish maid also was said to avail herself of her employer's tea, sweetened with the employer's sugar, and, in accordance with Irish notions of hospitality, to generously share it, as well as her employer's food, with her visitors ("Your Humble Servant" 1864, 56–57; "The Servant Question" 1865, 528; Bowker 1871, 497; Bridget 1871).[4]

Employers also found fault with Irish servant girls for the manner in which they spoke the English language, terming them "laden with an accent difficult to comprehend" (Bridget 1871). Information that an Irish maid was fired from her job because "the people said they couldn't keep her because they didn't want the children to pick up her English" wended its way back to Ireland, where it was eventually recorded in the archives of the Irish Folklore Collection (Neville 1992, 277).

A theme that repeats itself in employer complaints about the Irish Bridget is that she most definitely did not display the submissiveness expected of American women in the cult of true womanhood. Because there was a long tradition of assertive women in Irish culture, and because it is likely that it was the most spirited and ambitious of Irish women who came to America, the Irish Bridget was feisty in decided contrast to the ideal of the submissive woman. According to employers, Bridget was known for her "self-assertion" ("The Morals and Manners" 1873, 7). She was "insolent," "defiant," had a "temper," and "made it a point to be cross whenever there was company" (K. Sutherland 1852, 393–94). She was known for being "impudent" and for her "impertinence" ("Our Domestic Service" 1875, 273; Bridget 1871). She demanded "all her evenings out" and when told to be in by ten o'clock instead remained out until midnight (Bridget 1871; Bowker 1871, 497). Even the *Boston Pilot,* termed a "newspaper bible" for the Irish in America, testified to servant assertiveness (Potter 1960, 600). In a January 8, 1870, article, the *Pilot* reported that a servant girl filed suit against her employer because the number of people in her employer's family was greater than the number for which she had contracted—nine people rather than five. She won her suit, recovering an additional monthly allowance.[5] As late as 1934,

4. Pamela Horn states that servants in Britain who helped themselves to the employers' tea and sugar, and shared it with their friends and relatives, sometimes were taken to court for petty thievery by their employers (1975, 138).

5. Although the *Boston Pilot* article does not specifically identify the servant as being Irish, given the number of Irish servants and the Irish readership of the *Pilot*, I believe it logical to infer that the servant girl was Irish. The paper would have been more likely to specify the servant's ethnicity had she *not* been Irish.

an author complained of the faults and assertiveness of the Irish servant girl. It seems that an employer, attempting to fire a waitress with a "Hibernian temper," was dismayed that the waitress's initial response to her dismissal was to argue that "she will not leave and that, what is more, she will call in a policeman. (Her brother is on the police force)" ("A Dowager's Advice" 1934, 24).

Employers complained about the "uppishness" or "pretentiousness" of the Irish Bridget, who was said to scrutinize potential employment situations to see if they met with her notions of "gentility" and the exacting standards of her sense of "her own respectability" before agreeing to accept such employment ("Your Humble Servant" 1864, 54). Although it was clear to employers that "the ordinary mistress . . . occupies a higher sphere than the one where her servant dwells," to the annoyance of employers, the Irish Bridget seemingly was unaware of the distinction in class between mistress and maid ("Mistress and Maid" 1885, 442). Instead, as one employer declared, "servant-girls understand themselves to be politically and theoretically our equals" (Spofford 1977, 89). And so Bridget was known to make herself comfortable sitting on the couch in her mistress's parlor, where she expected the mistress to teach her how to play the piano (DeForest 1855, 329)!

The turnover rate of servants was high in America, as it was in Britain and Ireland, and it greatly displeased American employers. Irish servants drove their mistresses to distraction by quitting their employment at inconvenient times for what seemed to employers to be absurd reasons, such as marrying an unemployed fellow Irishman (Neal 1857b, 113; Bowker 1871, 497).

It was the religious difference that really created problems between them. In 1860, one American etiquette writer alluded to such problems when she advised mistresses to permit Catholic servants "the free exercise of . . . religion," and warned them, "Nothing is . . . so dangerous as to unsettle the faith of the lower classes" (Hartley 1993, 239). The warning was made because some Protestant employers did not consider Catholics to be Christians, and therefore felt the need to convert their servants to Protestantism. Such mistresses were often nonplussed by the refusal of Catholic servants to join in family prayers in the Protestant home, and responded by firing them. So Bessy Conway was fired for refusing to join in the evening family prayers of her Protestant mistress, Mrs. Hibbard, in *Bessy Conway,* Irish immigrant author Mary Sadlier's 1861 novel, which was written specifically for Irish servant girls (1863, 205–7, iii). As Sadlier indicates in her preface to this work, she sought to warn Irish girls, especially those girls going into domestic service, of the dangers awaiting them in America. Chief among the dangers was the possibility that they might lose their Roman Catholic religion (iii).

Irish Catholic servant girls' devotion to their religion annoyed their employers. Catholic servants demanded time off to attend mass *every* Sunday (not just on occasion, as would have suited employers) and every holy day of obligation (the number of which, to the employer's way of thinking, was excessive). As one author put it, the Irish Bridget demanded "the privileges of all the funerals, and every fast and festival of her Church" (Bridget 1871). Servants' religious devotion, which might otherwise have been seen as admirable, ended up causing employers dismay because it wreaked havoc with household arrangements and mealtimes. It caused employers to face the problem of who would do the work when the servant was out of the house. Employers learned to hate the inconvenience caused them by their servants' strict practice of Catholicism.

On February 2, 1852, a writer using the name Veritas wrote an article (one of a series) in the *Boston Daily Evening Transcript* titled "Trouble in Families: Servants as They Are Nowadays." In this article Veritas questioned Irish servants' motivation for religious practice, for in the churchgoing of the Irish Bridget Veritas saw not so much piety as an effort to stay on top of the latest news in the Irish community. Bridget's requirement that there be fish for her to eat on Fridays also annoyed Protestant employers, who rarely appreciated such Catholic religious practice as abstaining from eating meat on Fridays ("Your Humble Servant" 1864, 57). In consequence of their general dissatisfaction with them, on February 7, 1852, Veritas noted in the *Transcript* that "many families have positively refused to employ Irish servants at all, and especially those who are Roman Catholic." Despite historian Richard J. Jensen's 2002 claim that job discrimination against the Irish in the form of "No Irish Need Apply" (NINA) advertisements is a myth, some employers *did* phrase their advertisements for domestics to indicate obliquely or directly that no Catholics or no Irish need apply, *Irish* and *Catholic* being deemed equivalent terms (Dudden 1983, 70).[6] Some oblique advertisements

6. Jensen's work focuses on Irish males and employment; he does admit that NINA advertisements for domestic servants did appear (2002, 407). How common such NINA advertisements for servants were in the urban Northeast in this period remains one of the great unknowns. The definitive answer awaits a comprehensive review of newspaper advertisements in cities throughout the Northeast in this period. Jensen claims, though, that the presence of large numbers of Irish women in domestic service employment is proof that they really were

stipulated that Americans were wanted; one that appeared in the *Boston Evening Transcript* on July 2, 1852, for example, stated, "Wanted—A good American Woman, of kind disposition, to take charge of a young child." Some ads specified that only Protestants were desired, as did an ad that appeared in the *Transcript* on August 5, 1863, stating, "Wanted—A Protestant Girl, as Nursery Maid and House Servant." Other advertisements tackled the issue directly. For example, an advertisement in the *Transcript* on August 3, 1868, stated that a woman was wanted "to take the care of a boy two years old, in a small family in Brookline" (see ill. 8) It stipulated, "Positively no Irish need apply." Such "No Irish Need Apply" ads were not unique to the United States. During the nineteenth century employers in Britain, where many Irish girls were also in service, sometimes specified that "No Irish Need Apply" or "Must be of the Church of England" (Horn 1975, 39).

Middle-class American women, idolized in the cult of motherhood, often turned over to strangers of another class, culture, religion, and ethnic group the raising of their own children. This decision may have satisfied certain purposes, but it sometimes created conflict and anxiety in the mother. Witness Hannah Wright Gould, who confessed to her diary in 1851 that, while in attendance at a funeral, she let the fear cross her mind that her Irish nanny, Winny, might secretly be having Mrs. Gould's baby, Lizzie, baptized a Catholic (Dudden 1983, 69).

Tension in mistress-servant relations was exacerbated by the fact that many middle-class employers had not grown up in homes where domestics

---

not discriminated against (415). He thus ignores the fact that American employers did not want female Irish servants; they employed them only because they could not get the servants they wanted—native-born American girls. With regard to NINA and Irish males, Jensen contends that the materials he searched from the online collections of the Library of Congress, Cornell University Library, the University of Michigan Library, the *New York Times*, and the *Nation* turned up very few NINA ads. I would like to point out that Irishmen, who tended to work in manual labor–type jobs, would hardly have been likely to seek employment through perusal of the want ads of the *New York Times.* I am also unimpressed by Jensen's argument that the absence of copies of NINA signs and the absence of anti-Irish rhetoric in "the corporate records of the literature of personnel management" constitute proof that NINA is a myth (409, 412). I doubt that those who employed manual laborers would have retained such signs for the benefit of future historians, and I doubt that the authors of the literature he mentions would have concerned themselves with Irishmen involved in manual labor jobs.

Boston Post Office. 6t jy 29

WANTED—A good, reliable woman to take the care of a boy two years old, in a small family in Brookline. Good wages and a permanent situation given. No washing or ironing will be required, but good recommendations as to character and capacity demanded. Positively no Irish need apply. Call at 224 Washington street, corner of Summer street.
6t jy 28

WANTED—In a small private family in

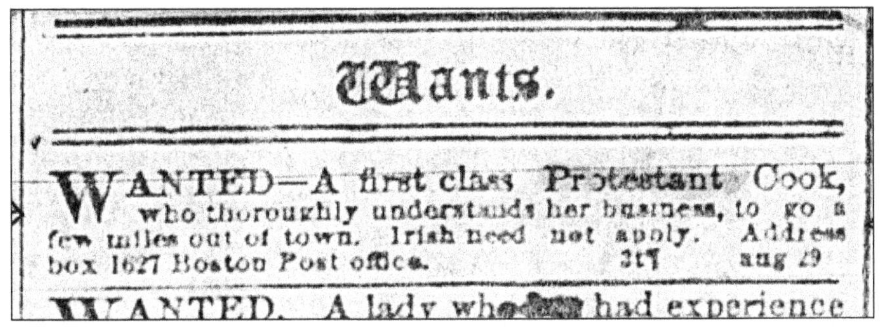

Wants.

WANTED—A first class Protestant Cook, who thoroughly understands her business, to go a few miles out of town. Irish need not apply. Address box 1627 Boston Post office. 3t* aug 29

WANTED. A lady wh[illegible] had experience

8. "No Irish Need Apply" advertisements (*Boston Evening Transcript,* August 3, 1868, 3; August 29, 1863, 3).

were employed. They were insecure about their position vis-à-vis servants, and in some cases were even afraid of them (Neal 1857b, 112). Some came to see the servant as holding the real power in the mistress-servant relation—if a mistress reprimanded her servant, or demanded too much of her, Bridget might quit, and then what would the mistress do (Spofford 1977, 30–32)?

The presence of young female servants also caused tension between the married American couples employing them. American mistresses felt that their husbands viewed difficulties with their Irish servants as emanating from the mistresses' lack of managerial skills, rather than viewing them as the servants' fault. They resented the implication that, if the husband took charge of the domestic staff, there would be no problems (K. Sutherland 1852, 392; Neal 1857b, 112–13; 1857a, 522). In addition, the fact that some husbands were sympathetic to the situation of the young servants living in their homes likely engendered the resentment of the mistresses, who saw themselves as the injured party in employer-servant relations (Browne

1852, 1). Then, too, while apparently not terribly common among the Irish, who had a reputation for chastity, out-of-wedlock pregnancies were not unknown among Irish servants, who found that promises of marriage made to them sometimes vanished before they gave birth. Blame was most often placed on the servant, whose life was often ruined in consequence, rather than on the employer (Dudden 1983, 214–16). In New York City, the Sisters of Divine Compassion, an order founded in 1886, worked with such young domestic servants who, after their pregnant state was observed, were sent away by their employers (Fitzgerald 2006, 224). Of course, not all Irish servant–male employer relationships smacked of scandal; some were genuine romances. The New England Protestant Pendleton family, for example, attributes the Catholicism of one branch of the family to Bedelia Maria Lear. Lear, who was born in Ireland, came from an orphanage in New York City to work as a housekeeper in Maine for James Watson Pendleton. They ended up falling in love and marrying in Belfast, Maine, in 1862. They proceeded to have five children who were raised as Roman Catholics (Pendleton 2002).

Irish servants in America were criticized for their love of fashionable dress, and it offended insecure middle-class Americans that their servants could dress so well that they could be mistaken for middle-class women. It was said that Bridget "is as fond of fine feathers as her mistress, and often carries a twelve-month's wages on her back. She will spend all her money for a silk dress, a lace collar, a velvet hat, and a flashy parasol, and not have a few shillings left to pay for a decent calico gown and a cotton neckerchief. Indoors and on duty she is as slattern as a beggar; outside on a Sunday or holiday she is as fine a lady as her mistress, and might readily be mistaken for her" ("Your Humble Servant" 1864, 55). In middle-class American culture, taste had long been equated with morality. So if Irish servants dressed in clothing so tasteful that they were mistaken for middle-class women, the equation was upset, to the confusion and annoyance of middle-class mistresses.

Americans displayed various reactions to their Irish servants. On February 11, 1852, in the previously mentioned series on servants in the *Boston Daily Evening Transcript,* Veritas suggested that better training would produce better servants, and so proposed a "Boston School for Cooks." Others, as Charles Dickens averred, made a joke of the whole matter of domestic service (1874, 585). This joking took on various forms. In 1860, one author of advice literature suggested, for example, that for private home entertainment,

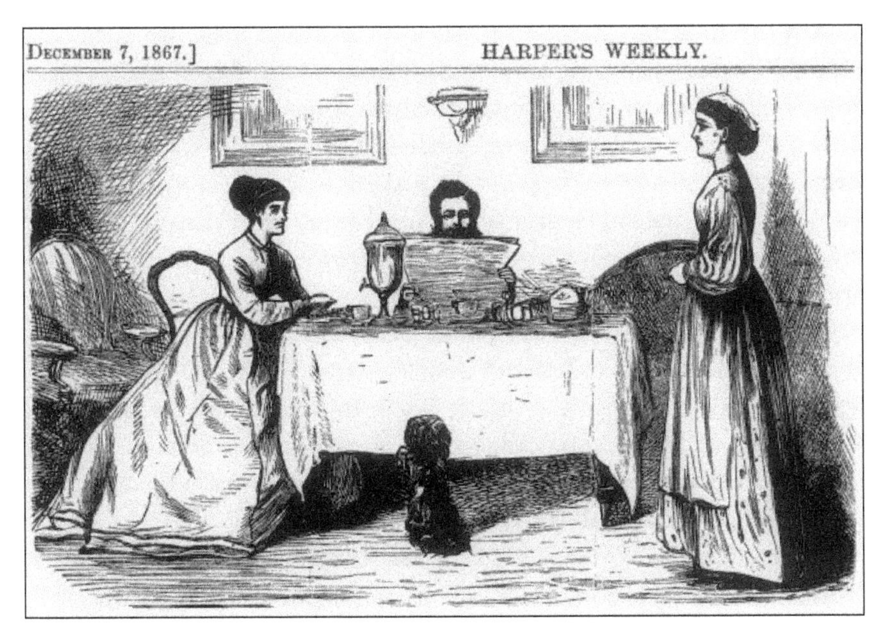

9. Bridget cartoon. The caption reads: "EGGS-CEEDINGLY CLEVER."
MISTRESS: Bridget, I told you to Boil the Eggs soft—and they're quite Hard!
BRIDGET: Soft is it, Mem? Why I've been Bilin' 'em this hour, and the Water won't get 'em Soft anyhow! (*Harper's Weekly,* December 7, 1867, 781)

a lady might wish to "personate a newly-caught Irish chambermaid" by using "the broadest brogue" and wearing "the commonest dress" (Hartley 1993, 210). Irish domestics were also satirized in cartoons (see ill. 9). In the magazine *Puck,* for example, the Irish maid was portrayed as "Queen of the Kitchen . . . in endless variations on the theme of the funnv, disorderly, hardworking but unpredictable servant girl . . . [who] lords it over her employer's family, fellow domestics and various hangers-on who frequent her kitchen for generous, unauthorized handouts and favors" (Appel 1971, 367; Murphy 2000). Interestingly enough, as early as the mid-1860s, the Irish were able to laugh at themselves, and simultaneously ridicule American mistresses. On September 9, 1865, the *Boston Pilot* ran this "Bridget" joke: "'Why Bridget,' said her mistress who wished to rally the girl for the amusement of her company, upon the fantastic ornamenting of a rich pie—'why, Bridget, did you do this? You're quite an artist how did you do it?' 'Indeed, mum, it was myself that did it,' replied Bridget. 'Isn't it puty, mum? I did it with your false teeth, mum'" (7).

On the American stage, portrayals of Irish maids presented the audience with stereotyped caricatures. Such depictions reinforced middle-class mistresses' feelings of superiority to the Irish servants they employed. The Russell Brothers, for example, were famous for their "Irish Maggie" story. It seems that Maggie, when "asked if she had put fresh water in the fishbowl, responded 'No, they ain't drunk up what I give 'em yesterday'" (Wittke 1956, 195). For upwards of thirty years, beginning in 1876, the Russell Brothers also performed onstage a very popular routine about female Irish servants (Maschio 1992, 81, 82; Wittke 1952, 215). With the development of an Irish middle class in America from about the 1880s, the popularity of caricatures of the Irish in the theater began to wane somewhat, and Irish resentment of such stereotypes increased. At a 1904 performance of Gus Hill's *McFadden's Flats,* an Irishman jumped from his seat protesting that the onstage portrayal of an Irish serving girl drinking wine "was an insult to Irish womanhood" (Wittke 1952, 220, 221; 1956, 263). In 1907, members of a United Irish Societies committee known as the "Society for the Prevention of Ridiculous and Perversive Misrepresentation of the Irish Character" heckled the Russell Brothers while they went through their routine on female Irish servants. Committee members protested that the Russell Brothers' portrayal of Irish women ridiculed "the honest, hardworking Irish Servant Girl." Later, objection was also made to the fact that the Russell Brothers raised "their dresses on stage" and included rear-end kicks as part of their routine (Maschio 1992, 85).

American employers also responded to Irish servants by increasing their physical separation from them by expanding the practice begun earlier of isolating servant quarters from family living quarters within the private home. For example, house plans in A. J. Downing's work *The Architecture of Country Houses,* first published in 1850, indicate servant bedrooms located in the attic or over the kitchen, away from family bedrooms. Separate servant entrances, separate staircases for servants, and separating kitchens from the principal rooms of a house represented planned designs to demarcate servant from employer. This setup, of course, was not a uniquely American phenomenon, as in both Britain and Ireland servant space was separated from family space, frequently by a green baize door (Horn 1975, 111–12; Hearn 1993, 19, 54, 68–69).

Employers also sought to strengthen the social distinction between mistress and servant in other ways. One way was to require that servants wear uniforms or livery. With their Irish servants they were often unsuccessful in this venture, for Irish domestics refused to wear the mid-1860s uniform of "white caps and gingham dresses" ("Your Humble Servant" 1864, 55). The uniform or dress recommended for servants in 1894 was "print dresses for morning work and . . . neat, dark costume for afternoons" (Springsteed 1894, 93). In 1904, Christine Terhune Herrick indicated that the servant uniform consisted of "caps, aprons, broad collars and cuffs, and the like," and she noted that "the tendency to introduce the wearing of livery into domestic service has grown within the past few years" (1904, 16, 88). Yet objection to a servant uniform had continued over time, for Herrick also pointed out, "In some parts of the country there are maids who object to anything that seems to suggest a livery or uniform" (16). It is difficult to determine exactly how many servants actually wore uniforms on a regular basis. In 1910, for example, it was said that the servant uniform, then consisting of "cap and apron," was worn "only on ceremonial occasions" (Rubinow and Durant 1910, 581). In the mid-1920s, however, *Vogue's Book of Etiquette* advised readers that parlor and housemaids should wear "striped calico gowns with aprons and caps in the morning; and . . . black gowns with aprons and caps in the afternoon" (1925, 261). The recollections of Mary Feely and Helen Flatley support the thesis that at least some Irish domestics wore servant uniforms in America from the late 1920s until the late 1930s. Of her uniform Feely said, "During the day, you wore white, plain white uniform. And at night, when you're serving dinner, you wore black with a white collar and cuffs . . . and white apron" (1996). Helen Flatley, on the other hand, who worked exclusively as a nanny, remembered that she "wore white . . . white shoes and lovely, lovely, white uniforms." Keeping such uniforms clean was not a problem for Flatley because "they were always washed, taken care of by the laundry. . . . [W]e had a lady who came in and did all the laundry" (1996b).[7]

To distinguish between employer and servant, mistresses also used unsubtle means such as addressing servants by their first names (at a time when very few workers were addressed this way), or calling them by their surnames only, with no honorific preceding the surname. The treatment of servants was designed to emphasize that their status was lower than the status of their employers. Lucy Maynard Salmon provided concrete examples

7. For information on servant attire in Britain into the twentieth century, see Horn 1975, 12. For information on servant attire in Ireland, see Hearn 1993, 19, 56.

when she noted in 1897 that servile behavior was required of a domestic while the servant

> receives and gives no word or look of recognition on the street except in meeting those of her own class; she is seldom introduced to the guests of the house, whom she may faithfully serve during a prolonged visit; the common daily courtesies exchanged between the members of the household are not always shown her; she takes no part in the general conversation around her; she speaks only when addressed, obeys without murmur orders which her judgment tells her are absurd, "is not expected to smile under any circumstances," and ministers without protest to the whims and obeys implicitly the commands of children from whom deference to parents is never expected. (1901, 158)

In 1878 one Catholic nun complained that some young girls aged twelve or thirteen, many of them likely Irish, who were placed out in service positions in private homes were overworked and when unable to complete the onerous tasks assigned to them were "stigmatized as being saucy, stubborn and disrespectful" (Fitzgerald 2006, 140).[8] It seems some employers wished to consider their servants to be robotic machines, rather than human beings. As one author pointed out, in the view of some employers, "the Irish Bridgets . . . are the machines" whose purpose is "to do a certain quantity of work of a particular kind" (Tomes 1871, 230).

Americans also looked longingly backward to an imagined past golden age of service, before the advent of the Irish to America, when servants were faithful family retainers known for their skill, loyalty, and long tenure with the family. To no avail, they urged that Irish servants be replaced with native-born American girls (Ellet 1857, 30; Spofford 1977, 159–61).

The major servant problem faced by American employers, especially from the late nineteenth century into the twentieth, was that the demand for servants was greater than the supply—there was a dearth of servants available to serve those who wanted them. The servant shortage, which was also a problem in Britain, elicited certain responses.[9] Some writers alleged

8. Given Maureen Fitzgerald's assertion that in New York City in 1871 more than 50 percent of the children in the Juvenile Asylum were born in Ireland, I believe it quite likely that many of these overworked girls were Irish born (2006, 117).

9. See Horn 1975, 151–56, on the responses that the 1900–1914 British servant shortage evoked.

that the servant problem was the fault of employers who treated their servants poorly. Such authors suggested that better treatment of servants, treating them respectfully, as human beings rather than as goods, would yield more contented servants, and thus happier domestic circumstances for middle-class Americans ("Your Humble Servant" 1864, 58; Bowker 1871, 501; Bridget 1871; "Mistress and Maid" 1885, 442–43; A. Miller 1905, 4). Others urged the application of business principles to domestic service as the solution to the servant problem, and one writer thought that contracts between servants and employers would improve matters (A. Miller 1905, 4; Frederick 1914). Still others saw a change in the conditions of service as necessary to solving the servant problem. In 1914, for example, Mrs. Christine Frederick suggested that the solution to the servant problem lay in having servants live out, in their own homes, and in 1915, C. Hélène Barker urged that housework be done in a businesslike work shift consisting of a set number of hours (Frederick 1914, 102; Barker 1915, 48). Others despaired of improving mistress-servant relations, and some thought the future lay in the standardization of housework, wherein it would become professionalized ("The Servant Question" 1865, 528; Pattison 1918, 58). One prescient author even foresaw the day that commercial services employing domestics would handle housework on a contract basis (Pattison 1918, 157). Still others believed that the solution to the servant problem could be found in smaller homes, where machines would replace the labor of servants ("The Passing" 1922).

Despite widespread criticism of Irish servants, their positive attributes were also recognized. Bridget was said to be possessed of a "strong arm and voluble tongue." She was "industrious," "pious," and chaste, and with her "sterling integrity" was rarely in trouble with the law. She also demonstrated her "affectionate nature" by being extremely generous to her indigent relations in Ireland ("Your Humble Servant" 1864, 57). In 1880, this generosity, which Irish servant girls continued to demonstrate from 1840 through 1930, led one writer to conclude that "there must be something radically wrong in a country so largely dependent on the alms of its scattered children" ("What Is Thought" 1880, 437). In 1906, another author lauded the good qualities of Irish domestics in the Boston area when she remarked that they were "strong in endurance, and . . . of a quick wit. . . . [T]he majority quickly adapt themselves . . . and are soon fairly competent cooks, waitresses or laundresses." The same author went on to maintain that "the Irish are, as a rule, honest, among the most moral of all nationalities." Indicating that their reputation as household workers had improved over time, she further declared that "agencies agree in pronouncing them excellent household workers" (M. Smith 1906, 7–8).

Not all American employers, therefore, castigated their Irish servants; some were actually sympathetic to their circumstances. In 1869, Catharine Beecher and Harriet Beecher Stowe reminded employers that their servants were young girls, on their own, far from home, without their parents, struggling to save money to send home to Ireland. The authors asked, "If our daughters did as much for us, should we not be proud of their energy and heroism?" (1994, 327). Stowe kept in touch with some of her Irish servants after they left her employ. In 1879, she wrote that on a visit to western America, "I was more than once sought out by those who, ten or fifteen years ago, were domestics in my house, now thriving mothers of families, and with children growing up in our schools to take rank as educated American citizens" (1879, 54). Harriet Prescott Spofford, too, was sympathetic to the plight of the Irish servant girl, especially any who worked as the sole maid in a household. She saw the Irish Bridget as the product of a "glad, gay race," as someone who was "fond of talking and laughing, fond of . . . quips and jokes, eager for pleasure." Spofford pointed out that the Irish maid-of-all-work "is bound down to nearly day-long solitude [in her work] . . . [so] it is no wonder that one day her heart fails her, and she ceases to care whether her work is done well or ill" (1977, 37–38).

The relationship between mistress and servant in the private home depended primarily on the amount of domestic work to be done, the level of skill of the domestic, and the personalities of the servant and the employer. There were good as well as bad employers, just as there were good as well as bad servants. But through their daily personal interaction with Irish domestics in the intimate sphere of the home, it appears that, as Catharine Beecher, Harriet Beecher Stowe, and Harriet Spofford did, some Americans came to see their Irish domestics as human beings rather than solely as alien strangers. It was through Irish women's work in domestic service in middle-class homes in urban northeastern America, then, that the Irish made their first inroads into acceptability in America. Nineteenth-century authors of popular American literature acknowledged what subsequent historians have overlooked—it was through their women, through "Princess Biddy," that the Irish conquered America ("Dinner" 1870, 708). Female Irish servants were "the pioneers in the general [Irish] conquest" of Americans, assigned the important task of "conquering the [American] hearth," to the point where employers feared that Irish domestics had become "heads of the [American] household" (Spofford 1977, 29–30). It was not political power that the conquering Irish Bridget acquired, but rather the affections of native-born Americans in the intimate sphere of the home. The Irish Bridget made the Irish human to the middle-class Americans with whom she lived and for whom she worked.

The Work World of the Irish Bridget

Domestic service was an important waged occupation for women, in general, in the United States throughout the period 1840 through 1930. Allyson Sherman Grossman claims that in 1870, 52.3 percent of employed women in America worked in domestic service in private homes. By 1930, however, the percentage had fallen to 17.8 percent. The percentage rose again by 1940, when 20.4 percent of American working women were employed in domestic service, but then dropped to 8.4 in 1950. That is, the number of servants in private homes increased from 960,000 in 1870 to 1,784,000 in 1910. Thereafter, the number declined to 1,360,000 in 1920, rose slightly to 1,909,000 in 1930, then rose further to 2,277,000 in 1940, after which the number of women employed in private household work declined to 1,459,000 in 1950 (1980, 18).

For Irish immigrant women, domestic service was a particularly significant occupation. In Boston in 1850, almost 72 percent of domestic servants were natives of Ireland (McKinley 1969, 152). Five years later, 1,600 Irish women worked in domestic service in affluent areas of Albany, New York, while in the same year more than 25 percent of Irish girls in the age bracket thirteen to twenty-five and between 50 and 66 percent of Irish girls in the age bracket eighteen to twenty-one worked as live-in domestics in Buffalo, New York (Rowley 1971, 288; Glasco 1975, 355). In Kingston, New York, in 1860, 94.5 percent of the Irish women whose occupations were identified worked in domestic service (Dudden 1983, 61–62). In 1880, 44 percent of New York City's domestic servants were Irish natives. In the same year, more than 40 percent of the servants in "Boston, Cambridge, Fall River, Hartford, Jersey City, New Haven, Providence and Troy" were natives of Ireland (Katzman 1978, 66). The 1890 census showed that of the 1,216,000 women domestic servants in the country as a whole, 154,553 were natives of Ireland (Desmond 1900, 522).

Some girls actually had experience in domestic service in Ireland before emigrating to work in this occupation in America, but the number who did so remains unknown. Bessy Masterson McManus's correspondence provides an example of a domestic servant in Ireland exploring the possibility of using her servant skills in the United States. From Kilfane, Thomastown, County Kilkenny, Ireland, on December 24, 1850, Bessy wrote to her cousin Michael Masterson in Kentucky that she and her husband had saved enough money for one of them to go to America, and she sought his advice as to which of them should go first to save money and then send for the rest of the family. In recounting her servant skills Bessy said, "I am Conciderd A perfect dairy maid and landrys and house maid also and Can dress plain dinners" (K. Miller Collection). Bessy's description also points out one of the previously mentioned major differences between service in Ireland and service in the United States—service in Ireland often involved outdoor as well as indoor work.

Indication that some servant girls emigrated from Ireland to work in service in America also comes from an 1884 report from Donegal, Ireland, "that female domestic servants were becoming 'scarcer every day' because as soon as they had saved up enough money for their passage they went out to America 'in search of service and husbands'" (Schrier 1958, 75). Lizzie Bracken's reference from the Bradley family in Tullamore, County Offaly, notes that she worked for the family for five years as "Cook and Laundress" before emigrating (see ill. 10) Other women disclosed that they, too, had worked in service in Ireland before coming to America. Rose Kelly, who came from County Derry, Northern Ireland, said that she worked as a domestic servant for a well-to-do Protestant family in Ireland before coming to the United States in 1925 (1995, 52). Ellen Brady (a pseudonym),[1] too, declared that she worked as a maid in Ireland before leaving for New York in the 1920s (1977, 18, 27).[2] Nora Joyce from

1. In the transcript of the Ellis Island interview, two names are used for the interviewee—"Kitty Flanagan" is first typed in and then crossed out and replaced by the handwritten name "Ellen Brady." I surmise that "Ellen Brady" is a pseudonym because Morrison and Zabusky 1980 used portions of this same interview; in that work, however, they used the pseudonym "Bridget Fitzgerald" for the interviewee. Morrison and Zabusky state that "except for a few well-known immigrants who gave permission for their names to be used, we have changed names and identifying details to protect the privacy of those we interviewed" (x).

2. The exact date of her immigration to the United States is never given in this interview. She says, "They checked your characters, so that's what they did with you when you came in the 20's to get a job" (27).

J. A. Bradley & Son.
Drapers, Grocers
& Seed Merchants.
Tullamore, June 4th 1887

Lizzie Bracken has lived in our service for the last five years as Cook and Laundress, and during the whole of that time she performed her duties to our entire satisfaction.

We found her most efficient and painstaking in her work: Strictly honest and upright in her conduct obliging & gentle in disposition Temperate & cleanly in her habits. She leaves us at her own request with the intention of emigrating to America: and we confidently recommend her to any one requiring a trustworthy, diligent and conscientious servant.

J A Bradley & Son

10. Letter attesting to Lizzie Bracken's character. *Courtesy of Julie Caulkins, Lizzie's great-granddaughter.*

the Aran Islands also stated that she worked in service in Ireland before coming to the United States. First, as a young girl, she did housework for summer vacationers on her home island of Inis Meán. Nora disclosed that from there she went to "Dundrum, Dublin for about two years, doing housework; do the wash and the cleaning." Then, in 1928, she came to an aunt in the Greater Boston area, where, through use of an employment agency, she secured her first place in service in America (O'Carroll 1990, 35, 37).

Plenty of servant jobs were available in America, and the Irish reported home on the availability of these positions. On September 14, 1848, from Williamsburg, Long Island, New York, William Dever wrote to his uncle in Ireland, "Servants at home ought to come here, Girls do very well." And on February 5, 1853, Anne Flood wrote from New York City to her family in Ireland about two girls who were "liveing out and doing very well." Caveats were sometimes added, however, to this encouraging view of opportunity for servant girls in America. In his letter of September 14, 1848, William Dever also cautioned that "proud lazy ladies will starve here" (K. Miller

Collection). As some of the Irish in America well knew, girls were required to work harder in the United States than they were in Ireland. In a letter she wrote from Taunton, Massachusetts, to her nephew on March 9, 1890, Margaret Kenney warned that "the People has got to work for what they get in this Country" (Schrier Collection). There were other reasons Irish girls were counseled against emigrating to work in service in the United States, as Mary Sadlier illustrates in *Bessy Conway.* In this novel, on her return to Ireland, the protagonist, Bessy, is asked by one mother if "would she advise any of her girls to go out to America." Bessy replies, "America is a bad place for young girls to go to, unless they have their father, or brothers, or somebody to look after them." Bessy continues, "Take my advice, Mrs. O'Hare, and keep your girls at home" (1863, 296).

Irish girls seemingly ignored Sadlier's advice, partly because America seemed so familiar to them. Through the relatives and friends who preceded them to America, including the ones who later returned permanently to Ireland, Irish domestics learned about this country and came to see the United States not as foreign but almost as a place just "away" from Ireland that was populated by their fellow Irish. It was from their fathers that Bridget McGeoghegan, who emigrated in 1923, and Ann Kelly, who emigrated in 1925, learned about America. Both of their fathers, who had lived in the United States but returned permanently to Ireland, told their children that they had loved living in America (McGeoghegan 1985, 18–19; Kelly 1991, 34). It was from her neighbors that Rose Kelly, who left home in 1925, learned about the United States. In Ireland, Kelly lived next door to two women (her mother's second cousins) who had lived in America. They told Rose one had to work hard in America, but they also told her they thought she was well suited for, and would enjoy, life in the United States (1995, 20–22). Mary Feely, who came to New York in 1927, also learned of America from her father, who had lived in the United States before permanently returning home to Ireland (1996). The source of Nora Joyce's preemigration information about America was her great-aunt. Nora, who came over in 1928, indicated that her great-aunt, who had lived in America but returned to Ireland to reside with Nora's family, told stories of life in the United States—how the floors in America shone like the dishes in their Irish dresser (O'Carroll 1990, 37).

Just how familiar with America the Irish felt is evidenced in the anecdote that Kathleen Magennis, who later worked as a waitress in a private club in New York, told of her landing on Ellis Island in 1921: "We're sitting in the big room, and this woman came in and she said, 'All foreigners follow me.' So I said, 'Mother, let's sit.' So we sat. So she came back and she says, 'Didn't you here [*sic*] what I said?' . . . I jumped up, and the tears are running down my cheek, and said, 'I'm not a foreigner, I'm Irish.' . . . Oh, that broke my heart. Anybody to call me a foreigner" (1994, 65, 80–82).[3]

In America, Irish girls also flocked to housework, as they were wont to call domestic service, because although most were inexperienced in it, as previously noted, their gender was deemed sufficient to make them eligible for this type of work. The fact that most of them spoke English gave them an additional advantage. Lillian Doran, who came over in 1912, replied to the question of whether Irish girls typically did service work when they immigrated to the United States by saying, "There was nothing else we could do" (1993, 38). Ellen Brady, who came to New York in the 1920s, confirmed this observation: "We [Irish immigrant girls] weren't equipped for any other job but housework" (1977, 36). When asked why she went into domestic service in America, Mary Feely replied, "What else could I do? . . . [T]here was nothing else that I could do except housework." Besides, working in service afforded immigrants some advantages: shelter (they lived in the employer's house) and food (which the employer provided). As Feely put it, "You don't have any expense when you're doing . . . housework. You get your room and board, and your uniforms" (1996).

The Stigma of Service

The occupation whose ranks Irish girls staffed had low status—there was a social stigma attached to domestic service in America. So strong was the stigma of service that native-born American girls would not engage in this work. They disliked domestic service because of "the lack of opportunity for advancement, the monotony, the unsystematized approach of employers, the length and irregularity of hours, the limited freedom, the isolation and loneliness, the role of subordinate and servant, and the employer's demand for deference and servility" (Katzman 1978, 44, 241–42).

Although most Irish people were probably aware of the low status accorded domestic service in America, they seem to have ignored or overlooked this fact, for Irish girls continued to fill the servant ranks in the United States throughout

3. George Potter says, "The Catholic Irish did not, in their own minds, consider themselves as 'foreigners' or 'aliens' in America" (1960, 169).

the period 1840 through 1930. Among the Irish who acknowledged the low status of domestic service in America was William Dever. Although in his September 14, 1848, letter to his uncle and brothers he commented on the opportunities that existed for servant girls in America, he also took note of the comedown experienced by some Irish girls who, for lack of another means of support, were compelled to work in service. As Dever put it, "I know independent young ladies at home & I have seen them here at service under them they once would not speak to." Irish immigrant servant Catherine McFarland was only too aware of the low esteem in which service employment was held. In a letter she wrote from Philadelphia to her mother in Ireland on March 5, 1855, she complained that some of her friends had written to her, but "when i told theme in my letter that i was liven at service the never answerd My letters since" (K. Miller Collection).

Over time, as Irish girls continued to populate its ranks, domestic service remained a low-status job for native-born Americans. Helen Campbell, who interviewed women for the *New York Tribune* to ascertain why they would not become servants, published her results in 1887. The answer given by one of the women indicates that it was the low status of the occupation and the loss of freedom it involved that made domestic work unattractive to her: "It's freedom we want when the day's work is done. I know some nice girls, . . . that make more money and dress better and everything for being in service. They're waitresses, and have Thursday afternoon out and part of every other Sunday. But they're never sure of one minute that's their own when they're in the house. . . . You're never sure that your soul's your own except when you are out of the house" (1889, 224).

For native-born Americans, the influx of Irish immigrants into domestic service in the second half of the nineteenth century caused both the status of the Irish and the status of service to decline further, as the responses to Lucy Maynard Salmon's 1889–90 survey on domestic service attest. One woman stated, "A great many very ignorant girls can get housework to do, and a girl who has been used to neatness and the refinement of a good home does not like to room with a girl who has just come from Ireland and does not know what neatness means" (1901, 147). Still another woman declared, "I . . . took a place as chambermaid. The work was all right and the wages good, but I'll tell you what I couldn't stand. The cook and the waitresses were just common, uneducated Irish, and I had to room with one and stand the personal habits of both, and the way they did at table took all my appetite" (Campbell 1889, 224–25).

An Irish girl's experience in domestic service depended on such factors as the personalities of servant, mistress, and members of the employing family; the amount of work required of the servant; and her experience and skill (or lack thereof) in executing the work. Despite its difficulties and low status, throughout this period, some Irish girls found service work to be quite acceptable employment. Mary Mcbride, for example, wrote home from Newburyport, Massachusetts, on October 23, sometime in the nineteenth century (she did not write the year on her letter), that "my Sister and I . . . have got an excellent situation and a fine Master and Mistress we like them very much" (K. Miller Collection). Ann McNabb, who came to America from Northern Ireland some five years after the famine-related death of her younger sister Maria, worked for a Mrs. Carr for twenty-two years as a cook and nanny. McNabb apparently had a close relationship with her employer, for she said, "Mrs. Carr's interests was my interests. I took better care of her things than she did herself, and I loved the childher as if they was my own" (Holt 1906, 144, 145, 146). Owen O'Callaghan's sister Bridget apparently found service work to be satisfactory, for in a letter he wrote from Philadelphia to his mother in County Waterford, believed to have been written on March 26, 1882, Owen told his mother that Bridget was doing well living in with a family that was "very nice people to live with." Mary Ann Rowe was comfortable in her situation, too. On October 29, 1888, she wrote from Dedham, Massachusetts, to James Wallace in Kilkenny, Ireland, that the people for whom she worked were "very nice people" and that her "mistress is so very carefull of me." And on May 14, 1899, Mary Cleer wrote from Utica, New York, to her uncle in Ireland that the man for whom she worked was "nice to his help" (K. Miller Collection).

Wages

Despite its low status, service work was attractive to Irish girls because, provided that they received their pay on time, the wages for domestic work compared quite favorably with wages for other female occupations, when one factors in the receipt of room and board (Salmon 1901, 93; Robinson 1924, 52). Servants had to watch out, however, for employers who, as one servant put it, would sometimes "forget, or pretend to forget, to pay" ("The Experiences" 1912, 779). Wages varied, depending on location, the particular type of domestic service in which the girl was engaged, and employer; servants who specialized earned more money than general servants, and wealthy employers paid better than families who were less well off. In New York in 1845, inexperienced all-purpose maids averaged about $4 a month, and experienced general housemaids earned around $5 to $6 a month, whereas cooks, nannies, and ladies' maids with experience earned between $8 and $10 a month (McKinley 1969, 19). In their American letters, Irish immigrants touted the salaries earned by servants in America. On September 3, 1883, for example, Patrick McKeown wrote from Philadelphia to his sisters in Ireland, "Single women can get along here better than men as they can get employment more readily than men. For instance liveing out girls or as the[y] are called at home servant girls gets from eight to twelve shillings per week and keep, that is from two to three dollars of American money" (Schrier 1958, 29). The responses to Lucy Maynard Salmon's survey on domestic service indicated that wages averaged around a little more than $3 per week, amounting to almost $168 on an annual basis (1901, 98). In 1916, the wages of the typical live-in maid were around $5 per week (Mayhew and Myers 1980, 344). In 1941 the wages were much the same—the average weekly salary of a domestic servant was only between $5 and $7 ("Katie Is Leaving" 1941, 10).

At the end of the nineteenth century, Salmon found the wages paid to domestic servants to be high when compared with other female employment, for live-in servants escaped the costs of room, board, and transportation to the work site that other female workers faced (1901, 93, 98). In 1910, Rheta Childe Dorr also found wages for experienced workers, averaging "over eighteen dollars a month," to be high. According to Dorr, such wages were higher than salaries paid to teachers, office workers, and shop and factory workers (1910, 252, 253). Thus, domestic servants could save their wages; Salmon calculated that the average domestic servant could save around $150 each year (1901, 99).

It is clear that Irish servants did avail themselves of the wage-saving opportunities housework provided. As already noted, the records of the Emigrant Industrial Savings Bank in New York City show that Irish immigrant servant girls were saving money, presumably their wages, as early as 1850 (Rich 2000, 2005). Records of the Philadelphia Savings Fund Society in the same year also demonstrate that Irish immigrant domestics, like twenty-six-year-old Sarah Crocket, were depositors. In fact, most of the Irish immigrant depositors in the society were women, and the overwhelming majority of those Irish women were employed as domestics (Beckham 2002, 230, 243, 244, 263).

As mentioned, Irish domestics remitted quite a bit of their American money to their relatives in Ireland. In addition, they used their wages to take care of family members in America. Bridget Ryan, who emigrated from near Thurles, County Tipperary, in 1895 and worked as a live-in cook in Troy, New York, provided financial assistance to various members of her sister's family. Among those relatives who benefited from her help was her grand-nephew Jack Casey, for Bridget used her wages to further his education, and he eventually became a judge (Casey 2006).

Allegedly, Irish servant girls also used their wages for certain causes, and raising money to relieve the Irish affected by the Great Famine was one of these causes. In *This Great Calamity,* historian Christine Kinealy cites an 1847 letter from Philadelphia appearing in Irish newspapers that contended that for Irish domestics in America, "their only desire at present appears to be to give every farthing they possess" for famine relief (1995, 163). In the 1860s, Irish servant girls sent money to New York in support of the Fenian cause, and, in consequence, Fenian leader John O'Mahony was subject to criticism for "robbery of the poor Irish servant girls" (Wittke 1956, 155). Likewise, New York–based Ellen Mahoney, head of the Fenian Sisterhood, was also criticized for looking to Irish servant girls for support of the Fenians (M. Kelly 2005, 57). In addition, it is alleged that Irish maids were among the "little people" in Philadelphia who provided financial support for Irish independence in the twentieth century (D. Clark 1973, 152).

In Britain, vails or tips were demanded by eighteenth-century servants, earning them a reputation throughout Europe for extorting money, and although this practice waned somewhat over time, some servants in nineteenth-century Britain still expected and received tips, particularly at Christmas (Horn 1975, 10–11, 100–101, 117). In Ireland, too, employers frequently gave tips as well as presents to servants at Christmas. Guests staying at an Irish residence sometimes tipped their host's servants, too (Hearn 1993, 52–53). The information available from servants themselves in the United States, however, does not address the issue of tips, but the literature written by American employers does, and indicates not only that tipping was common but also that the employing class objected to the practice.[4] Despite the fact that Christine Terhune Herrick claimed that "the matter of tips in this country has never assumed the importance it possesses on the other side of the water," in her 1904 work, *The Expert Maid-Servant,* she found tips to be an issue that needed to be addressed. Herrick said that when servants

4. Anne Frances Springsteed argued that to maintain their self-esteem, waitresses should not accept tips (1894, 128–29).

were required to shoulder more than their normal workload, they should be rewarded. She urged, however, that the reward take the form of "a gift, the granting of an unusual privilege, or by relieving the maid of a part of her own regular work," rather than a tip. According to Herrick, it was "not a good principle for the mistress to fall into the habit of bestowing tips for any extra service." Herrick found nothing objectionable, though, about a guest tipping his or her host's servant to compensate the servant for the extra work the guest's presence in the house entailed (1904, 120–22). In 1915, another author railed against the practice of guests tipping a hostess's servants, arguing that instead of relying on the generosity of her guests, the hostess might better simply pay her servants a decent wage (Barker 1915, 83).

Room, Board, and Work Space

Room was often touted as a benefit of domestic service that made the occupation more highly remunerative than its wages alone. Throughout the period 1840 to 1930, however, servant living space was often less than desirable, and usually provided a marked contrast with the living space of the employer. As noted in chapter 4, house plans from 1850 show servant rooms in the attic or over the kitchen. Attic rooms often lacked heat and running water. In some cases, the sleeping space provided to a domestic was not even a bedroom. It was reported that the room provided to one domestic "was nothing but a closet, in which there was neither light nor fresh air." In other cases, no sleeping space at all was provided for the servant; instead, she "was expected to make up a bed in the kitchen after her day's work was over" (Laughlin 1901, 757). Often, servants who worked as child nurses, like Helen Flatley, who came to New York City from County Mayo in 1928, did not have their own bedrooms, either, but, instead, "slept with the children" (1996a).

Harriet Prescott Spofford's 1881 comments on servant quarters support the view that they were hardly a real perquisite of domestic employment. About servant bedrooms Spofford said, "We have known it [a servant's bedroom] to be placed in a little black hole off the area kitchen, . . . but oftenest it is a garret at the top of the house, uncarpeted, half furnished . . . nothing wholesome or happy in it; nothing calculated to make a girl feel that she has a retreat . . . where she can . . . make a little home to herself. . . . [She has] seen the difference between our own rooms and that [of her quarters]" (1977, 39).

In 1887, one former chambermaid described the quarters provided to her when she was a servant as follows: "In that splendid big house the servants' room was over the kitchen,—hot and close in summer, and cold in winter, and four beds in it. We five [servants] had to live there together, with only two bureaus and a bit of a closet, and one washstand for all. There was no chance to keep clean or your things in nice order, or anything by yourself, and I gave up" (Campbell 1889, 230).

Although bathrooms were common in private homes in cities by the 1870s, and hot and cold running water could be found in most urban homes by about 1880, it was not a given that home owners ensured that plumbing reached attics where servants' bedrooms were so frequently located. Thus, for servants, cleanliness was an issue—they were supposed to meet the standards of cleanliness of the house in which they worked, without necessarily having access to its resources. Not all employers provided servants with towels, nor did all employers allow servants use of the family bathroom. Consequently, some servants had to use the kitchen sink for bathing, while others had to carry water for bathing from the kitchen to their rooms—a particularly difficult proposition when servants' quarters were in the attic (McKinley 1969, 251; Katzman 1978, 110).

In actuality, board or food was not always such a great benefit for domestic servants. Mrs. Elizabeth Ellet stated in 1857 that it was customary in the North for servants to eat after the family, with their meals consisting of "the remains of the family meals" (28). Sometimes the food provided to servants contrasted unfavorably with the food eaten by the family for whom the servant worked; it might have been of lesser quality or quantity. Lack of adequate nutrition to perform the physically taxing job of domestic service was a problem for some servants (Katzman 1978, 110).

The comments of Elizabeth Dolan (a pseudonym) on servant food in one house in which she worked serve to illustrate an employer's attempts to shortchange servants with regard to food, and a servant's successful effort to thwart such attempts. Dolan, who came from Ireland in 1912 at age sixteen, eventually wound up working as a cook for a Boston Brahmin family. There she refused to allow her fellow staff members to be given food inferior to what was served her mistress's family. According to Dolan, her mistress came to her saying,

> "I do not want you to buy"—I did the ordering—"to buy any roast beef for the help. They don't need roast beef. You can buy other things, but not roast beef." And I said, "The people today have to have roast beef. It's a must, at least once a week, for the blood." Mrs. Worthingham and me had quite some words over it, but, you know, I won out, and I ordered that

> roast beef once a week for the help. If it was good enough for her, it should be good enough for the help that was doing the work for her. (Morrison and Zabusky 1980, 44–45)

Cecelia Flanagan, who came to the United States in 1925, left her first service job in America because she didn't like the food provided to her. She said, "You had better food at home. . . . It was horrible. So I left myself. I got another job" (1994, 15). In her next job she worked as a cook! Again, the situation depended on the specific circumstances of the house in which one worked. In contrast to Flanagan, Bridget McGeoghegan, who immigrated in 1923, said of the family for whom she worked that "they had very good food" (1985, 30).

Not only did servant room and board often fail to match that of their employers, but their work space was often less than desirable, too. Although historic house museums in America frequently portray kitchens as clean, bright, and cheerful, the cheerful kitchen was more likely to have been the exception rather than the rule. Parker Pillsbury's 1869 description illustrates that kitchens were "low, dark, hot, subterranean . . . into which the sun never looked and never can. . . . [I]n many, if not in most of the large houses in cities, everywhere, the kitchen is a dismally dark, unventilated, uncomfortable, out-of-the-way place, with sink and all other odorous and disagreeable appointments festering about it" (88–89).

In 1881, the city kitchen was described as "a dark room, half underground, and half of its light dependent on a skylight, and with its sole window looking into a black area." The country kitchen apparently was not much better; it was characterized as "a larger and lighter room, with the cold pouring in at countless cracks, and the windows commanding lively views of the barnyard" (Spofford 1977, 38). It was in such depressing spaces that a servant spent most of her time.

How Servants Obtained Jobs

Regardless of whether the advantage that room and board represented has been overrated, Irish girls flocked to domestic service because there were plenty of job openings throughout this period as the demand for servants continually exceeded the supply. They secured service employment through the assistance of the Catholic Church, the Irish community, use of employment agencies called intelligence offices, relatives, word of mouth, and perusal of newspaper advertisements.

In the 1850s in New York City the Sisters of Mercy (an order founded in Ireland) provided a monthlong training program for potential domestic servants and by the end of that decade had placed in excess of twelve thousand females in service positions. Later, the Sisters of Charity in New York City opened an employment agency to place Irish mothers (though most Irish domestics were single, there were some who had children) in domestic service positions in households that would permit their children to live with them (Fitzgerald 2006, 58–59, 226).

One of the services provided by the Catholic Mission of Our Lady of the Rosary for the Protection of Irish Immigrant Girls in New York City was also to help Irish immigrant girls to obtain service jobs. The mission began operation in New York in 1884 under the direction of Father Thomas Riordan (Murphy 1992, 264). Encouraged by Charlotte Grace O'Brien's work, the mission aimed to protect Irish immigrant girls landing in New York City from the untrustworthy and sometimes evil people in the port area who preyed on their innocence. The mission protected Irish girls by having a priest available at Castle Garden (the point of entry to New York from 1855 through 1890) to counsel them, by setting up a safe lodging house in which they could stay until they obtained a job or were otherwise safely seen to, and by setting up a chapel for their use (John Nolan 1891, 780). With regard to its second purpose, no fees were charged to any girls for staying in the Home for Irish Immigrant Girls established by the mission, no matter the length of their stay. In 1899, almost two thousand of the more than twelve thousand Irish immigrant girls coming into New York availed themselves of use of the home for periods of time ranging from hours to weeks (Henry 1900, 16–23). In Boston, similar work aimed at aiding Irish immigrant girls was begun in the early twentieth century under the sponsorship of the St. Vincent de Paul Society and a lay group known as the Charitable Irish Society of Boston. Around 1910, working together, they hired a woman named Julia Hayes to meet and assist immigrant Irish girls at the port; one of the forms of assistance Hayes provided was to help the girls obtain domestic service jobs in private homes (Moloney 1999, 55–57).

The Irish community also helped Irish girls to land domestic service jobs. The *Boston Pilot,* for example, on September 2, 1865, advised that "Good Servants, desiring first class situations, will find *the Boston Daily Advertiser,* published at No. 12 State street, the best paper to advertise their 'Wants' in, for the reason that it circulates among the best Catholics of New England."

In the revised 1915 version of *Out of Work: A Study of Unemployment,* Frances A. Kellor devoted an entire chapter to discussion of "domestic service and intelligence offices." She portrayed intelligence offices as places where prospective servants were often treated discourteously, and indicated that they were of two types: the predominant type, aimed at a market of inexperienced immigrant girls, consisted of dirty, crowded places in seedy parts of the city, whereas the more genteel intelligence offices, for skilled workers, were located in the better sections of cities. The two major types of intelligence agencies subdivided further—for example, some focused on newly arrived immigrants, while others specialized in experienced immigrants, such as Scandinavian servants, and yet others dealt mainly with African American servants (216–17, 194–98). Kellor painted a dark picture of intelligence agencies, seeing them as taking advantage of prospective servant and employer alike. They charged the prospective servant a fee or a gift that was pegged to the value of the open position, while telling the prospective employer that no fee was charged the girl (208). Such agencies, Kellor claimed, were often more interested in the repeated placement of servants to increase the fees they obtained with each placement than they were in actually matching girls with employers for long-term stable employment. For example, she claimed that "one girl . . . had been placed ten times in one year, netting the office twenty dollars in fees, for it received a percentage of the wages each time, and a neat sum for lodging until she was placed again. If the employer who lost her returned to the same office for other girls, there were additional fees" (212–13). Worse yet, Kellor charged, some intelligence offices knowingly sent unwitting girls to work in "disorderly houses," that is, houses of ill repute (225).

Limited information is available on the servant's view of intelligence agencies, and the material that is available comes from the latter part of the period 1840 to 1930. Nevertheless, the little information that is available illustrates that servants themselves, unlike Frances Kellor, did not stress the negative aspects of intelligence offices and instead spoke neutrally and matter-of-factly about them. Theresa Gavin merely said that in 1912 she obtained her first position in service in the United States through an agency (1991, 30). Ellen Brady said that she obtained her first service job in America in the 1920s through an "employment agency. I went there and I had my references and I got a job." Explaining how they worked, she said that an employment agency "sent me out on the jobs. . . . [P]eople there interview you, see? They [prospective employers] go there. . . . And the agency interviews you first and then the agency tell the people . . . —that's about it. Well, they [prospective employers] don't ask you any questions, because they know all about you before they hire you. Because that's on the papers that you bring in with you" (1977, 21).

Rose Kelly said that in 1925 she obtained her first American domestic service position by going "to the office where you could get a job, and . . . I got the job right away" (1995, 41). Katherine O'Hara (a pseudonym), who immigrated to Boston from Ireland in 1930, indicated that she knew that some agencies dealt with domestic service positions available in wealthier homes. O'Hara said that shortly after her arrival in America, "I went into an employment agency . . . in Boston, and I got a job with a society lady in Brookline" (Morrison and Zabusky 1980, 46). It was desirable to work in a wealthier home because the pay was often higher, and it usually meant working with a larger domestic staff, which in turn usually meant less work for the individual servant.

Some Irish girls obtained service jobs through relations who had jobs waiting for them when they arrived in America. Sarah Mackey, who arrived in America in 1910, spent her first few days with an aunt in Elizabeth, New Jersey. Then, she said, "my sister got me a job with her. She was a cook some place and she got me as a waitress see, in a private home. Lovely, very nice." Indicating the assertive nature of Irish girls in service, she said of herself, however, "But, of course, . . . I didn't want to do anything anybody told me." Mackey said that a later employer called her "an independent Irish hussy" (1979, 11). A family member also lined up Margaret Convery with her first job. When she and her sister Bridget arrived in Philadelphia in 1914, they first spent a few days with their brother Dan where he boarded. Then Dan "got us work. . . . I worked for a lady that had . . . two children. . . . [I earned] three dollars a week" (1991, 47). Sarah Brady, on the other hand, who came to Boston from County Galway at age fourteen in 1912, said that in 1914, she got her first job as a nursemaid through someone she knew (1975, 4). But for Ann Sexton, it was also through family that she got her first job placement. Sexton said that her sister had a position as a nanny with the famous Rockefeller family waiting for her when she arrived in New York in 1922. Commenting on her lack of experience in this occupation, Ann said of her sister that "she had to break me in you know. . . . [S]he taught me how to handle the children, how to talk to them." Sexton said that she loved the two Rockefeller children who were her charges, but of some of the famous Rockefeller family whom she met in her employment she commented, "I wasn't impressed" (1986, 17, 5, 18). Through word of mouth and relatives, Ann Kelly obtained her first service job. When Kelly arrived in New York in the summer of 1925, her sister heard of a job available minding a child on Cape Cod. Kelly got the job and later said, "I went to Cape Cod with this family to take care of this little boy." Of this job she commented, "It was good opportunity for me and that summer happen to be a very hot summer. . . . Lot of people died in New York from the heat in 1925" (1991, 55, 56).

Newspaper advertisements factored into how Bridget McGeoghegan secured her first service position in America. Because her aunts in Boston all worked in domestic service, they looked at the newspaper to see what jobs were available for Bridget when she arrived in 1923; she answered one advertisement by going to a woman's house and got the job (1985, 36). Cecelia Flanagan, who also arrived in New York in 1925, got her second placement doing housework by looking through the newspaper. She said of herself, "I wasn't no dopey" (1994, 16).

The Reference

According to Pamela Horn, as a condition of employment, prospective employers in Victorian Britain demanded that the servant provide a reference, or "character," from a previous employer. No law compelled employers, however, to provide servants with the character that was essential to obtaining work. Malicious employers could refuse to provide characters, or could engage in character assassination in them, thus seriously impeding a servant's ability to get work. In consequence, it was not unknown in Britain for a servant to fabricate a character for herself. Although legislation in the late eighteenth century outlawed servants from providing deceptive characters (and also outlawed employers from trying to palm off poor servants on others by giving them good characters), apparently few servants were prosecuted for violating the law. Attempts in Britain in the early twentieth century to strengthen prohibitions against the provision of false characters were generally unsuccessful, as were attempts to pass legislation requiring that employers provide servants with characters (1975, 45–46).

Mona Hearn maintains that the situation was similar in Ireland. A good reference from the last employer was essential to securing employment; Irish newspaper advertisements for servants specified the need for a character. As in Britain, no law required employers to provide the all-important character, and spiteful employers could provide false-negative references, so that in Ireland, as in Britain, a servant might be driven to fabricate a character. In addition, Irish employers actually took physical possession of a servant's written character, requiring that a servant ask for its return when quitting the employer's house (1993, 28–29).

In America, unlike Britain and Ireland, it was rarely a condition of employment that a servant be required to obtain a reference from a previous employer. And, anyway, in the United States references for servants were virtually useless for several reasons. First, people's ideas about what constituted good domestic service varied, and domestic work that was acceptable in one household might not be acceptable in another. Second, both servants and intelligence offices were known to doctor references to improve them, or to fabricate them, and servants sometimes gave away or sold particularly good references to others seeking work. Some employers also gave good references to dispose of poor employees, gave poor references to servants they wished to punish, and refused to provide references to good servants they hoped to retain. Apparently, no one expected agencies specializing in immigrants or African Americans to provide references (Kellor 1915, 218–20; D. Sutherland 1981, 17, 64–66). Nevertheless, some girls who worked in service in Ireland before coming to America believed it necessary to possess a character. As noted, in 1887, Lizzie Bracken obtained a character from her Irish employer to take with her to America. And Ellen Brady said she was able to secure her first service job in America in the 1920s by bringing her references with her to an employment agency (1977, 21). Further testimony to some Irish girls' belief that they needed a character from their last Irish employer in order to secure a service job in America comes in the form of an anecdote recounted by historian Carl Wittke: "Biddy Malone . . . lost a certificate of character en route to the United States. . . . [A] friend . . . offered to provide her with another. He wrote that she 'had a good character before she left the 'ould country,' but lost it on shipboard comin' over" (1956, 195).

Housework

Housework was daunting work throughout the period 1840 to 1930, despite improvements in technology over time. In the early part of this period, before the advent of indoor plumbing, housework involved fetching water from a well and bringing it into the house, as well as draining slop jars. Because, throughout this period, if they employed servants at all, American households generally hired only one domestic servant, often it was to the sole servant, the "general servant" or "maid-of-all-work," that arduous housework devolved (D. Sutherland 1981, 94).[5] In 1901 it was pointed out:

> Families employing but one domestic servant . . . want as varied and elegant service as is enjoyed by families which employ more than one servant. They require of the one employee all the different kinds of service for which special workers are hired by families which employ more than one servant, and the expectation is . . . that each different kind of work shall be as well done as though the general servant were a specialist in each kind of work. . . . [T] he amount of work required [of a general servant] is much greater than that which is required of as special worker. (Laughlin 1901, 749)

Consider the morning duties Mrs. Ellet expected a maid-of-all-work in 1857 to complete before she ate her own breakfast:

> A servant should be trained to rise about half-past five . . . pass into the kitchen, . . . light the kitchen fire . . . and then proceed to prepare the room required for breakfast. . . . [T]he scuttle containing coal, wood, &c., must be brought up. . . . The stove must be polished . . . every morning, and thoroughly cleaned at least once a week. The fire may then be laid and lighted. . . . [T]he sweeping comes next. . . . Then comes the dusting. . . . The street-door steps should be cleaned, the mats shaken, the passage swept, and the brasses polished before the family come down. The breakfast is then to be prepared. . . . The servant next proceeds to the bedrooms, opens the windows . . . empties the slops, cleanses and rinses all basins, ewers, bottles, &c. wipes up all slops, and brings fresh water to supply all wants in each room. The beds are then to be made. . . . [T]he breakfast will have to be removed. . . . The servant will now get her own breakfast. (1857, 42–44)

In addition, the maid-of-all-work was expected to care for the lamps, cook and serve dinner as well as tea, answer the front door, and respond to the mistress's bell. She was also obliged to follow a set weekly schedule to take care of the myriad chores involved in cleaning and maintaining the bedrooms, kitchen, stairs, hallways, drawing room, and dining room (Ellet 1857, 44).

5. The article "Social Conditions in Domestic Service," citing data from an investigation conducted by Mary W. Dewson into the social conditions of domestic service, supports this contention: 109 of the 181 families involved in the investigation employed but a single servant (1900, 2).

If the employing family did not pay for the services of a laundress, doing the household laundry also fell to the maid-of-all-work. Mrs. E. F. Haskell's suggestion on how table and bed linens should be laundered, contained in her 1861 book *The Housekeeper's Encyclopedia,* illustrates the onerous nature of laundry work. Mrs. Haskell advised her readers to "prepare a boiler of rain water in the following manner: to every pail of water, take a small table-spoonful of sal soda pounded fine, enough hard soap to make a suds, and to five pails of water a table-spoonful of spirits of turpentine; wring out all the table and bed linen, and boil them without rubbing, a good half-hour hard, frequently pushing them down with the clothes stick. Then take them out, and rinse in three tubs of rain water, blue in the last." Mrs. Haskell called for folding clothes after laundering them, warning that "ironing should be finished as soon as possible after the clothes have lain three hours folded, as they soon become sour" (12–13). Ironing sometimes required a full day's work following laundry day. It called for "sprinkling and then ironing [cloth] with flatirons heated to the proper temperature, this ascertained by guess or experience. Ironing was an especially unpleasant job in hot weather" (Dudden 1983, 142).

In the execution of housework throughout this period, households generally followed a set routine with specific chores to be undertaken on specific days of the week. The weekly household routine suggested in Beecher and Stowe's *American Woman's Home* (1869), for which, in a house employing a single maid-of-all-work, the servant would have been responsible, demonstrates the multitude of chores involved in housework:

> Monday . . . is devoted to preparing for the labors of the week. Any extra cooking . . . the assorting of clothes for the wash, and mending . . . belong to this day. Tuesday is devoted to washing, and Wednesday to ironing. On Thursday, the ironing is finished off, the clothes are folded and put away, and all articles which need mending are put in the mending-basket, and attended to. Friday is devoted to sweeping and house-cleaning. On Saturday, and especially the last Saturday of every month, every department is put in order; the casters and table furniture are regulated, the pantry and cellar inspected, the trunks, drawers and closets arranged, and every thing about the house put in order for Sunday. (1994, 226–27)

Throughout this time frame, employer expectations for the maid-of-all-work remained remarkably similar. Compare, for example, the requirements previously listed for a maid-of-all-work in 1857 with the ones below that

Christine Terhune Herrick listed for a maid-of-all-work in 1904. According to Herrick:

> Early rising should be insisted upon. Six o'clock is none too early for a maid to be up in a house where breakfast is at seven-thirty or eight o'clock. By half after six the maid should be dressed and down-stairs. If the care of the furnace falls upon her, her first duty in winter is to open the draughts of the furnace and put on a little coal. While this is kindling she can go back to her work up-stairs. The kitchen fire must be lighted, the kettle filled freshly and set to boil, the cereal put over the fire, before the maid goes into the living-rooms to open the windows. While these rooms are airing she may brush out the front hall and sweep off the steps. (56)

Further, according to Herrick, the maid might have been expected to brush away dust in the drawing room, and most certainly she was expected to straighten its furniture, as well as to dust the dining room, all before cooking and serving breakfast for the family and eating some breakfast herself! The rest of the daily chores expected of her in 1904 included airing out beds and bed linen in the family bedrooms, making the beds, using a carpet sweeper on the bedroom floors, cleaning the bathroom, returning to the kitchen to wash the breakfast dishes and wipe the icebox shelves, setting the table for lunch, and getting lunch ready for the family. In the afternoons, on designated days, the maid's chores included laundry or ironing or both, washing windows, cleaning the woodwork adjacent to doorknobs, and sweeping the entire house at least once a week. Otherwise, in the afternoon, she was to complete such chores as shining the silver. Every day, before beginning preparations for dinner, she was expected to carpet sweep the hall. In addition, her chores included preparing the dinner, waiting on the family while they ate, and when the family finished dinner clearing the table and doing the washing up. Her other responsibilities included answering the doorbell (57–69).

Note the similarity between the schedule below for a domestic named Anna in 1941 and the 1857 and 1904 schedules for a maid-of-all-work, as well as the similarity between Anna's weekly routine and the weekly routine suggested by Beecher and Stowe in 1869:

> Monday; Anna prepares breakfast, does washing, sprinkles clothes, gets dinner. . . . Tuesday is ironing day. Anna also can do downstairs dusting, prepare and serve breakfast and a very fine dinner. Wednesday is thorough

> upstairs cleaning day—including the window sills and woodwork. Anna also vacuums rugs. Thursday is Anna's half-holiday. Before going she scrubs the bath and kitchen floors, and also remembers to straighten and defrost the refrigerator. Friday is Anna's day to polish the silver. Then she does the thorough general cleaning downstairs and prepares and serves dinner. A big day, for she also gets us breakfast and luncheon. Saturday—the time to bake cookies or cake for weekend pantry foraging. Also, Anna dusts and sweeps both the upstairs and downstairs. Sunday means, mainly, a good family dinner. After serving it, and dusting downstairs, Anna is off on her merry way. (Martin and Segrave 1985, 41)

Not only did the schedule of work remain fairly consistent for domestics over time, but the work continued throughout this period to involve long workdays and long workweeks. The workday of live-in domestic servants was longer than the workday of other employed women (Katzman 1978, 110), for in service work "it is the person who is hired and not, distinctively, the labor of the person," that is, servants were hired for their time, rather than for specific duties, so the employer expectation was that the servant should be "at all times subject to the call and direction of the employer" (Laughlin 1901, 759). Even during their few off-hours, servants were often still on-call to employers. In the nineteenth century and the early twentieth century, most servants labored for more than ten hours a day, with the norm being a workday of between eleven and twelve hours (Laughlin 1901, 756; Robinson 1924, 54; Katzman 1978, 111–13). Servants also worked seven days a week (Katzman 1978, 110). Time off was usually limited to one afternoon and one night, per week, usually Sunday and Thursday. If a servant wanted additional time off, she was required to obtain the express consent of the employer (Laughlin 1901, 757). This protocol led one Irish American woman to complain that employers wanted "girls on tap from six in the morning till ten and eleven at night. 'Tis n't fair" (Campbell 1897, 227).

Thus, as noted, in terms of the amount of work expected, the most common situation, that of a single maid-of-all-work, was also the worst situation for a servant. The ratio of staff to family was a key determinant in how taxing a servant's job would be, because more people meant more work. Hence, it is quite understandable why the servant referenced in chapter 4, of whom the *Boston Pilot* made note in 1870, sued her employers for more money when she found that the family consisted of more people than the number for which she had contracted.

The path to upward mobility in service was limited. One could try to move from being a single maid-of-all-work in a smaller house to work in a larger house, where the employer was ostensibly wealthier, paid higher wages, and employed multiple servants. Once in such a larger multiservant house, one could try to move up through the ranks within the house, say (likely through intermediary steps), from chambermaid to cook, for, as already mentioned, specialized servants earned better money. The best situation for domestics then was probably in a house that employed multiple servants; a given number of chores split among two or more people meant less work, and the possibility of more free time, for each of them.

Specialized servants not only earned more money but also had less work to do than single maids-of-all-work. In homes where two servants were employed, one usually served as cook. Besides meal preparation, depending on the particular household, the cook's duties might also have included being in charge of the furnace, sweeping the door steps, doing the washing up, and keeping the kitchen in good order. The second servant usually combined chambermaid and waitress duties. She was expected to dust, sweep, and air out the formal rooms before her breakfast; serve breakfast; and then, while the family breakfasted, make the beds. At the conclusion of the family breakfast, she was to clear the table and then eat her own breakfast, finish any remaining work in the bedrooms, clean the bathroom, and, if it was her job in the household to do so, do the dishes. The waitress served and waited on the family for dinner, and usually was responsible for dusting; care of the china, silver, and brass; washing windows; cleaning the woodwork; care of the lamps; answering the indoor servant's bell and the front doorbell; and turning down the beds at night. If the household lacked a laundress, it was usually expected that the cook would also serve as laundress. In homes with children in which three servants were employed, the third servant might have worked as a child nurse—with few exceptions, servants employed as nannies were not expected to engage in general housework. Otherwise, the third servant on staff could have served as a laundress or a combination chambermaid-seamstress. When multiple servants were employed they spelled each other, with, for example, the cook substituting for the waitress on her day off (Herrick 1904, 74–86).

As mentioned, most American households, if they employed servants at all, employed but one servant. Still, there were some truly wealthy American households in which all things were more elaborate that employed extensive numbers of domestics on their household staff that would have included a housekeeper, lady's maid, parlor maid, butler, valet and footmen, and so on, each with distinctive duties. Ellen Brady worked for very wealthy people in just such an elaborate household in New York, where more than fifty servants were on staff. Among the staff were a few Irish, whereas many of the others, including the footmen, were English. Wealthy people, Brady contended, "treat you [servants] like a human being," and their "children were so well mannered." Her description of her employment stands in marked contrast to what maids-of-all-work seem to have experienced in service for people of smaller means. Brady said, "The job was beautiful," although she added that eventually "it got boring." She described her post as that of a "useful girl." In this capacity, she said, "You work one day a week in each department . . . not the kitchen. You work with the butler, parlormaid, chamber maid, personal maid . . . and the footmen, and you learn everything." She noted that in this house, "I had my own bedroom . . . [a]nd a bathroom to [each two] girls." Servants in this house had their own cooks, too (three of them!), and their own dining room. Of the servants' food she commented, "We had better food sometimes than they [the employers] had themselves." While working for this wealthy family she was provided with a clean uniform every day. And although her time off was limited to one half-day per week, she was free from two to five o'clock every day before she was required to report back to work until approximately half past seven (1977, 25–40).

Technological Improvements

From 1840 to 1930, standards of cleanliness rose and improvements were made in the technology of the middle-class home in urban northeastern America. In some respects, improved technology lessened the drudgery of household work, but it certainly did not eliminate it; generally, household work remained tough physical work over the entire period. As mentioned in the Introduction, my research shows that, contrary to my initial expectations, although technological improvements eased the labor of domestic service, it did not completely revolutionize it, for the complaints domestic servants made about their work remained remarkably similar over time and space, as I will detail below and in chapter 7.

Technological improvements affecting the home began in the nineteenth century, but only in the 1920s, at the end of the period with which this book is concerned, was the full impact of improved household technology felt widely in American homes. One nineteenth-century technological improvement that lessened the work of servants was the establishment of municipal water systems in large American cities by the mid-1870s; many urban American homes had hot and cold running water by 1900. Not only were sewer lines installed in major cities by the late nineteenth century, but the homes of middle- and upper-income families were connected to these sewer lines as well. By the last decade of the nineteenth century, the bathroom with which Americans are now familiar, with a toilet, sink, and shower or bath, could be found in some American homes. In the mid-nineteenth century, only the wealthy expected their homes to feature interior water closets, but by 1900 it was the expectation of middle-class Americans in urban areas that water closets be incorporated into their housing. Thus, since by 1900 most urban areas had running water, servants no longer had to draw and carry water from wells, and since most urban homes were equipped with interior water closets whose pipes were connected to city sewer lines, servants no longer faced the unpleasant daily chore of emptying chamber pots.

Wire window screens, which first appeared in urban areas around 1869, were in widespread use by the start of the twentieth century. Screens had a positive effect on the workload of servants in that they helped reduce the annoyance of bugs, and lessened the amount of dirt coming into the home. The carpet sweeper, called "one of the most efficient technological innovations of the nineteenth century," began coming into broader use by 1880 (H. Green 1983, 76). It, too, had a positive effect on the work of servants, for the carpet sweeper not only removed the dust that often resulted from vigorous sweeping but also eliminated the need for servants to remove rugs from the interior to the exterior of the house to be beaten clean.

Wood and coal-burning cooking ranges were in use in American kitchens by the 1840s; many families, however, continued cooking over an open-hearth fire. Millard Fillmore, president of the United States from 1850 to 1853, inaugurated the White House's first cookstove only to find that his cook rejected its use (Mayhew and Myers 1980, 362). Gas ranges as well as coal stoves were in use in American kitchens by the early 1900s, as were combination ranges that made use of both gas and coal. Iceboxes were in widespread use by the mid-1880s, but not until about the second decade of the twentieth century did refrigerators come on the market, and General Motors began to sell the Frigidaire to the public around 1918 (Bacon 1943, 204; Schlereth 1991, 126–27). Various kitchen gadgets that lessened the work of food preparation also appeared or were refined over the course of the nineteenth century. They included "apple parers, pea shellers, fruit seeders, coffee grinders, potato slicers, egg beaters, [and] meat choppers" (D. Sutherland 1981, 194).

After the discovery of oil in 1859, kerosene, a petroleum-based product, came on the market as a fuel for lighting. It was a popular but smelly and volatile fuel. Gaslight brightened city streets after the mid-nineteenth century, but it was only in the last twenty-five years of the century that it illuminated the homes of wealthy Americans. By the end of the nineteenth century, electricity was beginning to elbow out other light sources. It was a boon to servants because no ashes were involved with electricity, one did not need to worry about proper ventilation with its use, electric light was more standard than flickering gaslight, and, most important, electricity basically eliminated the risk of fire or explosion. Although fewer than 10 percent of American homes had wiring for electricity in 1907, the number of Americans enjoying electricity increased thereafter, so that by 1920 almost 35 percent of American homes were electrified. By 1920, electricity was used for appliances as well as a light source. Although electric washing machines and vacuum cleaners were available by 1920, and their cost decreased in that decade, their limited use can be inferred from the fact that only 8 percent of household spending went toward household appliances in the 1920s. The use of small household appliances was more widespread in the 1930s, though, and during that decade the cost of electric refrigerators fell and electric stoves became more popular. Automatic electric washing machines became available late in that decade, but they did not come into general use until after 1945 (Cowan 1983, 93–94; Leavitt 2002, 114).

At the end of the nineteenth century gas was primarily used as a lighting source. Thereafter, however, as electricity made inroads over it in interior lighting, gas was marketed as a heating fuel and became widely used as a cooking fuel. In fact, "By 1930 gas cooking prevailed over all other forms in the United States" (Cowan 1983, 91).

Open-hearth heating had been replaced by heating stoves in most American homes by the mid-1860s. Coal-fired furnaces for central home heating became available after 1850, and gas-fired furnaces with automatic features were available by the 1920s. Starting in the 1880s, building contractors began installing heating systems, hot air or hot water, in houses. But because of the expense, installation of central heat was basically the purview of the wealthier segments of society until after 1918. Only in the post-1945 era did central heating come to be enjoyed by the poorer segments of American society.

Historian Ruth Schwartz Cowan argues that because improvements in household technology merely reorganized, rather than eliminated, household chores, the amount of time women spent on housework did *not* decrease. Instead, women's household work actually increased in some cases, because, for example, the production of manufactured cloth led to an increase in the amount of clothing people possessed, thus leading to more sewing and laundry (1983, 64, 65). By extension, then, in households where servants, rather than housewives, were responsible for the execution of housework, it was servants who found their work reorganized but not necessarily revolutionized. So while washing machines lessened the drudgery involved in laundry, given that larger wardrobes were available to people, the actual amount of laundry a servant had to do may have increased. Thus, despite technological improvements, servants' complaints show that they found housework remained taxing work throughout this period.

Servants' Complaints Regarding Housework

Irish servants found domestic service, especially as a maid-of-all-work, to be hard, unpleasant work. On March 5, 1855, Catherine Ann McFarland wrote from Philadelphia to her mother in Ireland, "If you new what i have to put upe with in ane ones kitchen." In an undated letter thought to have been written in the fall of 1871, Mary O'Hanlon complained that because all her chores had to be completed before she went to church, there was but one mass that she could attend on Sundays; she also complained that she had so much work to do that it was difficult to finish a letter. From New York City she wrote to her mother in Ireland that "I had to quit this letter 5 times & begin to make tea biscuit & set the teatable there was 12 for tea & what a lot of dishes & glasses its halfpast 8 now & I am just through dear mother" (K. Miller Collection).[6]

Hannah Collins's correspondence with her friend and fellow domestic Nora McCarthy shows that she, too, found housework to be hard work. On June 9, 1898, she wrote to Nora from Elmira, New York, "I am working every day and feels tired I don t have them Idle times like I used to in old Ballinlough." The following year, on May 24, 1899, she wrote to Nora, "I was glad you left that hard place I hope you will soon find another one that will be nice and easy I guess you are like myself for I never can get a nice

6. In Kerby Miller's annotated list of documents, he suggests that O'Hanlon was a seamstress or factory worker. My review of this letter, however, particularly the quote I use, convinces me that she was a domestic servant, at least at the time that she wrote this letter.

place. . . . I hope someday will come when I wont have to work so hard. . . . I do hate to get up every morning I am so tired." Two months later, in a letter enclosed in an envelope postmarked July 22, 1899, she wrote to Nora that "I am so tired and almost dead. . . . Nora I am sorry your place is so hard. . . . [N]othing but work all the time for us all." Again on November 17 of that year, she wrote, "I was so busy all the time since I wrote to you last cleaning house every day, but I am through now. and am so glad. as I had to clean all alone." Further, on January 23, 1900, she wrote to Nora, "I would have written sooner but we had company all the week and I was so tired she also had a card party Friday afternoon sixteen ladies Just think what work they made for me." Unsurprisingly, Hannah sought to limit the amount of work required of her. She quit one job where the employer left her "tired out" partially because, as she wrote to Nora on April 5, 1900, the employer "wanted me to stay in some evenings for her because she was out all the time I told her I was not a nurse girl to be taking care of kids they are old enough to mind them selves. Well I have another place." Hannah found housework so daunting that the main thing she did when her employer was away was rest. In a letter to Nora dated July 19, 1900, she wrote, "My lady has come home and is working me too hard as I didn't do a thing while she was gone but have a good rest I went to bed every after noon. . . . She was gone eleven weeks" (O'Malley Collection).

Hannah and Nora were not alone—letters written to Nora by other friends who also were Irish immigrant domestics provide further testimony to the hard work faced by servants, and to the fact that the work increased in proportion to the number of people living in an employer's house. In a letter to Nora enclosed in an envelope postmarked April 11, 1897, Mary Holland wrote from Boston that as a domestic, "I got to work hard enough." In like fashion, on March 17, 1897, from Lowell, Massachusetts, Mary Anne Donovan wrote to Nora that "I got plenty to do I dont be Iddle." And on April 20, 1897, when Mary Anne again wrote to Nora from Lowell, she said, "I am now working In a family of 4 2 children & the father & mother. . . . [T]hey Or quiet particular & Hard to be pleased . . . [so] I Am not quiet sure will I stay their or not." Earlier, in a letter enclosed in an envelope postmarked January 21, 1897, Noney Hayes had written from Boston to Nora that "I have eight in our family to work for so you Can Just Imagine what a snap I have" (O'Malley Collection).

Other Irish immigrant friends also complained to Nora McCarthy about their work in service. From Boston on January 20, 1897, Kate Monohan wrote, "Dear Nora I am to inform [you] that I changed places. . . . [I] has to work Much harder as there is ten in my family." One year later Kate was in yet another job, this time in Roxbury, Massachusetts, and in her letter to Nora of January 7, 1898, she had this to say about the job: "Its a purty hard place." Small wonder that domestic servants tried to improve their lot by changing jobs in a continual search for an improved employment situation. As Noney Hayes wrote to Nora from Boston, in her letter postmarked January 21, 1897, "Intend leaving my Place pretty Soon If you should hear of a nice plase would you Please Let me know" (O'Malley Collection).

Changing jobs was facilitated by having a "home" with Irish relatives in which to stay between jobs. As already noted, Hannah Collins had just such a home in Elmira, New York, with her cousin Mrs. Dempsey, whereas Nora McCarthy had such a home in Haverhill, Massachusetts, with her sister Mary Donovan. Other Irish girls just presumed they would return home to Ireland if things failed to work out for them as servants in the United States. Mary Feely, who began working in service in America in 1927, said she never worried about being out of work because "I thought, well, if I was laid off from my job, I could go home [to Ireland]" (1996).

Mary Malone found domestic service in New York State rough going because of her lack of preparation for it. In a letter dated January 24, 1877, and possibly written from Fairport, New York, she wrote to her brother in Ireland that "my wages is so little and I am not capable of earning big wages like other girls who can cook and the large washings and fine ironings. . . . I never got much in sight about house keeping" (Schrier Collection). Mary King Conroy, who left Ballyconneely, County Galway, in 1912 to do housework in Boston, "always talked about how hard they had to work and how not every house treated these girls all that well" (Greaney 1998). Margaret Convery, who came to the United States in 1914, said of her first job in housework, "I worked for a lady that had . . . two children. . . . I had to do everything. . . . I had to learn to cook, . . . and you done the wash, clean the house" (1991, 47, 48). Mary Boyle, who came to the United States in 1929, said her work as a domestic in America always involved child care as well as housework. Of one of the domestic jobs that she held, she said, "There was three children and housework and you did . . . from ceiling to floors, everything" (1995, 30, 31). Bridget McGeoghegan, who came to the United States in 1923 at age twenty-two, said of domestic work in America, "When you came to this country . . . you had to work hard. . . . I worked in a family. . . . She was a good lady . . . but, oh lord, she loved to work. She always said Bertha do not leave until tomorrow what you can do today. That was her daily cry. . . . [T]here was no such thing as hours" (1987, 7).

To properly appreciate the situation of Irish domestics, one must understand that most of them were young; in the nineteenth century, before the advent of compulsory education laws and child protective labor laws, some were very young. Helen Chapman wrote to her mother in October 1848 that Ann Mitchell, her Irish servant, was "not yet thirteen" (Coker 1992, 82). In 1911, I. M. Rubinow of the U.S. Department of Commerce and Labor found the number of domestics aged younger than sixteen large enough to indicate "a large child labor problem" (1911, 133–34). For transplanted young Irish girls, domestic service could have been a lonely experience, at least initially. It is probably no wonder, then, that Irish domestic Anastasia Dowling wrote home from Buffalo, New York, on January 20, 1870, that "I feel very lonesome here," noting that "the ways of this place is so diferent from home" (Schrier Collection). The separation from their families must have been very difficult for them. Mary O'Hanlon wrote from New York City to her mother in Ireland in an undated letter believed to have been written in the fall of 1871, "My dear mother after I came here at time I thought my heart would have broken thinking of you" (K. Miller Collection). And in her January 24, 1877, letter to her brother in Ireland, Irish servant Mary Malone also revealed that she was "verry lonseom and down harted" (Schrier Collection). In Elmira, New York, Hannah Collins was also homesick. In a letter postmarked September 7, 1898, she confessed to Nora McCarthy, "I get homesick and lonesome often." Though time probably diminished her lonesomeness, it did not completely eradicate it, for in her letter postmarked June 21, 1900, she wrote, "Well dear Nora I got so lonesome when I read your dear letter that I had to cry thinking of you and all our good old times" (O'Malley Collection). Loneliness made servants anxious for correspondence from home, and sad when none materialized. In Catherine McFarland's March 5, 1855, letter to her mother in Ireland, she wrote, "i doo feel so bad when the Mails Comes in and now letter i sit down and cry My fill" (K. Miller Collection).

At the end of the period 1840 to 1930 Irish domestics felt loneliness and homesickness as keenly as they did at its start. Mary Cox, who immigrated in 1925, said, "I did miss Ireland. I missed Ireland so much. . . . Most I missed essentially was my mother and father, my parents" (1991, 36, 37). Mary Boyle, who came to the United States in 1929, said that once the realization set in that she could not easily return to Ireland, "many times, many nights

I went to bed and cried myself sick" (1995, 21). Homesickness could also lead to errors in judgment that jeopardized a domestic's employment. In the early twentieth century one newly arrived and very homesick young Irish girl turned up inebriated at the Immigrant's Home in Boston after falling in with a bad crowd, previously unknown to her, from her hometown in Ireland. A threat of deportation helped her to shape up, and she was subsequently placed in service in a private home (Moloney 1999, 59).

Some Americans recognized the difficult position of the new young Irish immigrant who worked as a maid-of-all-work. Author Harriet Prescott Spofford pointed out sympathetically that in service, the Irish maid-of-all-work spent her day "bent over a hot cooking-stove, . . . bent over dish-pans and wash-tubs, and dusters and brooms; bent over back-aching ironing-boards and terrible scrubbing-brushes; her whole life enlisted for a continual warfare with dirt and discomfort" (1977, 37).

Unsurprisingly, the Irish Bridget was known for her reluctance to take jobs outside urban areas, where she would have been further isolated (Dudden 1983, 198). Another key to understanding the situation of the Irish domestic is to acknowledge the reality she faced—the house in which she worked was not a home or refuge; it was a work site. As Hannah Collins wrote to Nora McCarthy in a letter enclosed in an envelope postmarked July 22, 1899, "I aint got any home here." And as one employer told a servant, "If you take a servant's place, you can't expect to be one of the family" (Campbell 1889, 225).

In addition to loneliness and homesickness, domestic workers faced a difficulty usually thought of in terms of industrial workers—on-the-job injuries for which no compensation was provided and which might preclude them from continuing to support themselves. The hazards household workers faced that could lead to on-the-job injuries included dealing with "wet or polished floors; loose rugs; stairs and cellar and attic steps; climbing, reaching, lifting, carrying; fires, gas, electricity, fuel oils, cleaning chemicals; scalding fluids; hot irons; sharp utensils; fragile glass and china" (Watson 1932, 63). Irish storyteller Peig Sayers, for example, never made it to America because her friend Cait-Jim was injured while working in service in the United States. Cait-Jim wrote Peig that she would send her the passage money to come to America. Then, in a subsequent letter, Cait-Jim wrote to say that "she could not send . . . the money . . . for she had injured her hand and could do no work" (1974, 149–50). Two of Nora McCarthy's friends also suffered injuries while working in service. On February 13, 1897, Kate

Monohan wrote from Boston to Nora asking to be excused for taking so long in replying to Nora's last letter. Kate said, "My dear friend It was owing to a Sore hand which I had for a week or two past that I have not answered your letter Sooner I burned my fore fingers & could not handle my pen for Some time but they are all better now with the exception of one which is quite Sore yet." Earlier that same year, on January 17, Mary Anne Donovan had written to Nora that she, too, had been delayed in responding to Nora's last letter because she "had a Very Soar hand." Mary Anne went on to say, "I burned It so it kept me from Writing to any one It is getting better now" (O'Malley Collection). In the Boston area in the early twentieth century, the employers of an eighteen-year-old Irish nanny sent her out to purchase alcohol for them. While running the errand she was injured in an accident, the end result of which was that she lost her job, her life went downhill, and it was suggested that she be deported (Moloney 1999, 58).

On-the-job injuries could also be suffered in the particularly awful form of employer-inflicted beatings. On December 31, 1857, the *Hartford Daily Courant* reported that following throwing a cat at the head of an Irish servant named Bridget Kennedy, her employer, Marshall Pinney, kicked and beat her. Pinney was fined six dollars in court for his actions, which the judge termed "premeditated ugliness."

Illness of any kind could cause a domestic to lose or at least fear to lose her employment, so some just ignored their ailments. From Utica, New York, Mary Cleer wrote to her uncle in Ireland on May 14, 1899, that even though she had an abscess on her neck, "I worked through it all . . . done my work with my head on one shoulder. . . . I was afraid my head would never straighten" (K. Miller Collection).

Assertive Irish Servant Girls

Alexis de Tocqueville observed that in the American democracy in which "at any moment a servant may become a master," no distinct servant class existed (1990, 180, 181). He correctly pointed out, however, that American servants were left in a peculiar situation in which "by the laws they [servants] are brought up to the level of their masters," while, simultaneously, "by the manners of the country they are firmly kept below it" (183). As a result, Tocqueville declared, servants "do not themselves clearly know their proper place and are almost always either insolent or craven" (181). Irish servant girls illustrate the veracity of Tocqueville's observations. The assertive behavior of Irish servant girls, rooted in Irish culture and exacerbated by their democratic notions of equality, defied their American employers' expectations of submissive servant behavior. Irish servant girls most certainly did *not* accept the middle-class American view of them as the inferiors of the middle class.

On February 2, 1852, the first in a series of disparaging articles on Irish domestics appeared in the *Boston Daily Evening Transcript.* A woman using the pen name "Veritas" wrote the articles (to which reference was made in chapter 4), which she titled "Trouble in Families: Servants as They Are Nowadays." Veritas castigated Irish girls for demanding "the highest wages," wearing "absurd finery," requiring "great privileges," and insisting on church attendance more to keep up with current "gossip" than for the good of their souls. Veritas commented that it was no wonder that "many families . . . positively refused to take Irish girls at all, . . . especially such as are Roman Catholic." On February 4, she suggested that Irish Catholic servants be forbidden from attending early morning mass unless they first finished all their housework and "until it is proved by the good conduct of our servants that they positively go to church." Failing this advice, she suggested that employers "determine to employ none but German, Scotch or American servants." And on February 9, Veritas also complained that when the employing family faced illness or some other such problem, their Irish servants were loath to give up their afternoons off to help the family, and, instead, seemed to "choose these very occasions to ask permission to attend a ball or an Irish wedding!"

Veritas's comments sparked a response in the form of a series of letters to the editor that appeared in the *Boston Pilot,* a newspaper read by the Irish throughout America. The author of these letters was ostensibly an Irish servant girl calling herself "Bridget." Whether the author of these letters truly was an Irish servant girl, however, is open to question. The letters may very well have been written by someone else, such as the editor of the paper, to indicate the official Catholic Church "line" on the issues Veritas raised.[7] Nonetheless, the "Bridget letters" are important because they resonated with the readers of the *Pilot* who actually *were* Irish domestics. According to a correspondent to the *Pilot* from Wisconsin, Irish servant girls there

7. One or more people must have questioned, probably with good reason, whether Bridget was a real Irish domestic servant because the *Boston Pilot* printed this note on February 21, 1852: "We make it a rule not to insert communications unless the name is sent to us in confidence, or otherwise. This rule admits of a few exceptions. . . . But we are in possession of the real name and address of Bridget" (7).

supported Bridget's comments on mistresses. This correspondent, whose words appeared in the April 3, 1852, issue, wrote that girls "came to me in drifts to hear that letter [Bridget's letter] read, and many a blessing poor Bridget got. The only murmur I heard from them was, that she did not say half as much as she could" (4).

In her February 28, 1852, letter to the editor of the *Boston Pilot,* this "Bridget" wrote, "Servants talk over their mistresses, just as the mistresses talk about us. And servants generally come to know all the failings of their mistresses." In her earlier letter of February 21, Bridget suggested that Veritas was probably a nouveau riche woman who was insecure in her position when she commented, "These rich women that have risen from poverty, and are always looking round for fear that we'll [Irish servants] tread on the skirts of their dignity, make awful bad mistresses." Continuing in the same vein, in the same letter, she said of Veritas's suggestion that servant privileges be reduced, "That's just what you hear men and women, who have risen [?] from poverty, and are as vulgar as they [ever?] was, say about their workmen and servants. Cut their wages down; cut their privileges down. . . . [R]eal ladies . . . laugh at her . . . as loud as we servant girls do."[8] Bridget also guessed that part of Veritas's problem with her Irish servants might have been that she was jealous of their good looks! Calling Veritas "bigoted," in this same letter Bridget contended that Veritas wanted to keep Irish servants "from going to mass . . . because she hates us and our religion."

Bridget maintained that some people with limited means hired servants to keep up appearances. Such mistresses, according to what she wrote in her March 6 letter, "hire only one girl, or two at the farthest, and they can't always pay or feed them, while the girls have to do awful hard work, because these poor genteels is proud, and they want to keep up the outside appearance that people do that have four or five servants." In her February 14 letter, Bridget also accused the insecure, nosy mistress she felt Veritas was of eavesdropping on her servants, saying, "She likes to know what is going on in her house, so she *listens* to what we girls say in the kitchen."

Instead of being servile, Irish servant girls displayed assertive behavior. Their behavior can be attributed to two factors: they likely represented the most independent of Irish women of their time, and verbally assertive

8. The question marks refer to words that were unclear as I read a microfilm version of the newspaper.

women were an acknowledged presence in Irish culture. In fact, as James Reford's correspondence illustrates, the lack of servility demonstrated by Irish servant girls certainly offended some Protestant men from Northern Ireland. On April 9, 1873, Reford wrote from New Jersey to his sister in County Antrim that in America, girls "from the bogs of Conoght," some of whom he said were illiterate, invented a high-status Irish past for themselves, claiming they had had maids in Ireland, their fathers had owned large farms, and it was "a low day when they came to Amerky." He said that when they were interviewed for employment as domestics in the United States, they asked the potential employer such questions as "Have you got hot and cold water in the house . . . is My Bed room Carpeted . . . what privileges . . . " In Utica, New York, Irish servant Mary Cleer certainly displayed assertiveness. In a letter that she wrote to her uncle on May 14, 1899, she declared that she took care of a "mean" Welshman with whom she worked by taking "a pot of hot coffee" and giving "it to him between the two eyes." Through the intervention of her employer, she escaped arrest for the incident (K. Miller Collection). Mary Terry Kelly, who left Ring, County Waterford, for the Boston area in 1923, applied for a live-in domestic job with a family in the Back Bay area. She was offered the job contingent on her acceptance of the idea that she could go to mass only every other week. In reply Mary said, "I don't want it on those grounds. I'll take it on the condition that I'll go [to church] every Sunday, or I won't take it." The employer then acquiesced to Mary's demand, and she remained on the job for almost ten years (O'Carroll 1990, 49–50). Such assertive Irish girls also disliked reminders of their supposed lesser status. Mary Feely resented being required to use the servant staircase: "I didn't like . . . the idea of going down the stairs, the back stairs that went in the house and all that. Kind of annoyed me in the beginning" (1996).

Relations with Others

Unsurprisingly, since most American homes were staffed by a single servant, little is known about how the Irish Bridgets who worked in homes employing multiple servants got along with one another, or with non-Irish servants, in the houses in which they worked. Ellen Brady, who worked on an estate outside New York City that had a staff of more than fifty people, mentioned that the staff included an Irish housekeeper and an Irish laundress, and other people "from all over the world," as well as English footmen. It was not the ethnicity of the staff that concerned her, but rather their age. Ellen said, "It was mostly all old people" with whom she worked, so she was lonely; in her limited time off, she socialized with girls from her hometown in Ireland who also worked as domestics (1977, 28–36).

The quotations from native-born American girls cited earlier in this chapter demonstrate that being required to work with Irish girls made domestic service objectionable to them. The extent to which Irish girls were aware of such negative perceptions of them, and how they reacted to such perceptions, is not clear in the record. Indications of possible rivalry between Swedish and Irish domestics, however, can be found in comments made by Swedes. They proclaimed that their domestics were "more reliable and hard-working than Irish women" and were thus "more sought-after for domestic positions" (Lintelman 1991, 390). Nonetheless, some Irish domestics *did* make friends across ethnic lines. Rose McGurk, who came over in 1928, at age sixteen, said that she "mixed with all nationalities." She made great friends with a Polish girl she met while looking for a Catholic church on her first Sunday in domestic work in Brooklyn; the Polish girl, too, was in search of a Catholic church. In America, Rose also made friends with a Hungarian girl named Tessie (Aisling 2006, 9–12).

The ranks of domestic servants in America were populated by African Americans, as well as by Irish immigrants. How did the Irish Bridgets get along with African American domestics? It has been alleged that Irish immigrant and African American females competed for jobs in domestic service, and speculation has been made that Irish immigrants may actually have supplanted free black domestics in service in the North in the 1830s and '40s (Ernst 1994, 104; Wittke 1956, 126; Dudden 1983, 64). The hostility that scholars have identified as characteristic of Irish relations with African Americans in the United States may very well have permeated relations between Irish immigrant and African American domestics (Nelson 2007, 66, 67; Wittke 1956, 125).[9] Such hostility can be inferred from the limited evidence that exists showing that some Irish domestics refused to work in houses employing African Americans (Dudden 1983, 64–65). Yet evidence also exists showing more nuance in relations between Irish and African Americans, at least in New York City's Sixth Ward between 1830 and 1870. In that ward, not only did some Irish and African American women work together

9. Noel Ignatiev (1995) faults the Irish for moving upward and achieving status as "white" in America by joining in the oppression of African Americans instead of joining together in solidarity with them. His study, however, focuses on Irish *men*. Other scholarly "whiteness" studies, such as Jacobson 2000, Roediger 2002, and Roediger 2005, also give short shrift to women.

as washerwomen, but some Irish women are known to have married African American men (Hodges 1996, 107, 121–22).

Nevertheless, other Irish women evidenced obvious prejudice against African Americans. Consider the case of Irish immigrant Ellie Driscoll Enright, for example. Enright, whose fellow Irish immigrant friends worked as servants, ended up employing an African American domestic in her own home. Her comments reveal that she had absorbed racist American ideas, as well as American employer attitudes toward domestics, and that she failed to appreciate the irony of her situation. On May 5, 1900, she wrote from Washington, D.C., to a friend, Irish immigrant domestic Nora McCarthy, "What do you supose I got a Collored maid she is as black as the ace of spades but a good worker Washington is a great place for them the only thing about them they smell so bad and steal all the eye can see but mine is a cathelick" (O'Malley Collection). On the other hand, the attitudes of some Irish domestics toward African Americans (but not specifically African American domestics) in the twentieth century evidence more curiosity, ignorance, and fear than hatred. Lillian Doran, who came to the United States in 1912, said, "I never saw a black child till I come off the boat in New York, and I saw a bunch of them, . . . on the sidewalk, playing ball and skipping. I thought it was great" (1993, 27). Ann Sexton, who came to the United States in 1922, thought it was the powerful sun that turned people black in the United States—she did not realize that they were born with dark skin (1986, 10–11). Helen Flatley said that she had never seen a black man before coming to America in 1928, and that she was frightened by the sight of one (1996a). In short, relations between Irish domestics and African Americans present a mixed bag—many, but certainly not all, Irish were hostile to them and shared the racist attitudes toward African Americans that were held by members of general American society.[10]

The Irish Bridgets may have been looked down upon by native-born American girls, and they, in turn, may have looked down on African American domestics. Their relations with both African American and Swedish

10. Irish domestics' attitudes toward Jewish employers also evidence diversity. Famine-era Protestant Irish immigrant Ann McNabb was unapologetically anti-Semitic. She left her first job when she learned her employer was Jewish, declaring, "I can't eat the bread of them as crucified the Saviour." To no avail, her employer reminded McNabb that Jesus was Jewish (Holt 1906, 146). In contrast, Catholic Irish immigrant Helen Flatley, who came over in 1928, said that she worked for "Jewish people whom I dearly loved," and that "Jewish people, [were] the best" (1996a).

women may have involved competition for domestic jobs. They may also have made friends across ethnic lines. But since the most common domestic employment position held by Irish girls was that of the lone maid-of-all-work, their contact with domestics other than the Irish was probably limited. The lone maid-of-all-work typically faced a daunting workload and workday, because the ratio of staff to family was a key determinant in the amount of work she faced. Conversely, the workload was lighter for those girls employed in multiple-servant households. Since the Irish Bridget tended to be young and single, the isolated situation of a maid-of-all-work was all the more difficult for her, and contributed to her homesickness and loneliness. Yet despite the social stigma attached to domestic service, Irish girls staffed the servant ranks because service work met their immediate needs for employment, food, and shelter, and it enabled them to save their wages and remit money home to their families in Ireland. These Irish girls saw service as a taxing but temporary job, rather than a lifelong vocation. As we shall see in chapter 6, they expected to have some fun while single, and eventually to find husbands for themselves in America and, upon marriage, to leave service "for good" to stay home and raise children. Thus, with regard to their Irish servants, Americans misread the situation entirely in their belief that the Irish formed a social class of servants.

The Social World of the Irish Bridget

In an undated letter penned on January 9, sometime in the 1890s, Irish immigrant domestic Nora Hayes wrote from Hyde Park, Massachusetts, to her friend and fellow domestic Nora McCarthy, also residing in Massachusetts, "I have changed Places Sience I received your last Letter & do not intend to Stay only a Short time in this confounded whol I have had no Prevelages what-Soever not even any Company I fell thou I am in Prisonment" (O'Malley Collection). Nora Hayes's vehement complaints illuminate the difficulties a live-in servant had in maintaining a social life. Nevertheless, because service work often isolated the young Irish girl from her friends and family, the Irish Bridget determined to construct for herself a social life that revolved around maintaining written correspondence with family and friends, visiting friends, attending the Irish dances, and participating in religious services and devotions.

Correspondence

In the transatlantic correspondence of their American letters Irish servants indicated their continuing attachment to home and demonstrated that they maintained social lives that were partially anchored in Ireland. In an undated letter believed to have been written in the fall of 1871, Irish domestic Mary O'Hanlon wrote to her mother in Ireland, "You will think me foolish for writing you all this but its so like talking to you that I could write a week" (K. Miller Collection). Irish domestic Sarah Brady, who immigrated in 1912, said she "used to write continually" to her family in Ireland (1975, 3). And Helen Flatley, who immigrated in 1928, said, "I wrote, I wrote a lot," and remembered that from Ireland in return came "such lovely, lovely letters from my mother and she wrote to me all the time. And then when my other sister came out, Peggy, she wrote to both of us" (1996b).

In their correspondence, servants often asked the family at home for photographs. In the letter referred to above, Mary O'Hanlon also wrote,

"I would like to have your likeness" (K. Miller Collection). Sending photographs across the sea was a reciprocal process. In her May 24, 1895, letter to her sister in Haverhill, Massachusetts, Katie McCarthy of Ballinlough, Leap, County Cork, wrote, "Nora I would like very much to get your green horn picture if you could get it taken." Nora apparently obliged her sister, because Katie's September 5, 1895, letter to Nora indicates the profound effect receipt of Nora's photograph had on the family at home. "The picture looks exactly like you but you are not jolly looking like I was accustomed to see you," Katie wrote. "Mother and I cried our eyes out when we had seen you and you could not speak to us." When Katie showed the photograph to their father, "He says she is Nora and the tears rolled down his cheeks when you could not speak to him" (O'Malley Collection).

Irish servant girls also enclosed American newspapers in their letters to family and friends in Ireland, and in return mail received Irish newspapers. In a letter written to her sister Kate on October 1, 1870, Mary O'Hanlon reported not only that she "received a paper from P McCartram" but that she would also "send a paper or too to some parties." In the 1871 letter to her mother mentioned previously, O'Hanlon noted further, "Sure I sent Robert Gracey three papers on Saturday week" (K. Miller Collection).

American observers like author Harriet Prescott Spofford noticed how dear to Irish servant girls were shamrocks, symbols of their native land. In 1881 Spofford wrote, "They bring to one another a bit of the sod of the old land with a sprig of shamrock growing in it; they keep it in their windows or on the shelf with adoring care, as if it were the modern Lares and Penates" (1881, 56). Since shamrocks have been worn by the Irish on Saint Patrick's Day as far back as the late seventeenth century, the family in Ireland often enclosed shamrocks in correspondence sent around that date to their Irish domestic relations in America (Kinmonth 2006, 187). On March 1, 1896, Katie McCarthy wrote to her servant sister in America, "Dear Nora, Mother went out this evening picking Shamrock. . . . I hope you will have it in time." And on March 17, 1897, in the United States, Mary Anne Donovan wrote to her friend and fellow domestic Nora McCarthy, "I had a letter [from Ireland] on monday The 15 of March & the shamrock [was in the letter]." Mary Anne inquired of Nora, "let me no if you got the shamrock for Patrick's day" (O'Malley Collection).[1]

1. My review of Irish immigrant letters shows that it was fairly common for the Irish at home to send shamrocks to their people in the United States around Saint Patrick's Day; domestics were not the only recipients of these tokens from home.

Some Irish domestics maintained such transatlantic correspondence with home throughout their lifetimes. According to Maryellen McDonagh, for as long as she could recall, her mother, Kathleen Mannion, who had worked in domestic service when she first came to the United States in 1929, received a letter from her sisters in Ireland every month. In her return correspondence, Mannion always sent the family in Ireland clothing that Maryellen had outgrown. When Maryellen met her relatives in Ireland for the first time, one cousin remarked that she felt she already knew Maryellen since she grew up wearing her clothes (2002)!

The distance between Ireland and America was great, however, and so the connection maintained with the family at home in Ireland through correspondence could waver or be severed. Failure to receive return correspondence from the family in Ireland certainly occasioned much anxiety in the Irish girls in America. In a letter sent from Boston and postmarked October 2, 1896, Irish domestic Kate Monohan wrote to Nora McCarthy, "I did not hear from home for quite awhile I don't know what's the reason they don't write." From Elmira, New York, Hannah Collins wrote to Nora McCarthy in Massachusetts on March 7, 1900, "I am worried I had not a letter from home lately I should have got one a week go. I dont know what is the matter with them for they never delayed so long" (O'Malley Collection). Irish domestic Ellen Brady, who immigrated after World War I, dismissed such breakdowns in transatlantic communication between Irish servants and their families by observing, "You know how the Irish are. They don't write. . . . They never answer ya" (1977, 54).

Money issues also caused some Irish domestics, like Ella Ahearn, to sever the connection with home. Ahearn, who immigrated in the second decade of the twentieth century, said she kept up her correspondence with home until they asked her for money, "and I didn't have it to send to them, and then I quit writing to them. And then I changed addresses and I guess they couldn't maybe find me there. Sent it, but I think the mail went back" (1989, 45).

Since Irish servant girls also craved social lives in the United States, they determined to keep in contact with their Irish friends here. They did so through letters, such as the lively correspondence that Nora McCarthy's Irish immigrant servant friends maintained with her. They shared with each other news of the family at home in Ireland, and when the news from home was bad, they offered each other their condolences. After learning that Nora's sister Katie had died at home in Ireland, in a letter postmarked January 21,

1897, Noney Hayes wrote, "Norah I know must feel quite lonesome for Poor Katie Words cannot express to you how sad I fell for Poor Good natured Katie." They also shared general family news. On June 10, 1899, Hannah Collins wrote to Nora that she had received news from home that "they were all well and you will be surprised to hear that Auntie Norry was living with them now . . . the poor thing how lonesome she must be without any of her own children to look after her" (O'Malley Collection).

News about those from home who had married as well as those who had not was also a topic of stateside correspondence. In a letter sent from Elmira, postmarked May 27, 1898, Hannah wrote, "Nora dear you wished to know who Ellie Driscoll married I dont know but I guess its one of the Sullivans." The following year, in a March 15, 1899, letter, Hannah observed, "Nora, how very few got married around Ballinlough its a wonder your Cousins Jerry and Dennie McCarthy don't get married." They also discussed recent immigrants, with Hannah commenting in her May 24, 1899, letter to Nora, "I was surprised to hear Julia Hayes came out to this country." The following month, in a letter dated June 21, Hannah wrote from Elmira with news of another newly arrived immigrant: "Dear Nora, I seen a green horn the other night. he is from our place home his name is Jerry Donoghue he told us about our folks to home" (O'Malley Collection).

In their stateside correspondence, Irish domestics also shared with one another news of their American-based families and friends. On October 9, 1896, from Dorchester, Massachusetts, Kate Monohan wrote to Nora with news about her ill brother Pat, as well as news about her sister, Maggie, and brothers Michael and Con. And on August 17, 1897, again from Dorchester, she wrote to Nora to congratulate her on the birth of her niece Katie Donovan, saying, "I hope she will long enjoy her name" (O'Malley Collection).

Irish servant girls also confessed their homesickness for Ireland in their correspondence. From Boston on January 3, 1896, Kate Monohan wrote to Nora in Bradford, Massachusetts, "Dear Nora how did you enjoy yourself during the holidays I did not enjoy myself at all I cried my fill Xmas night when I thought of home." They also shared their happy recollections of home in their correspondence. From Elmira on December 18, 1899, Hannah Collins wrote to Nora, "I wish you a merry Christmas and a Happy New Year. . . . I only wish we could be together and have a good time as I well remember our Christmases home and how we used to spend them" (O'Malley Collection).

Dreams of each other and home also were featured in their letters. On December 1, 1898, from Elmira, Hannah Collins wrote to Nora, "I had an awful dream about you the other night. . . . [I]t was in this country but after a little while we were back again to dear Ballinlough. . . . I could not get that sweet place off my mind." Dreams were often connected with worry about the people at home. While a patient in the Boston Eye and Ear Hospital, on January 12, 1899, Nora McCarthy wrote to her sister Mary Donovan in Haverhill of her worry about the family in Ireland because "I been dreaming of them last night." And from Elmira on August 24, 1899, Hannah Collins wrote to Nora, "I kind of think Auntie Nory is dead because I have been dreaming so much of her lately" (O'Malley Collection).

From Somerville, Massachusetts, on January 17, 1897, Mary Anne Donovan (Nora's Irish friend from home and a fellow domestic, not Nora's sister Mary Donovan) fretted that she was "thinking from time To time if we would Ever see one another One hear & the other their." One way Irish domestics dealt with such fears and maintained their connection to each other was to share photographs. From Dorchester on October 9, 1896, Kate Monohan wrote to Nora in Haverhill, "About My picture, I have not taken any So far but myself & Maggie is going to have them taken soon I shall send you one but dont you wait for mine If you have yours send me one." Similarly, on January 17, 1897, from Somerville, Mary Anne Donovan wrote to Nora, "I never got my Pictures taken Since But I intend to please Nora send me one In your next letter." And about the same time, in a letter postmarked January 21, 1897, from Boston, Noney Hayes wrote to Nora in Haverhill, asking "if you got any tintype picture of yours I wish you would send me one in the next Letter" (O'Malley Collection).

In their letters to her, Nora's servant friends also found expression for the affection lacking in their daily work lives. Rather like the correspondence of white middle-class Protestant American women that Carroll Smith-Rosenberg analyzes in "The Female World of Love and Ritual: Relations Between Women in Nineteenth-Century America" (1985), Nora's friends' letters evidence intense female friendships. On May 12, 1898, for example, from Elmira, Hannah Collins wrote to Nora that "I thinks of you all the time. . . . I am sure you are a fine looking girl now I only wish I could see that Darling sweet face of your's it would do me lots of good." Hannah concluded the letter, saying, "Well my darling Nora I must finish by saying Good Bye," and signed the letter, "Your's loving Hannah," followed by, as she frequently did in her correspondence with Nora, several *x*'s, indicating kisses. In her September 23, 1899, letter to Nora, Hannah confessed, "I am always thinking about you. and I love you now as much as ever and you know how dearly I always loved you." In other letters, written between May and September 1898, Hannah addressed Nora as "My Darling Nora," "My Own Darling Nora," "My Own dear Nora," and "My Ever darling Nora." These letters sometimes contained little verses. On October 30, 1891, at the conclusion of her letter to Nora she wrote:

> Remember me when this you see
> Think me not unkind
> although your face I cannot see
> You are the dearest in my mind. (O'Malley Collection)

Nora's other fellow Irish domestics wrote to her in a similar manner, with Kate Monohan addressing Nora as "My Dearest Nora" in a letter sent from Boston dated January 3, 1896, and concluding letters with "kisses to darling Nora" followed by several *x*'s, as she did in her April 8, 1896, letter. Kate ended that letter from South Boston to Nora in Haverhill, saying, "Best regards from the one who loves you Good night Dear for awhile." She, too, included some original verse in her letters, for on August 17, 1897, she wrote to Nora from Dorchester, "If in the storm of life you need an umberella May you have to uphold it a handsome young fellow." Mary Anne Donovan also addressed Nora in a deeply affectionate way, for in a letter written from Somerville on January 17, 1897, she called her "My most loving friend"; Mary Anne concluded her letters with *x*'s (O'Malley Collection).

The affectionate language used in these letters symbolizes cultural continuity, for historically in the Irish language, people frequently addressed one another, male and female, in terms of endearment. As Irish servant girls' correspondence demonstrates, when the Irish made the transition in the nineteenth century from the Irish to the English language, they continued to use tender terms in their English-language speech, as they had in Irish. The highly affectionate language lonely Irish immigrant girls used with one another is also indicative of their deep need for emotional connection with friends from home. Loss of a friend's address was to be dreaded. As Mary Anne Donovan wrote from Lowell, Massachusetts, to Nora in Haverhill on February 15, 1897, "Dear Nora I suppose you have by this time forgotten me I would have written long Ago but I lost the address so I felt bad but to my surprise yesterday when I went in to my trunk I found it Inside a little box which you may Be sure I sought for eagerly" (O'Malley Collection).

Visiting

Despite contention to the contrary, in both the nineteenth and the twentieth centuries Irish domestics exerted themselves to ensure that their lives as live-in servants did *not* preclude them from maintaining ties with the Irish immigrant community (Hotten-Somers 2001, 187, 199). Through visiting back and forth, Irish domestics maintained contact, and therefore a social life, with their U.S.-based Irish friends and family. In a letter he wrote to his mother in Ireland from Philadelphia on March 26, sometime in the 1880s, Owen O'Callaghan, for example, mentioned that his sister Bridget, who worked as a domestic, "enjoys herself with the other Waterford girls" (K. Miller Collection). A servant's ability to have company in to visit in the house in which she was employed depended, however, on the acquiescence of her employer, and many employers were not partial to the idea. Even if the employer agreed to let a servant's friends visit, the servant generally had no place in which to entertain them, for as Rheta Childe Dorr pointed out in reference to Boston in 1910, few houses were "provided with a servants' sitting room. There was absolutely no provision made for callers" (1910, 266–67). Nonetheless, from the employer complaints on this topic found in popular American literature, we know that the social lives Irish servants constructed for themselves involved entertaining friends in the houses in which they were employed. In 1864, one author noted that Bridget, the sociable Irish domestic, "likes to entertain John the coachman . . . , or Patrick the livery-stable man . . . or the Widow M'Guire with her nine small children." While finding Bridget's friends amusing, the author acknowledged that employers disliked hearing "in the parlor the echo of the Irish howl, the loud Hibernian guffaw and rich brogue from the kitchen, and object[ed] to the daily entertainment of Bridget's hearty company at the expense of their larders" ("Your Humble Servant" 1864, 57). Or, as another employer put it, mistresses were not amused by "girls who entertain a brilliant circle of friends in their kitchens, at the mistress's expense," or by those who entertained "legions of 'cousins' on her employer's victuals" ("The Servant Question" 1865, 528; Dickens 1874, 585).

Wise employers, however, retained servants by meeting their needs, including their need for company. So some authors, like R. R. Bowker, advised employers to "allow them to receive friends in a proper manner"

(1871, 501). Noting the isolation of servant life, author Annette Jaynes Miller stated that while she never permitted servants to entertain friends during work hours, she did permit her servants to have company at night, and even apologized to them that "there is no place for them to entertain but the kitchen" (1905). And in 1909, recognizing that "they must have companionship," the wife of "A Thankful Husband" permitted her servant girls "to receive their company in the basement sitting-room, and to have a quiet game of cards or a cup of tea with them" (1909). Mary Feely's employer in the late 1920s and 1930s must have been of this school of thought. Her employer not only let her have visitors but let her feed them as well. According to Feely, although her servant's room "was tiny," she "always had a lot of food. . . . for the girls that come in" (1996).

Many employers were particularly opposed to servant girls having male visitors. Such employers forbade their servants from having "followers," as boyfriends were termed. As author Robert Tomes put it, the servant "is forbidden the companionship of her male friends, and is denounced as a trollop if she is caught passing a stolen word to the baker or butcher at the back door" (1871, 231). It is clear, however, that some employers *did* allow their servants to entertain gentleman callers, for in her 1917 book, *Simple Directions for the Cook,* Caroline Reed Wadhams advised cooks that "men callers should not be permitted to smoke where the smoke penetrates to the family living rooms" (1917, 10).

Nora McCarthy's servant friends were anxious to visit with her during their time off. On January 17, 1897, Mary Anne Donovan wrote from the Boston area to Nora in Haverhill, "I hope nora That you will Come To boston this summer." Mary Anne went on to say, "I had a Letter from Ellie Collins she is asking me to go to wakefield Some Sunday Nora If you might Come Down we would go For the fun of it to See the place I had Been their once Before." Kate Monohan also wrote to Nora, on February 13, 1897, stating that on the following Sunday she expected Nora to take the train to visit her in Boston, emphasizing, "I Sincerely hope you wont fail in Making your appearance." In the following year, on January 7, Kate demonstrated that visiting was a reciprocal activity, as she wrote, "Dear Nora I arrived home alright Saturday afternoon . . . but felt very lonesome for all my Haverhill folks I enjoyed my trip very much." In an earlier letter, postmarked April 11, 1897, Mary Holland wrote that she, too, wanted to get together with Nora: "Now Dear Nora I am very anxious to see you and Nelly I would go to see you Some time Soon if I only knew the way or perhaps ye Could Come to see me when you write Agane you please tell me what to do." How much Hannah Collins wanted to visit Nora is clear in her letters. In an April 5, 1900, letter to Nora she admitted, "I do be thinking of you every day and night and praying for that day to come when I will see you, or do you think we shall meet again." Hannah worried about the distance between Elmira, New York, and Haverhill, Massachusetts, saying in a letter written on June 21, 1900, "I would love to go to see you but I guess its too far" (O'Malley Collection).

The correspondence Nora McCarthy received from her Irish servant friends shows that they hosted visits from out-of-town relatives and friends, too. On October 9, 1896, from Dorchester, Kate Monohan wrote to Nora that her brother Pat was quite ill with bronchitis, so she was "going in town tomorrow to See him." Kate also told Nora that her brother Con was living in Connecticut, and declared, "I may go & see him for Xmas." The following year Kate made the trip, for on August 17, 1897, she wrote Nora, "I am to inform you that I was down in Connecticut to see Brothers Michael & Connie last Sunday." In that same year, on October 23, from Somerville, Mary Anne Donovan wrote to Nora that "I had Tim & Jamesy to see me several times. . . . [B]oston is a real nice place we has Lots of fun." In addition, Mary Anne noted, "I had hanna McCarthy down to See me last Thursday." And on January 8, 1900, Hannah Collins mentioned to Nora that Hannah's brother Patsy had come to Elmira for Christmas to visit his sisters Hannah, Mary, and Maggie. Hannah observed that "he only stayed a week," and "we are lonesome now after him as he said he don't know when he will come here again" (O'Malley Collection).

Since people from a particular area in Ireland often ended up living in a particular area in the United States, it was not uncommon for Irish domestics to have "unplanned visits" that occurred when they unexpectedly crossed paths with people from home. On April 8, 1896, for example, Irish domestic Kate Monohan wrote from Boston to Nora McCarthy in Haverhill, "Dear Nora you asked if I seen Many of the neighbours from home but my dear child there is more of the neighbours from home around here than ever you see at Leap on a Sunday at church" (O'Malley Collection). Rose Kelly, who immigrated in 1925, recalled that, to her surprise, on her arrival in Philadelphia, while taking the trolley to her boardinghouse, she ran into a girl from home. As Rose recounted it, "We got on the trolley car, . . . and we were just one block, . . . and on comes a girl, right from home with me, in Ireland. I said, 'Aren't you Bridget Mullen . . . ?' She said, 'Yes, I am. In the name of God, who are you?' Well, I said, 'I'm Rose Kelly. . . . ' So she said, 'Oh, you were only that height when I left.'" Later, Rose ended up getting together with Bridget. Rose said that eventually she "knew the half of Philadelphia" (1995, 37–39). Helen Flatley had a similar experience shortly after she immigrated to New York City in 1928: "I had a job taking care of one lovely little girl. And we went into the park one day, and believe it or not, this girl walked up to me and all she could do was open her mouth and say, 'I don't believe this. I don't believe this.' And sure enough, it was a girl that I went to school with" (1996a).

Employers not only disliked their servants having friends in but also disliked the upset in their routine caused by servants going out, calling the "afternoon out," for example, "the dread and abhorrence of every woman who employs a female assistant" (Neal 1857a, 519). But the life of a servant was often a tedious and lonely one, prompting one author to conclude in 1871 that it was no "wonder that she demands all her evenings out" (Bridget 1871). Their free time was very limited, as the case of nanny Annie O'Donnell demonstrates. Annie worked for the wealthy Mellon family in Pittsburgh in the early 1900s. In one of her letters she says that while on a trip to Manhattan with her employer, she could not get more than four hours free on one afternoon, and that time was insufficient for her to visit her boyfriend's cousins over in Brooklyn as she had hoped to do (Murphy 2005, 48). Their limited free time caused servants to crowd "as much exercise and excitement into one evening as ought to go to the enjoyment of a dozen," according to an 1894 report (Springsteed 1894, 95).

Having an active social life apparently did take its toll on the Irish girls involved in the hard work of domestic service. Hannah Collins, for example, complained to Nora in a letter written on March 7, 1900, "If I stay up one night you would think I had not slept for a week" (O'Malley Collection). Hoping to minimize the time servants spent outside the house, some employers interfered in the social lives of their servants by imposing curfews on them. Even though an 1871 report notes that such curfews were routinely ignored, employers apparently kept imposing them on their servants (Bowker 1871, 497). In 1917, Caroline Reed Wadhams warned servants, "On their evenings out, the cook and other maids should return not later than the hour set by the employer for closing the house for the night" (11).

Recreation

In *Cheap Amusements: Working Women and Leisure in Turn-of-the-Century New York*, historian Kathy Peiss discusses young single working women and leisure, noting that the dance halls and amusement parks they frequented represented a new commercialized recreation. Peiss contends that working women, especially the children of immigrants, "came to identify 'cheap amusements' as the embodiment of American urban culture, particularly its individualism, ideology of consumption, and affirmation of dating and courtship outside parental control" (1986, 6). Their recreation asserted "heterosociality," which some middle-class reformers felt compelled to squelch (7, 8). Although not the population under discussion in *Cheap Amusements* (Peiss concentrates mainly on those working women employed in factories, shops, and so forth), not only did Irish immigrant domestics evidence the desire for pleasure in commercialized recreation that Peiss discusses, but their recreation, some of which consisted of the cheap amusements of which Peiss writes, also provoked criticism from middle-class observers. For example, one author indicated in 1910 that employers dismissed the recreation of servants as being "limited to the park bench, the cheap theatre, the summer excursion boat, and the dance hall." This same author thought their limited recreational opportunities led servant girls to the dangerous practice of visiting with boyfriends in public, on park benches (Dorr 1910, 268–69).

Regardless of what their employers thought of their recreational opportunities, Irish girls wanted to have social lives—they wanted to have fun, and they reveled in their freedom to enjoy their recreation, which necessarily was removed from parental control. As Ellie Driscoll Enright wrote from Washington, D.C., to Nora McCarthy in Massachusetts on March 14, 1900, "Glad . . . to hear that ye were . . . having a good old time enjoying yourselves there is nothing better than to keep livley while we can as we are shure to be dead Long enough." In the same vein, later that year, on July 3, Ellie questioned Nora: "Tell the truth or not you glad to be away from there [Ireland] having a good old time among yourselves in this clean country" (O'Malley Collection).

Dances

Dancing played a prominent role in the social life of rural people in Ireland, and dances constituted an important component of Irish immigrants' leisure in the United States. Irish dances in America, unlike the dances discussed in *Cheap Amusements,* however, often had a distinctly Irish country flavor. Irish immigrant author Mary Sadlier featured them in her novel *Bessy Conway,* which, although first published in America in 1861, was set in the period just before the Famine. Of her protagonist, Irish domestic Bessy, Sadlier writes that as Bessy observes an Irish dance, with "the merry antics of the young men and the simpering shyness of the girls, as they gaily footed the floor to the tune of 'The Rocky Road to Dublin' . . . she could almost forget the thousands of miles that lay between her and the 'big barn' where many a time she tripped it on the bare earthen floor" (1863, 159). Of course, Bessy, the "perfect" servant, does not usually go to dances in the United States, and declines to actually participate in the one dance she does attend. In this novel, Sadlier portrays dances as "rascally shin digs" where at least one nice Irish girl, to her ruin, gets mixed up with an Irish man she would not have looked at twice at home in Ireland (192).[2]

Thursday nights were big nights in the weekly social calendar of Irish immigrants because, as Owen O'Callaghan reported from Philadelphia to his sister Maggie in County Waterford, Ireland, in a letter believed to have been written on September 17, 1883, "Thursday night [is] when all the girls are out"—it was the maid's night off duty (K. Miller Collection). According to John T. Ridge, in the late nineteenth century and early twentieth century, because many of their members worked as domestics, the ladies' Irish county organizations in New York City held their meetings on the servants' free evening, Thursday. And because their servant members usually had no place in which to entertain male friends, the ladies' county organizations also sponsored dances where they could meet suitable Irish men. The men's county organizations also sponsored dances, some of which were large-scale affairs. Such Irish county organizations, which thrived in New York City between 1880 and 1914, although initially separated by gender, by the post–World War II era dissolved in favor of county organizations that included both sexes (1996, 294–300). Ridge also tells us that in the early twentieth century, Irish town and local societies were founded for social purposes in New York City. Local societies formed by women, such as the Loughrea Ladies' Social Club, the Castleisland Young Ladies Club, the Glenamaddy Ladies Club, and the Gort Ladies Social Club, sponsored social

2. Sadlier implies that in the free atmosphere of America, where class distinctions were muted, Irish girls could meet unsuitable men at Irish dances and, without parental consent, make poor choices in husbands that could ruin their lives (1863, 185). The story is that poor Mary Murphy met Luke Mulligan (a ragpicker well beneath her class at home in Ireland) at a dance and married him, knowing that her parents would not approve. Her life went downhill afterward: her husband left her, her crippled daughter died in a fire, and she ended up dying on Blackwell's Island.

affairs aimed at providing young single Irish immigrants with opportunities for meeting suitable mates (2006, 45–53).

According to Hannah Collins's correspondence with Nora McCarthy, Nora was wont to go to dances, but Hannah was not. On November 17, 1899, Hannah wrote, "Dear Nora I was glad to learn that you had such a nice time at that dance. . . . I never bother with dance any more as I have never been to any dance since I been in the country only one and that was my Cousin's dance they had two years ago. I think they dance too funny in this country" (O'Malley Collection). Hannah's lack of interest notwithstanding, over time, going to Irish dances continued to play an important part in the social lives of the Irish girls who worked in domestic service. Mary King Conroy, who left County Galway for Boston in 1912, told stories about going to "dances in Lynn and Swampscott" while working as a domestic (Greaney 1998, 36). Margaret Convery, who immigrated in 1914, remembered that she began attending dances when some "girls from Mayo . . . come in one night, they were going to a dance and they asked me to go so I went with them." She described the attendees at such dances as "just regular Irish people" (1991, 54). Ellen Brady, who came over in the 1920s, remembered that when she worked as a servant, her recreation included going to dances, too (1977, 36). Mary Cox, who immigrated in 1925, said she used to go to dances in "an Irish dance hall . . . with fiddlers and accordion players." The dances were such an important part of her social life that she left one service job "because I thought I was too far away from the dances." Cox loved the dances, from which she came "home at three and four o'clock in the morning" because she "was up dancing all night" (1991, 35–36).

The Irish dance hall scene was particularly vibrant in New York City in the 1920s and 1930s (Ridge 2005, 45). When asked what she liked about New York City when she first came in 1925, Ann Kelly responded, "We had our county dance, you know you go and you meet all the people from home with you and have like a reunion" (1991, 57). Mary Feely recalled that when she first came to the United States in 1927, she used to go to "a dance hall in New York." Feely said "it was fun" and "was packed for years with all the Irish girls come there." She also commented, "You went to the dance, you meet somebody you knew a couple of years before that . . . [i]t wasn't a surprise meeting again" (1996). And Helen Flatley, who came over in 1928, said she, too, went to the dances: "In New York at that time, there would be . . . maybe ten or twelve dances in different parts of the city. . . . [T]hat's another place that you would [meet] people you knew in Ireland" (1996a). Flatley declared, "The dances were wonderful . . . our greatest joy because when you're young . . . you love to dance" (1996b).

Irish domestics' love of going to dances points to the fact that they valued having beaux. In her letters to Nora McCarthy, Hannah Collins made frequent mention of her boyfriend (and later husband), Tom Cloke, and inquired whether Nora had a boyfriend. In a letter postmarked May 27, 1898, for example, she wrote, "I got a fellow and he is this country born too Aint I smart he has got light hair and blue eyes his name is Tom Cloke so I will have a cloake to keep me warm in the winter nights dont you think I'm a great girl you must tell me about your fellow because I know you got one for they were always crazy about you" (O'Malley Collection). In fact, some Irish domestics met their future husbands at the Irish dances they attended, including Margaret Convery, Mary Feely, Helen Flatley, and Kathleen Mannion.

Fashion

Social occasions, including dances, provided Irish domestics with the opportunity of displaying the fashions they so loved. Mary Sadlier obviously disapproved of the fondness for fashion that Irish servant girls had. In *Bessy Conway,* she has Bessy write home to Ireland about servant girls and fashion: "Mary [Murphy] has a very good place . . . but I declare to you she has got to be so proud . . . there is no standing her, all on account of the bit of finery that she was never used to before, so it has fairly turned her head. . . . [I]t's rattling in her silks she is of a Sunday when she goes out, and a beautiful bonnet and veil that Mrs. Herbert [a member of the gentry in Ireland] herself might wear, and everything else to match that. . . . She spends all she earns on foolish dress." Mary was not alone, according to Bessy, who continued in her letter to say, "I know plenty of girls from our own county that have been years and years earning good wages and have nothing to show for it but dress" (1863, 135). The basis of Sadlier's objection to servant expenditures on dress was that spending their money in this manner would scare off prospective suitors who could not afford to keep the girls in such finery. Sadlier illustrates this point when she has Bessy respond to criticism of the plain calico dress she wears to an Irish dance by remarking that servants in Ireland did not waste their money on finery. Instead, by dressing plainly and saving their wages, Bessy claims that Irish servant girls at home were able to "make good matches among the farmers and tradesmen, and even shopkeepers" (163).

Fashion figured in Hannah Collins's correspondence with Nora McCarthy. On December 18, 1899, she wrote to Nora McCarthy, "I have a very nice new dress for Christmas its a plaid." The following spring, on April 26, Hannah wrote Nora, "I am glad you have a nice new suit. . . . I also have a new suit too it's a grey very pretty" (O'Malley Collection). Ann Sexton, who immigrated in 1922, acknowledged her concern with fashion, noting, "As soon as I got money, I bought pretty clothes" (1986, 19). And Mary Cox linked her interest in fashion directly to attending dances, declaring that after coming to America in 1925, she and her cousin "bought a flock of dresses and fancy clothes and everything. Then we went off to a dance in Tuxedo Park" (1991, 35).

Personal Hygiene

The love of fashion the Irish Bridget displayed would seem to indicate that maintaining good personal hygiene was important to her. The primary source material I collected in my research, however, does not really touch on this subject. I found no mention, for example, of how often domestics bathed. And, in all the information I reviewed, only twice was mention made of that most personal of hygiene issues for women: menstruation. Ellen O'Loughlin, only fourteen when she left County Clare to work as a domestic in Hoosick Falls, New York, was completely unprepared for her first menstrual period. She told her daughter, Mary Unger, that, not knowing what to do, she went to her female employer and told her what happened. Her kind employer then took Ellen to a physician, who explained all to her (Unger 2006). When she came to New York City from County Cavan in 1922, Ann Sexton had a horrible experience related to menstruation. Because some type of skin disease had broken out shipboard, before landing, all aboard who were not American citizens were taken to a place Sexton called Hoffman Island. There, while menstruating heavily, she was not given any material to absorb the flow, but instead, with others, was forced to stand naked while being hosed down. Sexton said she "nearly died with embarrassment." The nurse present recognized the ordeal Sexton was undergoing, saying to her, "You poor little kid, this is terrible" (1986, 13).

Other Recreation

In the 1890s, some Irish servant girls like Mary Holland enjoyed solitary pursuits such as watching the boats come into Boston Harbor (Holland to

McCarthy, May 3, 1897, O'Malley Collection). Other of their recreational pursuits entwined with their Americanization process. For example, it was not only the young middle-class American woman who enjoyed the freedom and fun offered by the bicycling craze of the 1890s. Irish domestics such as Hannah Collins's sister Mary were interested in "learning to ride a wheel," too (Hannah Collins to McCarthy, June 21, 1899, O'Malley Collection). And, as the nineteenth century turned into the twentieth, Hannah Collins's correspondence to Nora McCarthy reveals that the social lives of Irish domestics also included going to weddings, playing cards, and sleigh riding (May 20, 1898; August 24, 1899; March 7, 1900, O'Malley Collection). Hannah's letters also offer proof that, as employers claimed, Irish servant girls *did* use parks for recreational purposes. On July 5, 1899, Hannah wrote to Nora that she spent the Fourth of July holiday at a park where there was "a nice lake." The following year, according to Hannah's letter of June 1, on a Decoration Day excursion, her boyfriend took her "all over . . . and to the Lake" (O'Malley Collection).

In the twentieth century Irish servant girls continued to spend their leisure time in parks. Irish domestic Ellen Brady commented that in her free time she went "to the park, walk around" (1977, 36). Irish domestics also participated in the new commercial amusements of the twentieth century that American scholars have connected with the Americanization process (Peiss 1986, 30–31; Kasson 1978, 39–40, 108; Nasaw 1993, 45). For example, Ellen Brady also enjoyed going to Coney Island and the movies (1977, 25, 35). For recreation, Irish domestic Helen Flatley loved going with her fellow Irish on boat cruises of several hours' duration that went up the East River or the Hudson River, and going on picnics at Bear Mountain (1996a, 1996b). Flatley also "learned how to have dinner out" in restaurants as a form of entertainment (1996a). If there were no parties, Irish domestics like Mollie Ryan in Albany spent their free time at the Ancient Order of Hibernians Hall (Arnold 1996). And the recreation of those girls who worked for the very wealthy in multiservant households sometimes included taking part in so-called servants' balls provided for them by their employers. According to Ellen Brady, at such affairs, held in hired halls, "you'd dance, and eat, and you'd sing. It's just like a party for young people or old people" (1977, 31, 32).

From 1840 through 1930, vacations, as middle-class Americans now know them, were not available to most working-class Americans, including domestic servants. For Hannah Collins, a vacation was the rest she got when, overtired from housework, she went to stay or "vacation" with nearby relatives. On August 25, 1898, Hannah wrote to Nora, "I left my place two weeks ago I got my vacation and I am staying at Mrs. Dempsey's house I dont think I will go back there [to her employer] any more for Its hard and I was tired out" (O'Malley Collection). Instead of paid vacations, the vacations of servants were likely to be "working vacations" in which the domestic accompanied the employer's family to a summer resort where she was expected to continue with her duties. Accordingly, on different occasions, Kathleen Mannion, who immigrated in 1929, accompanied her employers to Nantucket and Cohasset, Massachusetts. Then with another family, she spent the entire summer at a lake in New Hampshire (McDonagh 2002).

Some Irish servants harbored hopes of vacationing in Ireland, although it appears that most ended up having to wait until well after they were married to accomplish this goal. How many made such visits remains unknown because this information was not systematically collected and categorized. Hannah Collins hoped to make a visit to Ireland, for she wrote to Nora McCarthy on June 9, 1898, that before she got married, "I will have to see dear old Ireland first." It is unclear whether she accomplished this goal. Hannah was realistic about her chances of doing so, for the following year, on August 24, she wrote, "I would love to go back to see them again but I suppose I never will still I may." Katie McCarthy's correspondence from Ireland indicates that some Irish girls did return from America for a visit to Ireland, but whether they were domestics is unclear. She mentions Maggie McCarthy from Lowell, Massachusetts, who came home to Ireland in October 1894 and expected to return to America in the spring of 1895 (to her sister Mary Donovan in Haverhill, October 14, 1894); Julia Hayes, who came home for the summer of 1895 (to her sister Nora in Haverhill, May 24, 1895); Maggie Hourihane, who was expected to come home for the month of August 1895 (to Nora, June 16, 1895); and Ellie Driscoll and Julia Coughlin (to Nora, August 1, 1895), who also returned to Ireland for visits (O'Malley Collection). Irish domestics like Lillian Doran, Mollie Ryan, Helen Flatley, and Kathleen Mannion did return to Ireland for visits before they married in the United States. Doran, who immigrated in 1912, declared, "I made three trips to Ireland before I got married" (1993, 41). Mollie Ryan, who immigrated in 1925, returned to Ireland in 1930, intending to stay permanently, but changed her mind and came back to America (Arnold 1996). And Flatley explained, "I went back. I was only here five years when I just saved every penny I could to go back. And I did go back. Then I stayed a month or so over there and then came back here again" (1996a). Likewise, Kathleen Mannion returned to Ireland in 1937, planning to make her stay permanent but changed her mind and came back to the United States (McDonagh 2002).

Religion

As already noted, in 1852, in response to a series of articles critical of Irish domestics that were written by "Veritas" that ran in the *Boston Daily Evening Transcript* in February 1852, an alleged Irish servant girl calling herself "Bridget" wrote a series of letters to the editor of the *Boston Pilot*. In one of those letters, which appeared on February 21, 1852, Bridget testified to the importance of Catholicism for servant girls, saying, "If it wasn't for the Church we couldn't get along at all." Representatives of the Catholic Church used various means to support Irish servant girls, including providing them with advice designed to strengthen their resolve to maintain their religion in America and teach them how to conduct their work and personal lives. Charles Fanning avers that in 1853, Father Hugh Quigley, an Irish immigrant priest who ministered to immigrants in the rural area northeast of Troy, New York, wrote a novel, *The Cross and the Shamrock; or, How to Defend the Faith, an Irish-American Catholic Tale of Real Life,* specifically "'For the Entertainment and Special Instruction of the Catholic Male and Female Servants in the United States'" (1997, 123). In this work Irish servant girl Anne Connell argues with her mistress for permission to attend mass. She is unsuccessful until the mistress's husband intervenes on her behalf. Impressed by the good that comes of Anne's attendance at mass, he tells his wife to cease attempting to convert Anne to Protestantism and to stop interfering with Anne's practice of Catholicism. Fanning indicates that the novel was very popular—more than 250,000 copies of it were sold (125–29).

There must have been an audience for Father George Deshon's *Guide for Catholic Young Women, Especially for Those Who Earn Their Own Living* (1868) because it went through at least thirty-one editions. In this book Deshon directly addresses servant girls, urging them to practice their religion if there is a Catholic church nearby; if not, he urges servant girls to say their prayers (1978, 65, 72). He recommends reading the Catholic version of the Bible, and provides instruction on how to effectively resist mistresses who try to force their servants to read the Protestant version of the Bible (82–85). He reminds servant girls that they should not lie about breaking their employer's dishes, and that they should not eavesdrop on conversations of the employing family (263–65, 223). Girls who spend their money on fashion are criticized in this book, as are bold women (245, 237). Deshon tells girls not to spend their time worrying about whether they will marry, and reminds them that there is a vocation to the single life (276, 274). He also warns that if they marry a drinker, trouble will follow (282–83).

In her didactic *Advice to Irish Girls in America* (1872), the nun of Kenmare (Mary Frances Cusack [Sister Mary Francis Clare]) urged Irish servant girls to resign themselves to their lot, emulate the Blessed Virgin, wear a scapular, and through their good example possibly convert to Catholicism the Protestant mistresses for whom they worked (64, 196, 197, 160–61). When considering marriage she suggested that if a servant girl's fiancé drank, she should get him to "take the pledge." Once married, she declared it was the wife's duty to "have his meals always ready for him, and . . . [a]ttend to any little thing that you know he wishes" (148–49).

In 1881, American author Harriet Prescott Spofford pointed to the continuing importance of Catholicism for Irish domestics when she commented that within a Catholic church, Irish servants were "at home once more; it is the atmosphere of the sweet old land that breathes about them; they have there the shadow of home. . . . [S]trangers in a strange land, the church is father and mother, home and country, too!" (1977, 60).

Since most Irish servants were Roman Catholics, they were pleased to obtain positions located near Catholic churches. In 1888, Irish domestic Mary Ann Rowe attested to this fact when she wrote home to a friend in County Kilkenny that "I am within two or three minutes walk from the church. There is a splendid church here . . . and three priests. I can go to mass every Sunday and to confession whenever I want to" (K. Miller and Wagner 1994, 76). Conversely, Irish servants were loath to take positions distant from Catholic churches. In the early 1900s, wealthy people from Albany, New York, who summered in nearby Loudonville, had difficulty retaining Irish servants because the servants could not easily get to a Catholic church for mass. Servant turnover became such a great problem that it prompted Mrs. Leo Adt, a non-Catholic, to approach William Byrne, a state senator and fellow resident of Loudonville, to ask him to contact officials of the Catholic Diocese of Albany to request the services of a priest to say mass on Sundays. The upshot was that St. Pius X Church was founded in 1916 as a mission chapel in Loudonville, catering to Irish servant girls (*The St. Pius X Parish* 1976, 3).

For Irish servants, practice of the Roman Catholic religion was entwined with the social lives they constructed. Veritas, who wrote those critical articles in the *Boston Daily Evening Transcript*, accused them on February 2, 1852, of being intent on churchgoing mainly because they wanted to keep up on the latest gossip. It is true that the church served as a contact point for servants to keep in touch with the Irish community, and thus churchgoing was integral to maintenance of their social lives. Hannah Collins alluded to the important place going to mass on Sunday held in the social life of a servant when she wrote to Nora McCarthy in a letter postmarked October 20, 1898, that "you has a great old time mashing the fellows when you go to Church I wish I was there" (O'Malley Collection). Before and after mass, young people could chat and laugh while they socialized together in gatherings outside the church, and during mass they could eye each other, admiring the figures each cut while dressed up for church on Sunday (Spofford 1977, 59).

Catholic parish fairs also served as social occasions. According to Colleen McDannell, Catholic fairs, which were fund-raisers for parishes, had their heyday in the 1870s and 1880s, but took place from at least 1834 through the end of the nineteenth century. Besides "doing good" for the church, these fairs were also social occasions for the parishioners, serving as special events for the Irish Catholic women (the "ladies") of the parish who organized and ran the fairs. These "ladies" included married women as well as single women, and domestic servants likely numbered among them. The ladies of the parish negotiated with merchants to obtain the donated goods featured at the fairs. These items included chromolithograph "holy pictures" and other artwork featuring the Blessed Virgin Mary (especially as Our Lady of Lourdes), the Sacred Heart of Jesus, and saints like Saint Joseph, as well as portraits of Irish scenes and Irish heroes like Daniel O'Connell. At the fairs, Irish women also staffed the booths displaying the donated items, and sold raffle tickets for the goods. Probably the largest of all such fairs was the 1878 fair held in the nave of the as yet unopened St. Patrick's Cathedral in New York City; the recorded attendance was in excess of twenty thousand on its opening. It ran for forty-two days and raised more than $172,000 to finish construction of the cathedral. The large amount of money raised by such ladies' fairs was crucial to parish expansion, including the building of churches and schools. More germane to the social lives of Irish domestics, however, is the fact that such fairs were fun for the women who ran them and all who attended them. The fairs featured elaborate decorations, musical entertainment, and food and drink; in short, ladies' fairs provided just the festivity that the word *fair* implies (1996, 236–50).

The church figured not only in the social life of its members but in their emotional life as well. Through Catholic devotions, such as saying the rosary, religion provided solace for immigrants, including Irish domestics, who labored far from home. One can imagine that for young Irish domestics it must have been comforting to think that, although they were separated from their own mothers in Ireland, they still had a mother in America, the Blessed Mother Mary, who was accessible to them through prayer, especially through saying the rosary. And so it is unsurprising that Bessy, the Irish servant girl protagonist of Mary Sadlier's *Bessy Conway,* is delighted when Fanny Powers, another Irish girl, joins the domestic staff of the house in which Bessy is employed, because in the evenings, they could kneel down and "say their beads" together (1863, 151, 152).

Their religious beliefs consoled Irish immigrants. For those who feared (most of them rightly so) that they might never again see the family in Ireland, the belief that the entire family, the Irish family and the American family, would be rejoined in heaven in the next life must have provided powerful consolation for their separation in this life.[3] In her letter of March 14, 1900, written from Washington, D.C., Ellie Driscoll Enright offered Irish domestic Nora McCarthy just this type of consolation upon learning of Katie McCarthy's death in Ireland: "Poor Katie I hope she is in heaven . . . I hope we will meet [again] in heaven" (O'Malley Collection).

Of course, not all Irish domestics were devout. Mary Sadlier makes that point in *Bessy Conway* when she writes that some Catholic domestics who worked with Bessy not only were lax in the practice of their religion but resented "goody-goody" Bessy's efforts to monitor, and get them to improve, their religious practice. Sadlier has Bessy reply to her fellow servant Bridget's assertion that it was impossible for Bridget to get to mass on Sunday because of the amount of work expected of her, by asking, to Bridget's fury, "Why didn't you get up and go to six o'clock Mass, . . . you'd have been back at seven, and have plenty of time to do your work." Bessy, who

3. Ann Rossiter also points out that although religion appears to have been an important source of consolation for female Irish emigrants, this topic has not been researched and analyzed by scholars (1993, 194–95). My review of Irish immigrant letters, however, shows that religion, specifically the two ideas that the dead would be happy in heaven and that one day the family would be reunited in heaven, provided consolation not only to Irish domestics but to Irish people in general, whether they were male or female, Catholic or Protestant.

(of course) had already been up and out to the eight o'clock mass, found that her "helpfulness" was singularly unappreciated by her colleagues (1863, 79–80). Other Irish servants like Mary Feely were conscientious about fulfilling their obligation to hear mass every Sunday and on holy days of obligation, but were not overburdened with religious fervor. When she was single and worked as a domestic in New York from 1927 through the 1930s, Feely did not care to spend what little free time she had participating in Catholic organizations. Instead, she said that during her free time she "would rather go to a dance" (1996).

Most Irish servants were Catholics, but there were Protestant Irish girls who worked in service in America, too. The exact number of Protestant Irish servants remains unknown, however, since religion is not a topic of inquiry in the U.S. Census. Religious differences served to sharply divide the Irish. Anna McGuffey Morrill (1845–1924), who spent most of her life in Cincinnati, grew up in a household that employed four Protestant Irish maids, all of them Famine immigrants. One of them, named Mary Anne, was "an ardent Orangewoman" wont to worrying that, "even over here in America, 'Thim Catholics' would hurt her" (1993, 6).

Such Protestant Irish servants sometimes sought to distinguish themselves from Catholic Irish by calling themselves Scots (or Scots-Irish), as did Anna, the servant colleague Lillian Pettengill discusses in her 1903 autobiographical work, *Toilers of the Home*. When asked her background, Anna first tells Lillian that "I'm Scotch." It is only after Lillian says how much she likes Irish people that Anna finally confesses to being "Scotch-Irish" (270–71).

Leaving Service

Irish domestics did not view themselves as constituting a servant class and did not expect to spend their entire lives in service. For most of them, service was a temporary experience, a stage of life, before they moved on to something else. After all, neither occupational advancement nor occupational security was characteristic of domestic service. According to one author writing in 1909, there were three main reasons Irish girls disappeared from the ranks of servants: "to be married, or to go home to old Ireland, or to take care of a sick relative" (A Thankful Husband 1909, 1231). The second and third reasons could overlap, as the case of Mary King Conroy illustrates. In 1912, Conroy left County Galway for Boston. She remained in the United States for ten years, after which she returned to Ireland to take care of her father.

11. Bridget cartoon. "Bridget announces that she is engaged to be married" (*Life,* February 25, 1904, 186–87).

While caring for him, she met and married her husband, Martin Conroy, and so remained in Ireland to raise a family (Greaney 1998, 36).[4]

It is likely that most Irish girls left service to marry (Glasco 1975, 357) (see ill. 11). It was easier to marry in the United States than it was in Ireland, because a dowry was not a prerequisite to marriage in America. On February 9, 1850, the *Boston Pilot* cited a letter printed in the *Newry (Ireland) Examiner,* in which an Irish girl from Buffalo, New York, wrote to her mother in Ireland that "I would advise all the handsome girls in Gourtbane to come here, as it makes no matter with girls here whether they have money or not; the boys here do not look for a fortune; but every boy a handsome wife."

Marriage also offered an escape from the hard work that was domestic service. Hannah Collins was initially ambivalent about marrying, for she wrote to Nora McCarthy on October 1, 1898, that "I am not in a hurry I

4. Aine Greaney mentions that when Conroy's daughters immigrated to Boston in the mid-1950s, she joined them there and remained in Boston until her death at age 107 (1998, 36).

would rather live single yet It's a hard thing to get married to be bound to a man all the time." By the following year, however, taxing domestic work apparently effected a change in her attitude so that marriage now represented deliverance, for on May 24 she wrote to Nora, "I have to work all the time I hope someday will come when I wont have to work so hard that is when I will be Mrs Cloak that warm name." Still, because married people were *not* expected to send home remittances, Hannah felt obligated to postpone marrying, telling Nora in a letter postmarked February 21, 1900, "I have to send some money to my dear Parents once & a while and if I get married I cant send them any" (O'Malley Collection).

As mentioned above, some Irish domestics met their future husbands at the Irish dances they attended. Others, such as Lillian Doran, met their Irish-born husbands at weddings; Ellen Brady met hers at a party (1993, 38–39; 1977, 37). Bridget McGeoghegan knew her husband from home—he was the first to come see her when she first immigrated to the United States in 1923 (1987, 2). And Rose Kelly met her Irish-born husband, Owen Loughlin, through his sister Kathleen, with whom she worked in service in Irvington, New York (1995, 46, 47).

Irish immigrant men in the United States have been portrayed as drunken louts, brutes, and wife beaters, with "'drunken' [used] as a modifier for 'Irish'" (D. Clark 1973, 103). Yet in contradiction to this conjoining of drink with Irish men in the American mind, Irish men were active in temperance societies that were popular in Irish America, as they were in Ireland.[5] As I mentioned in chapter 1, Father Mathew even brought his famed temperance campaign to the United States.

The American stereotype of Irish men between 1840 and 1930 tended to be a negative one—they were seen as alcoholics and wife beaters. Unsurprisingly, poverty and cultural dislocation may have provoked some Irish immigrant men to increase their drinking, which, in turn, probably did cause discord in some Irish homes in America. The American view of the Irish as drunken wife beaters, however, probably owes much to American

5. Colleen McDannell argues that male participation in temperance societies in America reflected the efforts of the Catholic Church to define masculinity, or the Catholic true man. The church defined masculinity as encompassing churchgoing and attention to the family and domestic affairs. The Catholic true man belonged to church sodalities and societies, such as temperance societies and the Holy Name Society, instead of hanging out at pubs with his fellow men (1986a, 27, 29).

disapproval of drinking alcohol. The Irish attitude toward drinking alcohol was very different from the American view, for as previously detailed, drink had long been an important and accepted part of Irish culture—not that drunkenness was acceptable, but drinking was. Another reason that the stereotype of Irish men as drunken louts was so pervasive might be because of the *way* some of them drank. That is, putting aside those men who really were alcoholics, many Irish men in the United States may have continued the drinking pattern that was "evident in Irish rural society during the nineteenth century, and [was] described by temperance critics as 'circumstantial drinking.'" In this pattern, there are "periodic drunken bouts associated with special occasions like markets, fairs, weddings and religious festivals, [that are] separated by long stretches of total sobriety" (Malcolm 1986, 11, 49–50). In other words, many Irish immigrant men in America may have been episodic drinkers, or what Americans today call "binge" drinkers. That is, they may have imbibed alcohol only occasionally, on ceremonial occasions, or when tragedy struck (as when children died), but when they did drink, they may have overimbibed. Thus, American observers, seeing them at their worst, when drunk, would view them as drunken louts, *in general,* whereas their women might have viewed the same behavior very differently. If a man was otherwise a hardworking, loving husband and father, a woman might overlook his getting drunk once in a while.

Regardless of the negative stereotypes, anecdotal evidence suggests instead that, whether they drank or not, the ranks of Irish men included loving husbands who got on well, and socialized, with their wives. Consider, for example, Hugh Augustus (Gus) Shalvoy's memory of his Famine-era Irish immigrant grandfather's relationship with his Irish immigrant grandmother. Owen Shalvoy, from the Nobber area of County Meath, and his wife, Margaret Scollin, from Drumshanbo, County Leitrim, both came to Danbury, Connecticut, where they met and then married in 1854. In a May 17, 1978, letter to his granddaughter Karen Shalvoy Elias, Gus recalled of his grandparents, "I used to hear him saying, when playing checkers with her, about my pretty young maid from Connaugh" (Lynch-Brennan Collection). The Shalvoys lived long enough to celebrate their fiftieth wedding anniversary in 1904, an event that rated coverage in the Danbury newspaper.[6]

6. Owen and Margaret Scollin Shalvoy were my maternal great-great-grandparents. County Leitrim, from which Margaret Scollin Shalvoy hailed, is in the province of Connacht.

Irish immigrant housewife Mary Malone McHenry also demonstrated she thought highly of her Irish immigrant husband, Martin. On April 11, 1870, she wrote home to her parents in Ballygub, County Kilkenny, Ireland, from Middle Granville, New York, describing her husband as being "craked about" the children, and being "a fraid of his Life that anney thing will happen [to] them." In that same letter Mary described her brother, Dan Malone, who then boarded with her, as also "cracked about the children." Eighteen years later, on December 7, she wrote to her parents that although she and Martin had a large family of children to care for (eleven at that time), she was still enclosing a Christmas gift of money for them, so "ye must think I have a kind husband he want to send something" (Lynch-Brennan Collection).

Irish domestic Helen Flatley remembered the Irish boys who went to the dances in New York in the 1920s as "such lovely, lovely, young men." She recalled that when she was young, her girlfriends "were all going out with a bunch of Irish guys, just like my husband" (1996b). Irish domestic Bridget McGeoghegan certainly remembered her Irish-born husband with great fondness: "I'd marry the same man all over again. I had him for fifty-two years so, he's gone for ten, died ten years ago" (1987, 33). And Irish domestic Rose Kelly remembered her Irish-born husband, Owen Loughlin, as looking like "a Spaniard with black, curly hair." According to Rose, Owen "was a very good man" who she thought was the most "honest man in the wide world. He was so honest" (1995, 47). Irish men, therefore, included good, kind men as well as the stereotypical drunken louts. Into the twentieth century, Irish immigrant women tended to marry their fellow Irish men. They married Irish men because both came from the same religious and cultural background—they were familiar to each other. They also married Irish men because many were good men who made good husbands and fathers,[7] or, as Hannah Collins succinctly put it in a December 16, 1898, letter to Nora McCarthy, "a sweet little Irishman he is the best of all" (O'Malley Collection).[8]

7. McDannell suggests another reason that Irish women married Irish men. She avers that in America the Catholic Church wanted the Catholic true man "to shift his allegiance from his male peer group to his family," and Catholic advice literature emphasized "the importance of a tight, nuclear family founded on 'American-style' companionate marriage" (1986a, 27, 29). Thus, the behavior the church encouraged might very well have made Irish men in America more attractive as husbands than were Irish men in Ireland.

8. Hannah Collins was disappointed that her boyfriend, Tom Cloke, was not Irish born, for she wrote to Nora McCarthy on October 8, 1899, "I guess Tom is alright but you know

A Life of Service

Despite the fact that domestic service offered little opportunity for occupational advancement, and did not provide occupational security, some servants did remain for years with certain families. In 1888, at about age fourteen, Sarah Byrne immigrated from Ireland and went directly to work as a servant in the Park-McCullough House in North Bennington, Vermont, where she remained employed until her death in 1944, acquiring along the way a spouse in the form of fellow employee William Green, who worked as a coachman and chauffeur (Park McCullough House Association) (see ill. 12). Bridget Ryan, who came to Troy, New York, from near Thurles, County Tipperary, in 1895, never married and remained in live-in service for the course of her entire American life. She worked as a cook for the prominent Warren family in Troy for years, until her death at age eighty. One night in 1949 her grandnephew Con Casey drove her home to the Warrens from a visit to her family on her Friday night off, and she died in his arms as he went to help her out of the car (Casey 2006).

Maureen West's research on Mary Maguire presents us with a little-known model of the Irish domestic in America. The date of Mary's emigration from County Cavan, Ireland, is unknown, but she was working as a servant for the Shattuck family in Massachusetts in 1880. In 1885, Mary returned to Ireland, where she married Cathal Dolan. Over the next ten years she remained in Ireland and had seven children. Beginning in 1895,

---

he did not come from Ireland I often wish he did but he is awful nice to me and gives me a good time." In an earlier letter to Nora, written on August 25, 1898, Hannah noted that although Tom was not Irish born, his mother was—she hailed from Tipperary (O'Malley Collection). Of course, another reason Irish women married Irish men can be attributed to what has been termed the clannish nature of the Irish—Irish people in America stuck together. Irish people who married outside the group, therefore, sometimes suffered opprobrium in consequence. When Kathleen Magennis emigrated from Northern Ireland in 1921, she worked as a waitress in a private club in Brooklyn. When she married Gerardo Lamberti in 1923, "none of the Irish would come to see me at the church because I was marrying an Italian" (1994, 86). Likewise, there was trouble when Bridget and James Maher's son married a girl who was not Irish. Irish immigrant domestic Bridget (Delia) Collins, who immigrated in 1904, later married Irish immigrant James Patrick Maher. When it came time for their son, Michael Maher, to marry, he picked a girl who, although Catholic, was half Italian and half German. So upset were the Maher parents that their son was marrying a girl who was not Irish that the bride said her wedding was more like a wake than a wedding (Varley 2001).

HALL FARM EMPLOYEES
H. P. Mc CULLOUGH

Name Sarah Byrne Green
Date of Birth 1874
Nationality Born in Ireland
Year Employed about 1888- 1944
Years of Service 56 Yrs. Died in 1944
Monthly Compensation
Occupation HouseKeeper & Cook.

12. Sarah Byrne. *Courtesy of Park-McCullough House Association, North Bennington, Vermont.*

however, she periodically returned from Ireland to America to work for the Shattuck family in Andover, Massachusetts, leaving her children in the care of female relatives. Starting in 1898, she brought some of her children with her to work for the Shattucks in America. Between 1895 and 1907, Mary Maguire Dolan went back and forth between her home in Ireland and the Shattuck home in America. She died in Ireland, in the Cavan Hospital, in July 1922 (2004, 2–4).

13. Catherine Larkin Vaughn. *Courtesy of her granddaughter Nancy Graham Moreland and her great-granddaughter Deirdre Farrell Romanski.*

Catherine Larkin, born in 1885, worked in service in Claremorris, County Mayo, before coming to the United States (see ill. 13). Larkin, from Ballinrobe, County Mayo, came to the Troy, New York, area, where she worked as a domestic until her marriage in 1914. Because her husband, George Vaughn, died when her youngest daughter, Florence, was only four years old, Catherine returned to service work to support her family. The second time around, however, she worked days for various employers, coming back home to her family each night. Her daughter Florence Graham remembers that her mother was a very smart woman, who insisted that her employers pay for her carfare (2006).

In general, employers could not be relied on to take responsibility for servants as they aged. Some, such as Ellen O'Loughlin, who when married in America was known as Nellie Cronk, worked in service until their old age, but not in one house as the longtime servant of a single employer. Instead, Nellie lived out in service with various employers from 1893, when she came to America at age fourteen, until the week before she died at the age of nearly eighty, even though she was married and had a child.[9] Nellie's daughter, Mary Unger, said her mother had to continue in service work because the family needed the money; Nellie's husband, it seems, was frequently "on strike" (2006). For those servants, however, who, as they got older, became increasingly unable to perform taxing housework, often prospects were dim. Like most members of the working class in this period, they could expect to be discharged without any sort of pension, and therefore could end up in almshouses (Dudden 1983, 208–9). Such was the fate of Margrett Baggs, a domestic from County Tipperary, Ireland, who, in 1880, after thirty-three years in America, at age sixty-six, entered the Rensselaer County Poor House in upstate New York. The notation on her record states the reason for her dependence as "old age and no home" (New York State n.d.).

Irish immigrant domestic servants were young social creatures who wanted to have good times, and who expected someday to leave service through marriage. They were not passive victims of the circumstances in which they found themselves, but rather showed agency in managing to construct multifaceted social lives for themselves, despite the conditions of live-in domestic life that militated against their doing so. When they married, they usually picked Irish men because they were familiar—both were products of rural, peasant Irish culture. As shall be discussed in the next chapter, their experience in domestic service was an acculturating one for Irish girls, one that affected not only them but also the families they later established.

9. When older, Nellie Cronk lived in with some employers, and also did domestic service as day work for other employers.

Was Bridget's Experience Unique?

Acculturation and Upward Mobility

Scholars of Irish immigration agree that domestic service provided an acculturating experience for Irish domestics and facilitated the rise of the Irish into the American middle class (D. Clark 1977, 59; Diner 1983, 94; Janet Nolan 1989, 94; K. Miller, Doyle, and Kelleher 1995, 55). Domestic service offered Irish women "a first-hand peek at how Americans lived"; onlookers said that it was Irish women who "brought the family 'up,' civilized them by introducing the manners and accouterments of the middle class" (Diner 1983, 140). Contemporary observers agreed, finding that the families of former domestics benefited from the women's experience, claiming that the care former domestic servants took "of their children's diet and health" showed "the superiority of domestic service over factory training for developing intelligent home-makers" (More 1971, 13).[1]

Famine-era Irish immigrant Ann McNabb's recollections show that participation in domestic service proved to be an acculturating experience for her sister Tilly. Ann asserted that Tilly's American employer, Mrs. Bent, "larned her to cook and bake and to wash and do up shirts—all American fashion" (Holt 1906, 145). Sixteen-year-old Irish immigrant Ann Mitchell really took to heart the lessons in cleanliness and respectability she learned in the approximately three years she worked in service for Helen

1. In contrast, Faye Dudden argues that the middle-class mores to which servants were exposed in their work were probably useless to working-class life (1983, 230). I disagree with her contention. With regard to domestic servants in Victorian Great Britain, many of whom were Irish, Leonore Davidoff and Ruth Hawthorn make an argument similar to Dudden's, although they acknowledge that in service women probably learned how to organize their housekeeping day (1976, 88).

Chapman. Ann saved all her wages to bring her siblings to America. When they arrived in New Orleans in 1850, she insisted on going to meet them. Her mistress said:

> I found out after she had left, that her anxiety was to get them made a little decent, before they were seen here. She took all the money she could raise with her and on her arrival found them with a crowd of immigrants renting a room and buying some bread each day. They were bare headed, bare footed, almost naked. She went to work and really I never saw such a sum of money go farther. She had friends in New Orleans who wished her to stay with them, but she was so fearful they would find out about her family that she stayed with the family in all their dirt and discomfort. She went about town getting each of them some things absolutely necessary, set the Irish women to work, made each of the children sunbonnets, palm leaf hats, and frocks, got shoes, jackets and pantaloons for the boys, and when they arrived, though she was terribly ashamed of them, I thought they looked remarkably well. She sat up nights and worked her fingers to the bone. All this was done in two days, the time of the steamer's stay in New Orleans and by a young girl of sixteen. (Coker 1992, 189–90)

Owen O'Callaghan, too, testified to the acculturating affect employment in domestic service had on his sister Maggie. In a letter believed to have been written on either December 12, 1884, or December 12, 1888, he wrote from Philadelphia to his brother in County Waterford, Ireland, "Maggie is a regular Yank now Youd think by seeing her she was a native" (K. Miller Collection).

Speaking of learning the tasks required in domestic service in America, Margaret Convery, who immigrated in 1914, said "they tell you how to do it" and "you have to learn in a hurry" (1991, 53, 52). In the same vein, Ellen Brady, who came to the United States in the 1920s, commented, "You watch, you use your head, you pick it up. How to set a table, how to arrange fruit, how to arrange flowers." She added, "You watch, you see. You know how to set your wine glass, there's your water glasses, with different kind of glasses you're gonna put up. If you're going to serve fish, you gotta know where your fish fork goes, where your salad fork goes, where your butter plate goes, your bread plate goes, your napkin goes. . . . [Y]ou dust and make the beds their way, dust their way, do this that way, their way, you know" (1977, 26–27). According to Rose Kelly, who came to America in 1925, her acculturation began shipboard, before she even landed in the United States: "When I was in the ship . . . I watched the people, what they were doing, and I figured that's what I would be doing in America . . . you know, the way they waited on the table" (1995, 35). And Helen Flatley, who came to the United States in 1928, pointed out that in domestic service, she "learned a lot of the ropes" (1996a).

Irish immigrant women's experience in domestic service also affected the families they established once they left domestic service to marry. Colleen McDannell argues that, to the extent possible, in their own homes they tried to reproduce the conditions of the middle-class homes in which they once worked (1986b, 73). According to the recollections of relatives of former domestics, this was the case. Maureen Maher Varley recalls that her grandmother Bridget (Delia) Collins Maher, who came to the United States in 1904 and worked as a domestic, had a parlor that went unused except for important family occasions. Nonetheless, despite the little use it got, she insisted that her daughters clean the parlor and polish its furniture every Saturday (2001). And Maryellen McDonagh recollects that her mother, Kathleen Mannion, who came to the United States in 1929 to work in service, "kept a very clean house." In addition to keeping a nice house, McDonagh remembers her mother insisting that she and her siblings display proper manners (2002).

The Roman Catholic Church in America supported and encouraged Irish acculturation through the social services it provided (D. Clark 1973, 91). Patrick Donahoe also encouraged Irish acculturation in the *Boston Pilot,* the newspaper he edited. In the *Pilot,* which was read by Irish people across the United States, not merely those Irish resident in Boston, Donahoe encouraged female subscribers to read *Godey's Lady's Book,* one of the foremost magazines of its time for middle-class Protestant American women. On May 29, 1852, the *Pilot* contained this note: "The Godey's Lady's Book for June, like all the numbers of this Magazine, is beautifully embellished and contains 112 pages of reading matter, music, embroidery &c. Orders to be addressed to L.A. Godey, Esq., Philadelphia, Pa." (6). Similarly, on November 24, 1855, the *Pilot* ran a brief notice that "Godey's Lady's Book, for December, is beautifully embellished, and filled with entertaining reading. This magazine commences its fifty-second volume in January. A fine old age—and yet the ladies are constantly interrogating the proprietor to know if he is unmarried" (5). And on September 4, 1875, the *Pilot* also encouraged its subscribers to read magazines such as *Atlantic Monthly* and *Scribner's* that were ostensibly written for a middle-class Protestant American readership (6).[2]

Other signs that the *Pilot* encouraged acculturation can be found in the advertisements it contained for books and postsecondary education. As early as 1855, the paper ran an advertisement for what I term "Irish books" such as Irish immigrant author Mary Sadlier's novel *The Blakes and the Flanagans* (October 27, 1855, 2) and famed Irish novelist William Carleton's *Willy Reilly and His Dear Coleen Bawn* (November 24, 1855, 5). But the *Pilot* also directed its Irish readership to the fare read by middle-class Protestant Americans. On November 6, 1875, the paper ran a review of Nathaniel Hawthorne's *House of the Seven Gables,* terming the work "one of our favorite stories—one of the best stories in English literature" (6). And on September 5, 1885, Lew Wallace's popular novel *Ben Hur* was advertised in the *Pilot* (4). By the 1860s the *Pilot* ran advertisements for Catholic schools such as St. Joseph's Academy in Troy, New York, and St. Mary's Academy in Notre Dame, Indiana (January 7, 1860, 6; October 7, 1865, 7). As early as January 8, 1870, an advertisement for that quintessential Protestant American institution of higher education, Harvard College, also appeared in the *Pilot* (7). In addition, on September 4, 1875, the paper advised readers that Catholic young men could obtain a good education at Cornell, in Ithaca (6).

Other advertisements that ran in the *Boston Pilot* also indicate that it encouraged the aspirations of Irish immigrants for an improved material life. By 1865 advertisements for goods associated with middle-class Protestant Americans, such as frames for cartes de visite, paper hangings, and carpets, appeared (November 4, 1865, 8; October 7, 1865, 8; October 2, 1875, 7). Ads for books of instruction on playing pianofortes also ran in the paper, and that famous department store, R. H. Macy of New York, advertised as well (January 8, 1970, 7; November 6, 1875, 7).

The piano and the parlor, those symbols of respectability, also became the icons of the Irish home in the United States. Working-class Irish families who managed to purchase both pianos and parlor furniture generally did so through an installment plan (More 1971, 139–46). Dr. Patricia O'Malley remembers that her grandmother former domestic Nora McCarthy "had a

2. Colleen McDannell also notes that the *Boston Pilot* encouraged its readers to read *Godey's* and that "Catholics read Protestant literature, whereas Protestants most likely did not read Catholic works" (1986b, 103).

piano in the front room" of the house (1997). Irish aspirations, especially Irish women's aspirations, to possess such symbols of gentility were a source of amusement even for the Irish themselves, as the writings of Finley Peter Dunne show. In "The Piano in the Parlor," for example, Dunne writes of Mrs. Donahue, who refuses to have her daughter, Molly, play any Irish tunes on the piano, insisting instead that Molly "give us wan iv thim Choockooski things" that are "so ginteel" (Fanning 1997, 285).

Although the *Boston Pilot* encouraged acculturation through some of its notices and advertisements, it simultaneously encouraged maintenance of an Irish Catholic identity in America through other advertisements it ran for home decorations that had specifically Irish or Catholic connotations. Such advertisements appeared as early as October 27, 1855, when the paper ran an ad that "Messrs. John Murphy & Co., have published a beautiful engraving of the Immaculate Conception, from the original, approved by His Holiness, the Pope. It can be had at Donahoe's 23 Franklin street" (4). On September 4, 1875, the paper advertised the availability of "The Centennial Chromo of [Daniel] O'Connell," the Irish hero (5). Later that year, on November 6, a chromolithograph of the Sacred Heart of Jesus, termed "a work of art . . . that should adorn the parlor of every Catholic house," was also advertised (8). Such images of the Sacred Heart "became a hallmark of the Irish Catholic family" home in America (McDannell 1986b, 68).

By the 1870s, having a wife who did not work for wages outside the home was a signifier of membership in the American middle class. After marriage, Irish women in America, including former domestics, tried to follow this model set by the middle class; they, too, tended not to work for wages outside the home. Instead, to assist with family finances, they engaged in such remunerative endeavors as taking in boarders. Betty Arnold recalls that in Albany, her mother, Mollie Ryan, a former domestic, took in boarders (1996). As wives and mothers, women dominated the Irish home in America as, in certain matters, they had in Ireland. They handled family financial matters and had aspirations for their children. In noting that "the big push. . . . the big deal, [was to] get them into high school," Dr. Patricia O'Malley indicates that education was central to the ambitions that former domestics, like her grandmother Nora McCarthy, had for their children (1997). Maureen Maher Varley, too, recalls that her grandmother former domestic Bridget (Delia) Collins Maher stressed to her the importance of education, strongly encouraging Maureen to stay in school (2001). This stress on education for the children dates to well before Nora McCarthy's immigration in 1895 and Delia Collins Maher's arrival in the United States in 1904. The concern of Irish domestics with their children's education was evident as early as 1846, when former domestic Minerva Padden Donovan wrote to a previous employer's son that she and her husband were pleased that they were able to "keep them at school through the summer season which we have not been able to do for the last three years before" (P. White 1967, 188).

Irish women's emphasis on education fostered group occupational and social mobility. Women were key to the movement of the Irish into the American middle class. Illustrative of this rise and the female role in it is that few daughters of domestics followed their mothers into service, much to the dismay of Americans like Mary Gove Smith, who commented in 1906, "It is unfortunate for the occupation that the second generation usually feels domestic work beneath its dignity" (8). Instead, teaching school became the occupation of choice for second-generation Irish females. By the first ten years of the twentieth century, Irish American females became "one of the largest ethnic groups among public school elementary teachers, constituting one quarter of the teachers in Providence and Boston and fully a third of the teachers in New York and Chicago" (Janet Nolan 1998, 78).

Sociological scholarship supports the idea that Irish women were successful in ensuring that their children were educated. Using data from the National Opinion Research Center's General Social Survey, Andrew M. Greeley contends that by the 1910–20 era, "Irish Catholics had already exceeded the national average in college attendance and graduation and professional and white collar careers" (1988, 231). This point affirms an observation made in 1900 that there were "more lawyers, doctors and authors among the second generation of Irish-Americans than there are saloon-keepers, and more teachers than policemen" (Desmond 1900, 523). Over time, the Irish continued to move upward on the social scale, were set back by the Great Depression, but bounded back from it to become "the most affluent gentile ethnic group in America" (Greeley 1988, 231).[3]

Not that it was a straight trajectory for Irish women from domestic service to life in the middle class. Not only was it those domestics who never married

3. Andrew Greeley reports, "There are 15,238 respondents in the General Social Survey of whom the ethnic question was asked; 771 are Irish Catholics, who are 16 percent of the Catholic population. The surveys have been taken every year since 1972 with the exception of 1979 and 1981" (1988, 229).

who faced dim futures, but some domestics who married fared poorly, too, for some husbands proved unable to provide their wives with the better life the women anticipated marriage would bring. As mentioned in chapter 6, Ellen O'Loughlin, known by the name Nellie Cronk as a married woman, was engaged in domestic service until shortly before she died when she was near eighty (Unger 2006). Likewise, Catherine Larkin was compelled to go back to service work after her husband, George Vaughn, died and she was left with four daughters to raise (Graham 2006). One female author observed in 1907, "It is a sad thing to find an attractive, ambitious wife who is a good manager, but completely discouraged because of small and irregular income due to drink, unemployment, illness, or lack of enterprise on the part of her husband" (More 1971, 137). In her 1914 book, *Mothers Who Must Earn*, Katharine Anthony illuminated the situation of women whose husbands could not provide them with the better married life for which they had hoped. Anthony studied 370 married women living in the middle West Side neighborhood of New York City. Of these 370 women, 95 were Irish-born, making the Irish the largest single ethnic group represented in the sample (54). Most of the women in Anthony's sample worked as domestics before marrying and had expected their paid employment outside the home to end when they married. As married women, however, they found that circumstances forced them to earn wages to support their families. Such compelling events included the injury or death on the job of husbands, the incapacitation of husbands by illnesses like tuberculosis, or the improvidence of some husbands and desertion by others. According to Anthony, many women in such situations went back to the occupation they had left for marriage, namely, domestic service. As married women, however, some performed domestic service as day work rather than live-in work, whereas others worked as scrubwomen in public places. Such women had narrow, hard lives that included little or no social life, and for them the rise to the middle class proved illusory.

Irish mothers pushed their children to Americanize, but not at the expense of their Catholic religion or their Irish identity. The Irish acculturated themselves but retained their religion and certain Irish attitudes. Irish mothers in America raised their children to be proud of being Irish, although they apparently failed to provide them with much information on the immigration experience or on Ireland. Whether consciously or not, however, Irish women passed down certain Irish cultural notions, as exemplified by the fact that "American Irish families are still predominantly Catholic" (Horgan 1988, 46, 72).

Despite the contention of some scholars that ethnic identity is a fragile, illusory thing in contemporary America, other scholarship supports the notion of the persistence of Irish identity among Irish Americans.[4] One case study of Irish Americans conducted from 1978 to 1981 in Boston, for example, indicates that certain Irish attitudes have continued over time, one of them being parents' maintenance of "close ties with married daughters in the United States" (Ikels 1985, 263). And sociologists Michael Hout and Joshua R. Goldstein acknowledge that the Irish in contemporary America retain "an unexplained subjective 'closeness' to Ireland" (1994, 79). The

4. The question of ethnic identity among white Americans continues to interest scholars. Based on a survey conducted in the Capital District (Greater Albany area) of New York, Richard D. Alba concludes that ethnicity in contemporary America is merely "symbolic ethnicity," that is, it represents "a vestigial attachment to a few ethnic symbols imposing little cost on everyday life." He contends that such symbolic ethnicity indicates that as a result of assimilation a new ethnic group he calls European Americans has emerged in the United States (1990, xiii–xiv). He argues that for this group, ethnicity is dependent on voluntary identification (4, 20). He states that these European Americans have redefined the American experience to be about immigration and says that these people are proud of their ethnicity (314–15). What Alba fails to come to grips with, however, is that these Americans still define themselves in relation to a specific European country from whence came some (it need not be all) of their ancestors. Alba fails to convince this author that at any time soon white Americans are likely to identify with the term European Americans. Reginald Byron based his work on the same geographic area as Alba, based on a survey conducted between January 1991 and April 1997, in an effort to see if measurable evidence of a distinctive Irish identity could be found in contemporary Albany. He finds Albany "as Catholic, and as Irish, as any city in the United States," but says his work led him to "question the notion of Irish-Americaness [*sic*] itself" (1999, 38, 16). Byron, like Alba, concludes that the individual determines the importance of his or her ethnic identity, and that ethnicity is basically irrelevant to the everyday lives of Irish Americans. By his measures (knowledge of Irish history and so on), the people surveyed retain no distinctive Irishness. He admits, however, that "Ireland still continues to exert a strong emotional attachment" for these people (78–83). This emotional connection to Ireland is key. Although by Byron's standards the Irish in Albany are not particularly Irish, the point is not how Byron perceives them but how they perceive themselves, and they perceive themselves as Irish because they were raised to do so, again bringing up the notion of the importance of mothers as transmitters of a sense of Irishness. Irish women in America seem to have impressed on their children the importance of Irish identity, whether they felt the need to pass on what, by objective measures, might constitute Irish culture or not. Both Alba's work and Byron's work really raise more questions about what it means to be an American (which neither clearly defines) than what it means to be an Irish American. If Byron's people still think of themselves as Irish Americans, what or who is the (plain) American against which, in opposition, they define themselves as *Irish* Americans?

Irish in America, it seems, retain a sense of themselves as Irish, as a special kind of American. In pushing their families upward into the middle class while retaining their religion and certain Irish cultural attitudes, in America, Irish women pioneered the way by which their families would show there was more than one way to be American—one could be American yet retain a distinct, if nebulous, sense of oneself as Irish. As Marjorie R. Fallows puts it, "What the Irish have demonstrated is that American life can encompass difference without insisting on eradicating it, and that an ethnic group can adopt an American identity without completely renouncing its historical sense of peoplehood" (1979, 150).

Other Domestic Servants over Time and Space

How does the experience of the Irish Bridget compare with the experience of women from other ethnic and racial groups who have also worked in service in the United States? Were the experiences of women from other groups similar to the Irish experience, or was the Irish experience unique? A review of the demographics will set the context for answering this question.

The 1870 federal census was the first to try to accurately record all female employment, and it showed that domestic servants were concentrated in two areas of the United States: urban areas where immigrants, the Irish in particular, dominated the occupation and the South, where African American women were dominant. According to this census there were 145,956 Irish-born servants, 42,866 natives of Germany working as servants, and 11,287 natives of Sweden, Norway, and Denmark working as servants. Of foreign-born servants, it was the Irish who prevailed in the northeastern states of Connecticut, Maine, Massachusetts, New Hampshire, New Jersey, New York, Pennsylvania, and Rhode Island, as well as the states of California, Illinois, and Ohio. In contrast, of those individuals born outside the United States, it was German servants who were dominant in Indiana, Iowa, Nebraska, and Wisconsin, whereas Scandinavians were preponderant in Kansas and Minnesota ("Our Domestic Service" 1875, 277). By 1900, 60.5 percent of Irish immigrant women worked in domestic service in the United States, 42.6 percent of German immigrant women were domestic servants, and 67.6 percent of wage-earning Swedish immigrant women also worked in service (Katzman 1978, 49, 67).[5]

5. The article "Our Domestic Service" reports that Chinese men worked in service in large numbers in both Nevada and California (1875, 276). David Katzman provides statistics

Americans may have coveted Frenchwomen as maids, but so few immigrated to the United States that their numbers in domestic service were negligible. And few Jewish and Italian immigrant women worked as domestic servants in America in the nineteenth and twentieth centuries. Mary Gove Smith believed few Jewish women entered domestic service because their families did not want them living outside their homes; she also contended that not only did Italian women consider household work demeaning, but they also disliked "the isolation, confinement, and concentration of effort" entailed in domestic service (1906, 8). It is notable, too, that the Italian migration was heavily male, rather than female, and the Italian women who did immigrate tended to be married women, making them unlikely to work in domestic service, which usually required living in the employer's house. If Italian women worked outside the home, they often worked in the needle trades; in addition, some Italian immigrant women also ran small shops and opened restaurants, specializing in Italian foods. The Jewish migration to the United States was more equalized by gender than the Italian migration, but Jewish women tended to immigrate in family groups, unlike the Irish. Rarely were Jewish women the major wage earners for their families, and when employed, they generally worked in the garment industry (Vecchio 2006, 121–25; Steinberg 1981, 160–61).

Scholarship

Scholarly investigation into the experiences of domestics other than the Irish varies by group. Scholarship on German immigrant domestic servants in the United States in the nineteenth and twentieth centuries, for example, is sparse, at best. Only one scholarly work on German immigrant women in domestic service in the United States appears to exist: Silke Wehner-Franco's 1994 German-language book, *Deutsche Dienstmädchen in Amerika, 1850–1914* (German Servant Girls in America, 1850–1914). Laurence A. Glasco, however, published work dealing with German immigrant domestics in Buffalo, New York, whereas Carol K. Coburn has written on third-generation

---

from the 1900 census, which put "servant" and "laundress" in two separate categories (1978, 67). Therefore, the figure for the Irish in 1900 is derived by adding the 54 percent classified as servants to the 6.5 percent of the Irish classified as laundresses, to obtain the 60.5 percent total of Irish in domestic service. The same method was used to calculate the percentages for German- and Swedish-born domestics.

German American domestics in Block, Kansas. Joy Lintelman, on the other hand, has produced some rather detailed work on Swedish immigrant domestic servants in the late nineteenth and early twentieth centuries.

African American women have a long history in domestic service in the United States. And in the early part of the twentieth century, the number of African Americans in service in the urban North grew as southern blacks migrated. Concomitant with the increased presence of African Americans in domestic service in the North, the number of Irish immigrants working in domestic service in the cities of the Northeast declined. "Bridget, the stereotyped, full-time, live-in servant of the nineteenth century, left the scene, replaced by Beulah, the part-time black maid of the twentieth" (Strasser 1982, 176–78). By 1920, African American women constituted the major servant group in the urban North, and by 1944, they constituted more than 60 percent of domestic workers (Katzman 1978, 273; Palmer 1989, 13). For this reason, until very recently, most scholarly study of domestic service has focused on African Americans. One scholarly study of African Americans in domestic service was conducted early on—Isabel Eaton published her work on African American domestics in Philadelphia's Seventh Ward in W. E. B. Du Bois's *Philadelphia Negro* in 1899.

Since women began entering the American workforce in large numbers in the 1980s, domestic service, viewed in the second half of the twentieth century as an occupation on the decline that was expected to almost disappear, has instead resurged as an occupation, as working women have sought assistance with the housework they face in the home after a full day's work outside of it. With this resurgence in domestic service, scholarly interest in the topic has blossomed, as historians, sociologists, ethnologists, and geographers have studied the occupation. And this resurgence, it has been argued, has created a situation in which "privileged women have delegated their menial household duties to other women" rather than uniting in opposition to "the devaluation of household labor" (D. Roberts 1997, 51, 52).

Most of the scholarly literature consists of case studies of domestic servants from particular groups, in certain geographic locations in the United States, in specific time frames. Margaret D. Jacob's work, for example, focuses on Native American (American Indian) female domestic servants in the San Francisco Bay area from 1920 through 1940. Evelyn Nakano Glenn's work concerns Japanese women in northern California and shows that, agricultural work aside, domestic service was the usual occupation of both Japanese immigrant women and their American-born daughters until World War II. Vicki

L. Ruiz points out that domestic service was the major occupation of Mexican women in the United States from 1900 to 1950, and her case study concerns undocumented Mexican national women working in domestic service in El Paso, Texas, in the 1980s. Also in the 1980s, Mary Romero studied American-born female Chicana domestics working in the Denver, Colorado, area, and in the mid-1980s, Shellee Colen studied West Indian immigrant domestic workers in New York City. From 1986 to 1988, Pierrette Hondagneu-Sotelo investigated undocumented Mexican immigrant women working in domestic service in the San Francisco Bay area of California. In the mid-1990s, she undertook a case study of Latina domestic workers in Los Angeles. In the late 1980s, Leslie Salzinger studied two Latina cooperatives for domestic servants in the San Francisco Bay area of California. Others who have produced scholarly work on domestic service in the United States in the late twentieth and early twenty-first centuries include Doreen J. Mattingly, who studied Mexican immigrant domestic workers in San Diego from 1993 to 1994; Jennifer Bickham Mendez, who conducted a case study of a commercial cleaning service in California in 1994; Michael J. Pisani and David W. Yoskowitz, who completed a case study of Mexican immigrant domestics in Laredo, Texas, in 2000; and Rhacel Salazar Parreñas, who studied Filipina domestics in Los Angeles.

In the 1980s Irish immigration, mainly illegal immigration into the United States, particularly to New York City, resurged, and, once again, many Irish females entered domestic service in private homes, oftentimes as nannies (Rossiter 1993, 192; Corcoran 1996, 462, 473; Almeida 2001, 4, 78). Although Mary P. Corcoran (1996) and Linda Dowling Almeida (2001) touch on the topic, there appears to be but one actual and very limited study (the sample consists of only three female Irish immigrant domestics) focusing specifically on Irish domestics in New York City in the early 1990s; this study was completed by Sharon McGowan as her senior project for Bard College in May 1992. The Irish women McGowan interviewed worked as both live-in and live-out nannies who, while primarily hired to provide child care, were also expected to do housework (39). To eliminate confusion as to which set of Irish immigrant domestics I am making reference, those from 1840 to 1930 or those of the 1990s, hereafter I will call the Irish domestics of the late twentieth century the modern Irish domestics.

Commonalities and Distinctions in Servants' Experiences

In the annals of migration history, women moving to work as paid domestic servants have formed "the largest single female category of migrant labor"

(Harzig 2007, 39). As an occupation, domestic service has been an integral part of the rural-to-urban migration for many women. Most Irish, German, and Swedish immigrant domestics, for example, migrated from rural areas of their home countries to work in service in urban America. In contrast with the past, the modern Irish came from all over Ireland, not just from rural areas (Almeida 1992, 200). Nonetheless, one of the three Irish domestics in McGowan's study of the modern Irish had rarely been outside her home county, rural County Armagh, before she moved to the United States (1992, 38).

Many African American domestics migrated from the rural South to urban America to work in service. And German American girls migrated from rural to urban parts of Kansas to work as domestics (Coburn 1991, 110–14). In contrast, the Latina domestics from the Amigos cooperative that Leslie Salzinger studied in 1988 were from urban areas (1991, 143). Likewise, Pierrette Hondagneu-Sotelo claims that the Latina immigrant domestics in Los Angeles whom she studied in the 1990s hailed from cities in their home countries (2001, 58).

Domestics' reasons for migrating to work in service in America, too, have been consistent over time and space. They migrated for economic reasons—to improve their lives—and they entered domestic service because it was the best occupational venue available to them. A review of the literature also indicates that certain employers' reasons for hiring domestics—to provide the employer with more leisure time and to fill the employer's status and emotional needs—also have remained much the same over time and space, regardless of the ethnic or racial group to which the domestic belonged (Parreñas 2001a, 184; Rollins 1985, 192; Kaplan 1987, 95). In addition, as mentioned above, a key factor in modern domestic service, however, is that many employers themselves are employed outside the home and so hire domestics to help them deal with their "double day"—the housework and child care duties that await them at home when their paid employment day ends.

To varying degrees, most domestics considered in the scholarly literature have faced class and ethnic, as well as cultural or linguistic, differences with their employers. According to the literature, historically, domestic service has been an occupation deemed especially proper for women of color, and so race and color have intersected negatively with domestic service. This was the case for Irish immigrants, who were initially viewed by white native-born Americans more as a separate race than as an ethnic group ("The Morals and Manners" 1873, 7; D. Clark 1973, 129). Japanese, Latina, American-born

Chicanas, West Indians, and American Indians are all examples of women who have dealt with the intersection of race and color with domestic service (Glenn 1986, xi; Hondagneu-Sotelo 2001, 13–14, 18–19, 55–56; Romero 1992, 71–72, 93–95, 98; Colen 1989, 172, 189; Jacobs 2007, 181–82). The experience of African American women in domestic work, in particular, has entwined with racism, as can be inferred from the statement one nineteenth-century Philadelphia employer made, showing a preference for African American servants "because they look more like servants" (Eaton 1973, 484). Even one modern Irish nanny felt the sting of believing that her employers thought her inferior to them in class because she worked as a nanny (McGowan 1992, 78).

The literature also demonstrates that Irish immigrant domestics were not the only women to confront discrimination in recruitment and advertising for domestic work. Mexican domestics, too, faced such discrimination. As recently as the 1980s, an ad in an El Paso, Texas, newspaper read "Wanted: European housekeeper" (Ruiz 1987, 71).

Over time and space, regardless of the worker's ethnic or racial background, certain aspects of live-in domestic service have remained fairly consistent. For example, despite technological improvements, housework remains hard, physical work. Also, a supposed advantage of live-in service is that it provides the domestic with room and board, and, indeed, even modern Irish domestics have appreciated these benefits of live-in service (McGowan 1992, 59). German immigrant girls found the food provided to them in service in the United States superior to what they were given in Germany (Wehner-Franco 1994, 241–46). Yet with regard to board or food, Phyllis Palmer discloses that employers often provided servants of color with food that was inadequate in amount, leaving them hungry (1989, 83). Similarly, Shellee Colen mentions that inadequate food was provided to West Indian immigrant domestics in New York City in the 1980s (1989, 181). And Pierrette Hondagneu-Sotelo declares that the food provided to some Latina domestics in Los Angeles in the 1990s was sometimes of very poor quality or was so insufficient that they felt compelled to buy their own food (2001, 33–35, 217). The lodging provided to German immigrant domestics, like what was provided to Irish domestics, was often in attics (Wehner-Franco 1994, 246–51). Palmer notes that the live-in domestics she studied were sometimes provided rooms that were unappealing, consisting, as they sometimes did, of a room over the employer's garage (1989, 83). American Indian domestics, West Indian domestics, and live-in Latinas in Los Angeles, too, found it objectionable that sometimes they were expected to share a bed or a bedroom with the children for whom they cared (Jacobs 2007, 181; Colen 1989, 180–81; Hondagneu-Sotelo 2001, 31). In contrast, modern Irish domestics have approved of their quarters—one described the bedroom of her own that was provided for her as quite "lovely" (McGowan 1992, 67).

In general, employers have used physical space to separate themselves from servants. Employers of Irish domestics, for example, presided over houses in which, by design, servant spaces were separated from family spaces. Some employers of German American domestics separated them from the family by making them eat in the kitchen (Coburn 1991, 114). Employers also physically separated themselves from their African American domestics by relegating them to the kitchen when the domestics were not busy with chores in other rooms (Kaplan 1987, 97). It rankled live-in West Indian domestics, too, that they were not permitted to eat meals with the family for whom they worked, but rather were expected to eat in the kitchen (Colen 1989, 181). Whether they would or should eat with their employers was an issue for Latina domestics in Los Angeles, too (Hondagneu-Sotelo 2001, 182, 204). Not all servants desire inclusion at the family dinner table, though. One Filipina domestic in Los Angeles refused her employer's offer to have her eat her meals with the employer's family, saying she would be more comfortable eating alone because "this is where I sleep, but it is not the same as being in your own home" (Parreñas 2001a, 166). Her comment points to an aspect of live-in domestic service that has been true over time and space: the house in which a domestic lives is her workplace, not her home. That fact was made clear to one modern Irish domestic who, although she was permitted to eat with the employing family, found that she was expected to clean up after meals all by herself (McGowan 1992, 69). Another scholar makes an ironic observation with regard to employers attempting to confine domestics to particular areas of the home. It appears that some exhausted employers in contemporary Los Angeles, who are unwilling to expend the emotional energy that personal interaction with their live-in Latina domestics would require of them, confine *themselves* to their bedrooms to avoid dealing with their lonely employees (Hondagneu-Sotelo 2001, 173–74).

Most live-in domestics, including the modern Irish, have shared the experience of working long hours and being on call to their employers (Wehner-Franco 1994, 176; McGowan 1992, 73; Hondagneu-Sotelo 2001, 142, 145). In addition, most live-in servants have had very limited time off. German immigrant girls usually had Sunday afternoons off, and then in the last quarter of the nineteenth century, their time off was increased by the addition of a half-day holiday during the week (Wehner-Franco 1994, 178). Swedish immigrant domestics, the African American domestics in Philadelphia's Seventh Ward, and the domestics of color that Palmer studied got the same limited time off, usually Thursdays and Sundays, that Irish domestics had gotten (Lintelman 1989, 17; Eaton 1973, 468–69; Palmer 1989, 77). And in the 1990s, some Latina domestics in Los Angeles got only Sundays off, whereas some Filipinas had no days off at all (Hondagneu-Sotelo 2001, 227; Parreñas 2001a, 169). Latina domestics in Los Angeles, like the Irish servants of old, also have found that their employers do not want them entertaining friends inside the employer's home (Hondagneu-Sotelo 2001, 32).

So live-in domestic work is isolating and lonely work today, as it was in the past, with modern Irish nannies being reported as tending to be more homesick than other European nannies, and domestics' complaints of being treated as if they are invisible echo over time and space (McGowan 1992, 61; Hondagneu-Sotelo 2001, 32, 63, 66, 196, 197, 210; Mattingly 1999a, 52; Mendez 1998, 130–31; Macdonald 1998, 35; McLaughlin and Kraus 2002, 274). It is no wonder, then, that Hondagneu-Sotelo found that Latina domestics in Los Angeles sought some personal relationship with their employer to validate their humanity, while time-pressed employers wanted a more distant, businesslike relationship to minimize the amount of emotional energy they expended on their domestics (2001, 11).

German immigrant domestics and their more modern sisters in service have experienced employer attempts to cheat them of their wages ("A German House Servant" 1925; Romero 1992, 128; Ruiz 1987, 70; McGowan 1992, 62; Jacobs 2007, 165, 180). In addition, the African American and West Indian experiences in domestic service, the Latina experience in service in Los Angeles, and the experience of modern Irish domestics all mirror the Irish experience between 1840 and 1930 in that they rarely included paid holidays, vacation, or sick leave (Martin and Segrave 1985, 150–51; Kaplan 1987, 94; Colen 1989, 186; Hondagneu-Sotelo 2001, 108; McGowan 1992, 73, 74). Chicana domestics in Denver, too, failed to receive the benefits of paid vacations and Social Security because most of them worked off the books, as did many Japanese domestics (Romero 1992, 129, 148; Glenn 1986, 175). Despite the fact that by the 1970s certain protections covered domestic workers, many employers failed to extend Social Security coverage, minimum wages, and unemployment insurance to African American domestics; this situation was complicated by the fact that enforcement of such requirements is not easy (Martin and Segrave 1985, 60, 74, 128, 144; Dill 1988, 35; Coble 2006, 7). With regard to West Indian domestics in New York and Latina domestics in Los Angeles, the problem today is not the lack of governmental regulation of domestic service. Instead, the problem is either ignorance of the required regulations or failure to comply with them, both of which are exacerbated by the fact that the rules governing domestic service are generally not enforced (Colen 1989, 173; Hondagneu-Sotelo 2001, 12, 21).

Employer fear that domestics will steal from them is apparently widespread. Like employers of Irish servants, the literature indicates that employers of Swedish, Japanese, African American, West Indian, Latina, and Mexican domestics all feared their employees would steal from them (Bowker 1871, 497; Lintelman 1991, 384; Glenn 1990, 362; Harris 1982, 18–19; Colen 1989, 185; Hondagneu-Sotelo 2001, 47, 163; Ruiz 1987, 70).

Employer ridicule of domestics has not been limited to the Irish, either. Like the Irish domestics who were the butt of "Biddy" and "Bridget" jokes, Mexican national domestics in El Paso were the subject of derisive "stupid maid" stories (Ruiz 1987, 69–70). In addition, across the board, it appears that domestics have faced possible sexual harassment or exploitation at the hands of their employers' husbands, for Irish, Swedish, German American, African American, Mexican, and Latina domestics all encountered this problem (Dudden 1983, 214–17; Lintelman 1991, 385–86; Coburn 1991, 114; Kaplan 1987, 101–2; Bolden 1976, 146; Harris 1982, 4–5; Rollins 1985, 150–51; Ruiz 1987, 67, 70; Hondagneu-Sotelo 2001, 66).

Over time and space, immigrant women have also accrued a similar benefit from their work as domestics—the ability to save money to support their families. Like the Irish, Swedish servants sent money home, as did Japanese and West Indian immigrant domestics in New York City (Lintelman 1989, 15; Glenn 1990, 354; Colen 1989, 186). Latina and Filipina domestics in Los Angeles and Mexican immigrant domestics in San Diego sent home remittances, too (Hondagneu-Sotelo 2001, 65; Parreñas 2001a, 160, 249; Mattingly 1999b, 68).[6] Nineteenth-century African American domestics in Philadelphia's Seventh Ward were known to provide key economic support to

6. According to the *New York Times Magazine*, so great are the remittances sent back to the Philippines by its emigrants (male and female, domestics and others) that the remittances total "$15 billion a year, a seventh of the country's gross domestic product" (April 22, 2007, 53).

their families, and African American women who migrated from the South to Washington, D.C., to work in service also sent money home (Eaton 1973, 459–60, 462; Clark-Lewis 1987, 209).

In general, scholars agree that throughout the nineteenth, twentieth, and twenty-first centuries, domestic service has been a low-status occupation that stigmatized its workers.[7] One hallmark of the demeaning nature of the work that has incensed domestics over time and space is being required to scrub on their hands and knees ("A German House Servant" 1925; Glenn 1990, 358; Mendez 1998, 122; Ehrenreich 2001, 83). Interestingly enough, however, regardless of their employers' perception or treatment of them, most domestics, including modern Irish domestics, like the Irish of 1840 to 1930, do not seem to have accepted the idea that they were lower-status beings because they worked as domestics (McGowan 1992, 58). In fact, Swedish immigrant girls did not concur with the low status accorded domestic service in America (Lintelman 1991, 389). Instead, they believed they had improved status as servants in the United States compared to their past positions as domestics in Sweden. Another reason Swedish women did not feel demeaned in service is that the Swedish community viewed domestic service more positively than did native-born Americans (Lintelman 1989, 11–16; 1991, 382–93). German immigrant girls, too, did not feel that they lost status working in service in the United States, for they found conditions in America far better than they were in Germany (Wehner-Franco 1994, 136–38).[8] And it is clear, too, that German American girls thought that their status rose, rather than fell, in domestic service (Coburn 1991, 114).

7. Alana Erickson Coble argues that in the twentieth century, the use of household appliances gave housework "technological cachet" in consequence of which "respect for housework rubbed off on paid domestic labor in the form of greater respect for their work and for them." Further, she asserts that "in the 1990s, the employer truly respected . . . her help." Not only does Coble fail to provide convincing evidence to support her argument, but her contention stands in decided contrast to the conclusion of most scholars that housework was and remains low-status work. In fact, Coble admits that "some stigma [is] still attached to the occupation" (2006, 3, 111, 6).

8. W. W. Whitelock (1906) also avers that the conditions of domestic service in the United States were far better than conditions in Germany, so the majority of German domestics probably found life as a domestic better in the United States than it was in Germany. Nonetheless, in "A German House Servant" (1925), the author argued, "A cook's vocation in the United States is presumably not much pleasanter than in Germany, in spite of the higher pay and the more comfortable room."

According to Bonnie Thornton Dill, although the African American domestics she studied "were keenly aware of the low social status of their occupation, . . . they rarely presented themselves as defeated by it. Instead, they portrayed themselves as having been actively engaged in a struggle to assert their individual worth" (1988, 36). Even West Indian domestics who had held higher-status jobs in their home countries before coming to America did not feel that working as domestics made them lesser beings than their employers. They, like the Irish of 1840 to 1930, saw domestic service not as a lifetime career but rather as a "stepping-stone" to other employment and a better life (Colen 1989, 173, 187, 189). Some of the Latinas studied in the San Francisco Bay area in 1988 ostensibly moved down the class ladder from higher-status work in their home countries to domestic work in the United States, but they, too, refused to see themselves as having fallen downward occupationally. Instead, they were proud of the good work they did and the good pay they earned (Salzinger 1991, 139). Some of the Latinas studied in Los Angeles also had formerly held higher-status jobs in their home countries. Although they disliked working as domestics, they also "take pride in their work, and . . . are extremely proud of what their earnings enable them to accomplish for their families" (Hondagneu-Sotelo 2001, 150–51, 12). Most of the Filipina domestics studied were educated, and some came from families that employed maids in the Philippines. Working as domestics would seem to have caused them to slip down the occupational ladder, and they were sensitive about it. They comforted themselves, however, that while their occupational status declined, they gained financially in that they earned more than professionals in the Philippines. Indicating how important it was for them to hold on to their view of themselves as having some status, Filipina domestics called themselves "the educated domestics" to distinguish themselves from other domestics such as Latinas and African Americans (Parreñas 2001a, 150, 19, 174).

Their own ethnic or racial community constituted an important support for domestics. During their limited leisure, American Indian domestics and Swedish servants, like Irish immigrant domestics, kept in close contact with their ethnic communities (Jacobs 2007, 179; Lintelman 1989, 11; 1991, 389, 393). Also, between jobs, Swedish domestics, like Irish domestics, found housing with friends in their ethnic community (Lintelman 1989, 13, 14). The Japanese community, too, provided support for Japanese domestics, and the African American community did so for African American domestics (Glenn 1986, 179; Dill 1988, 47–48, 50). In addition, the West Indian community supported and encouraged the domestics from its ranks (Colen 1989, 188). Modern Irish domestics found in their fellow Irish immigrant women a community of helpers willing to offer advice on how to improve their pay as domestics (ask for hourly wages) and improve their working conditions (choose live-out as opposed to live-in work) (McGowan 1992, 91, 95).

All of the domestic servants cited in the literature, not just the Irish, showed agency. Their attempts to unionize, although unsuccessful, demonstrate such agency. From 1870 through 1940 efforts to improve working conditions in domestic service through organizing unions were made, but they foundered because certain aspects of the occupation and those who staffed its ranks did not lend themselves to unionization. These aspects included the isolation and youth of servants, the fact that most domestics did not expect to spend their whole lives in service but instead saw their work in service as temporary, their diversity (in terms of race, ethnicity, and religion), the "collective 'peasant' mentality antithetical to collective action" that many servants are alleged to have had, and the fact that, on the whole, up to the 1930s, organized labor was uninterested in unionizing female domestics (Van Raaphorst 1988, 13, 98, 101, 166–67, 179).

Since employment contracts clearly spelling out expectations have historically been, and continue to be, uncommon in domestic service, mismatches between the employer's and the domestic's expectations of what will be entailed in the job have led in the past, and continue to lead, to tense employer-employee relations. So when German, African American, Japanese, Latina, West Indian, and American Indian domestics, as well modern Irish domestics, were very unhappy in their work situations, like the Irish in 1840 to 1930, they voted with their feet and quit ("A German House Servant" 1925, 464; Dill 1988, 39–41; Glenn 1990, 363; Hondagneu-Sotelo 2001, 61, 155; Colen 1989, 187; Jacobs 2007, 186; McGowan 1992, 85). Immigrant Mexican cleaners in San Diego, too, found that quitting was their "bargaining chip" in dealing with employers (Mattingly 1999a, 64).

Through their agency, African American domestics are acknowledged as having effected a positive improvement in the occupation. Unlike young single Irish, German, and Swedish immigrant domestics, African Americans in the twentieth century tended to be married women for whom service was often a lifelong occupation. Since African American women had their own families, they preferred to return home at the conclusion of a day's service work rather than to live in with their employers. As a result, African

American domestics are credited with engineering the transformation of domestic service from mainly live-in to mainly live-out, or day, work (Eaton 1973, 468, 504; Katzman 1978, 92, 198–99, 273; Palmer 1989, 68). In doing so, they gained increased individual freedom, decreased their detachment from their families and the African American community, and reduced their hours of employment. African Americans, however, were not alone in bringing about the switch to day work. Married Japanese American domestics from 1905 to 1940 also preferred day work because it afforded them the flexibility of earning money while simultaneously fulfilling their family responsibilities in their own homes (Glenn 1990, 355, 357–58). Chicana domestics in Denver in the late twentieth century, as well as undocumented Mexican immigrants in San Francisco in the late 1980s and modern Irish domestics, have all found day work preferable to live-in service (Romero 1992, 143, 145–48; Hondagneu-Sotelo 1994, 54, 59; McGowan 1992, 90, 95). Latina domestics in Los Angeles in the mid-1990s, too, preferred day work as cleaners to live-in work because it permitted them to have a family life. Their preference highlights the fact that most live-in domestics are single, whereas many live-out domestics are married (Hondagneu-Sotelo 2001, 38, 49–50). Nonetheless, with regard particularly to contemporary live-in nannies, some are mothers to children left behind in their home countries (Hochschild 2002, 15, 20–26).

Japanese domestics in the period 1905–40 also demonstrated agency in insisting on working on a task, rather than a time, basis. Further, they purposefully selected employers who would be absent from the home when the work was performed. In doing so, they derived greater occupational autonomy because absent employers have little opportunity to interfere with a domestic's execution of the work (Glenn 1990, 362–63). For similar reasons, late-twentieth-century Chicana domestics, too, preferred to work for employers who were absent from the home while they worked (Romero 1992, 153). And in the mid-1990s, many Latinas in Los Angeles, too, worked alone in private homes for absent employers (Hondagneu-Sotelo 2001, 78, 121).

Chicana domestics working at the end of the twentieth century also showed agency in their struggle with employers "to restructure the work as a small business by transforming it from wage labor to an occupation involving labor services." In this transformation, while working for multiple employers on a set schedule, individual Chicanas "define the work on the basis of a contract—by the house or the apartment—rather than as hourly work." In defining themselves as "expert cleaners or housekeepers" Chicana household workers sought to distinguish themselves from servants per se (Romero 1992, 147, 155). According to one scholar, this flat-rate job-work form of domestic service represents yet another transformation in the nature of the occupation (Hondagneu-Sotelo 1994, 51).

When the Irish worked in domestic service in the Northeast from 1840 to 1930, in comparison with factory pay, the wages domestic service offered were good. Over the first half of the twentieth century, however, salaries for domestic servants increasingly lost ground against wages paid to factory workers, making domestic service both low-status and low-paid work (Chaplin 1978, 110; Martin and Segrave 1985, 68–69). More recently, however, domestic work has again been cited as offering attractive pay. For Chicana women in the 1980s, "In comparison with other jobs they had held, domestic service usually paid more" (Romero 1992, 12–13). A similar point was made by Doreen J. Mattingly in her 1990s case study of Mexican cleaners in San Diego; she noted that the hourly wages of the domestic workers she studied exceeded the minimum wage (1999a, 55). In the mid-1990s, Latina domestics in Los Angeles found live-out work to pay better than live-in work, and found that the wages earned in live-out housecleaning compared favorably with factory pay (Hondagneu-Sotelo 2001, 44, 51). And, as previously noted, Filipina domestics earned more as domestics in Los Angeles than they would have earned as professionals in the Philippines (Parreñas 2001a, 19).

Irish domestics who spoke English would certainly seem to have had a decided advantage over non-English-speaking or limited-English-speaking German, Scandinavian, Japanese, Mexican, and Latina immigrant domestics. Former Irish domestic Mary Feely, who came to the United States in 1927, apparently believed that her English-language facility was an asset because she mentioned that the girls who did housework who "come from Sweden and Norway and Germany . . . didn't speak a word of English when they come here. But they learned. Some of them took care of the kids for a couple of months until they learned enough that they could get by on" (1996). German immigrant girls, however, did not necessarily see their lack of English-language skills as a problem in domestic service with one exception—working as a cook, which required consultation with the employer on meals (Wehner-Franco 1994, 110–11, 189).

Research into contemporary domestic service indicates that English-speaking ability is an asset, for English-speaking cleaners in San Diego in the 1990s earned more than those without English-language facility, partly because they were better able to seek out new jobs and to negotiate wages with employers (Mattingly 1999a, 63). For Latina domestics in Los Angeles in the 1990s, too, the acquisition of better-paying domestic jobs was linked with English-language facility (Hondagneu-Sotelo 2001, 36, 45, 51). Filipina domestics in Los Angeles saw their English-language ability as an asset in their work (Parreñas 2001a, 178–79). Interestingly enough, however, other scholars claim that the language barrier was sometimes advantageous to domestics. For example, since Japanese women could not understand their employers, they were said to be oblivious to "insulting or denigrating comments" (Glenn 1990, 361). Similarly, in the late 1980s, a novice Mexican immigrant domestic in San Francisco was advised by a more experienced domestic that the language barrier was an asset because the domestic could "simply smile" at, rather than be compelled to speak to, an employer whose conversational attempts might have wasted the domestic's time and money (Hondagneu-Sotelo 1994, 57).

Unlike some other countries, the United States has never had a government program to recruit foreign domestics to live and work here (Hondagneu-Sotelo 2001, 20–21).[9] Irish women in the period 1840 to 1930 came to this country first and then found their way into employment in domestic service, and these Irish women were *legal* immigrants. In this respect, their position is greatly distinguished from the situation of some more recent domestics, including modern Irish domestics. Undocumented immigrants are much more likely to work as domestics than are legal immigrants, for service is one of the few employment options available to them (Mattingly 1999b, 66). Undocumented domestics generally earn less as domestics than their legal counterparts (Hondagneu-Sotelo 1994, 59). Recent undocumented immigrants employed as domestics include West Indian, Filipino, Mexican, and Central American immigrant women. Also among the undocumented are the modern Irish, some of whom are quite well educated (Rossiter 1993, 192; McLaughlin and Kraus 2002, 36; McGowan 1992, 39).[10] Regardless of their education, class, race, or ethnic background, undocumented domestics earn less money than

9. That is not to say that there has been no direct government involvement in domestic service in America. Margaret D. Jacobs shows that through the Bureau of Indian Affairs, the federal government placed Indian girls in live-in service in the San Francisco Bay area from 1920 through 1940. As part of this program, the bureau also employed female agents known as "outing matrons" to supervise these Indian girls (2007, 166).

10. The *Irish Voice* reported that in 1994, illegal Irish immigrants outnumbered illegal Mexican immigrants in New York State (January 4–10, 1995, 17).

do documented domestics, and are more vulnerable to employer exploitation than are legal immigrant domestics (Rollins 1985, 151).[11]

At least to some extent, domestic service functioned as an acculturating occupation not only for the Irish from 1840 to 1930 but also for German and Scandinavian immigrants and for German Americans. In the twentieth century, however, according to the literature, domestic service did not serve to acculturate many women of color, including Japanese and African American women (Glenn 1990, 345; Dill 1988, 34; Rollins 1985, 55). Latinas appear to constitute an exception to this rule, for Latina domestics in Los Angeles in the 1990s found that, in some respects, domestic service functioned as an acculturating occupation for them (Hondagneu-Sotelo 2001, 48–49).

Every woman's experience in domestic service is dependent on a number of factors, including her personality, her employer's personality, the personalities of other members of the employing family, the amount of work required of her, and her experience and skill in executing the work. Good employers exist along with the bad, and some employers have been more partial to servants from one group than to servants of other groups. American employers lauded Swedish domestics, leading proud Swedes to believe their domestics were superior to Irish domestics (Lintelman 1991, 390). A 1906 report indicates, however, that Swedes may have overestimated the esteem in which their domestics were held. Though praising them for being "hard workers, industrious, honest, efficient," the author of this report went on to say that Swedish domestics are "not as rapid as the quick-motioned Irish girl" (M. Smith 1906, 8).

Most of the employers Isabel Eaton interviewed regarding African American domestics in Philadelphia's Seventh Ward in the late nineteenth century indicated they favored them over white servants, with one employer commenting that they were "much cleaner than the Irish both in their work and in their persons." Another employer ventured that "the Germans drink and the Irish order you out of the house, but the colored people are more respectful and anxious to please." Yet another employer pointed out the reality, however, that "there are good ones and poor ones. . . . [I]t varies with the individual, not with the race" (Eaton 1973, 484–88).

11. Similarly, Cooper finds that undocumented live-in domestics in contemporary England can find their experience tantamount to slavery (2004, 291).

Religion was important not only to Irish domestics but to Swedish immigrant, German American, African American, and West Indian domestics as well (Colen 1989, 188). Irish servants were actively involved with the Roman Catholic Church, and so, too, Swedish servants were great supporters of their church. Protestant Swedish churches in America counted domestics "as their best members" (Lintelman 1991, 391). German American servants in Kansas were good supporters of the Missouri Synod of the Lutheran Church, particularly its Ladies' Aid Society, which they turned into a money-generating organization (Coburn 1991, 111, 117). Their churches were the center of recreation for African American domestics in Philadelphia's Seventh Ward (Eaton 1973, 469). And the desire of African American servants to participate in their churches was one reason that they favored day work, which made religious practice much more possible than did live-in service (Clark-Lewis 1987, 210–11; 1994, 136, 169–70). For African Americans, the church "provided a place in which domestic workers could achieve status based upon their participation, making their occupational performance relatively unimportant" (Dill 1988, 50). Modern Irish Catholic domestics report that they have *not* experienced discrimination on the basis of their religion (McGowan 1992, 93). Otherwise, except for one scholar remarking that many Latina domestics (especially Guatemalans) in an organization of domestics in Los Angeles are not Roman Catholics but rather are evangelical Christians, recent scholarship makes little or no mention of the relationship between religion and modern-day domestics (Hondagneu-Sotelo 2001, 225–26).

About 33 percent of German immigrants to America were Roman Catholics, the remainder mainly Protestants, Lutheran, or other (Conzen 1984, 22). Some of the Catholic German immigrant girls worked in domestic service, so Irish girls were not the only Catholics to populate the ranks of domestic servants in the United States from 1840 to 1930. Whereas a large number of advertisements for servants, especially after the 1880s, specified particularly that German *Protestant* girls were wanted, nothing in the literature indicates that German Catholic servants faced the same sort of conflict with their mistresses over religion that Irish Catholics encountered (Wehner-Franco 1994, 112).

A review of the literature on domestic service evidences many similarities and some distinctions in the experiences of domestics over time and space in America. The Irish Catholic experience in domestic service from 1840 to 1930, however, appears to be distinguished from the experience of all other domestic servants, in at least one respect—only Irish Catholic women appear to have dealt with discrimination on the basis of religion in this occupation. Irish immigrant domestic servants strongly resisted the efforts of their white middle-class Protestant employers to interfere with their religious practice and to dissuade them from their Catholicism. Consequently, after dealing with Irish immigrant domestics, employers no longer felt so free to interfere with a servant's religious beliefs. By the beginning of the twentieth century, after the full onslaught of Irish Catholics into domestic service had been felt, religion ceased to be a point of contention between employers and domestics in the United States (Katzman 1978, 164).

The Irish, then, can be credited with making domestic service in the United States more modern in that, as a result of their experience with American employers, religion became irrelevant to the occupation. Thus, in at least this one respect, the experience in domestic service of the Irish Bridget from 1840 to 1930 was unique.

Epilogue

The newspaper headline declaimed "Housework Gap Shrinks." The story, which appeared in the March 6, 2008, *Albany Times Union,* quoted a report issued by the Council on Contemporary Families claiming that "more couples are sharing family tasks than ever before, and the movement toward sharing has been especially significant for full-time dual-earner couples." The report also confirmed, however, that men do not yet share equally with women in housework and child care. This information, affirmed by scholarship, is likely no surprise to the many middle-class women employed outside the home who have chosen to pay other people, mainly other women, to provide them with household assistance. Even though men are helping out more, it is still primarily women who serve as the chief executive officers of their families—that is, they manage their households, they arrange their families' social lives, they oversee their families' schedules of activities and appointments, and they remember birthdays and anniversaries and take care of the gift giving attendant to such occasions. Women continue to bear primary responsibility for this type of household work that sociologist Pamela Smock terms "invisible," according to the *Times Union* article cited above. With much to do in running a household, and limited time in which to do it, many women who work for wages outside the home have decided that if "something has to go," it is going to be housecleaning. Thus, these middle-class women hire people to help them specifically with the seemingly never-ending housecleaning that plagues them as they deal with their "double day." Consequently, the occupation of domestic service has resurged in conjunction with the influx of American women into paid employment outside the home that began in the 1970s and 1980s. This resurgence in domestic service apparently is not unique to the United States, for Sheila McIsaac Cooper has identified a similar phenomenon in domestic service in England, in the same time frame, for similar reasons (2004, 277, 287).

One of the problems in discussing contemporary domestic service is the ambiguity of the term. Different types of work in the private home get lumped together under the general rubric of domestic service. Cleaning, child care, cooking, and personal service tasks (for example, picking up after the employer, laying out the employer's clothing, getting the employer's bath ready) are all termed domestic service. Even if one defines domestic service to mean only cleaning tasks, in the private home one can employ people in several different ways to accomplish such tasks. For example, one can hire an individual to perform housework for a flat fee rather than for an hourly rate. Cleaners, as these workers are called, tend to work for multiple employers, and set their own schedules. They act as independent contractors, and usually perform the work in the absence of the employer. Although such work offers flexibility and sometimes decent money, often the pay is under the table and carries no benefits such as sick and vacation leave. Also, this independent-contractor, day-work type of domestic service is considered low-status work. It tends to be performed by female workers (some males also work as cleaners—for years I paid a man to clean my house) who are often distinguished from their employers by being of a lower social class or of a different race or ethnic group from the employer.[1]

The commercial cleaning service is another type of domestic service available to contemporary Americans. For a set fee and a set amount of work, it is usual for such commercial cleaning services to send out teams of bonded employees (usually female, but sometimes including males) to clean private homes. In general, such commercial cleaning services fully equip their cleaner-employees for their work, and the employees usually perform the work while the employer is absent from the home. Although workers may or may not receive benefits when working for commercial cleaning services, it is low-status and often low-paid work. Females who are of a lower social class than the employer but may be of the same race tend to perform this type of work. Such a commercial cleaning service called "The Maids" is available in the Albany, New York, area. The name of this commercial cleaning service, however, highlights the ambiguity of the term *domestic service,* for its

1. Such domestics are not always of a lower class or different race than their employers. In an article titled "Dirty Laundry" that appeared in the *New York Times Magazine* on January 28, 1996, Louise Rafkin said that she is white and found work as an independent-contractor by-the-job cleaner or domestic preferable to her previous employment "teaching American literature to undergraduates."

employees only *clean* private homes; they do not do other personal service work, yet the company name conjures up images of true personal servants.

In addition, today, as in the past, some people, mostly females, are paid to perform tasks in the private homes of others that can include one or more of following: child care, cooking, and cleaning. These tasks are synonymous with those of domestic service, yet often neither the employee nor the employer thinks of such people as servants. Instead, employees consider themselves to be *helping* their employers. Because the pay for this work is often under the table, it offers no benefits, but it is not necessarily considered low-status work. Such workers are comparable to the "help" that Faye Dudden (1983) contends began to disappear in the 1830s with the advent of immigrants to live-in service work in the United States. "Help" never totally disappeared from the American scene, however—it is still here, and it is here to stay, for in the present as well as in the past people have hired help, usually on a day-work basis, to come into their homes. Unlike domestics, "help" tend to be treated as equals by their employers, and suffer no social stigma for their work, because they are usually of the same class and race as their employer. Teenage girls (and sometimes boys) who babysit or serve as "mother's helpers" for neighbors and family friends are examples of modern help.

And, as in the past, domestic service also continues to be available to American employers in its historic live-in, seven-days-a-week form that can include cleaning, child care, cooking, and personal service tasks, or can be specialized so that a servant performs only one of these tasks. In contemporary America live-in cooks, maids, and nannies are often of a lower social class than their employers, and may be of a different race as well. And in contemporary America, women employing nannies on a live-out basis are not necessarily truly wealthy, as working women have reached out to nannies to help them deal with the difficulties of balancing paid work with motherhood (Kaylin 2007, 54–55).[2] Women's experiences with live-in service in America today can run the gamut from pleasant to the horrible, exploitative, slavelike conditions experienced by some undocumented workers. On December 3, 1997, for example, the *Irish Voice* reprinted a 1989 article reporting that a priest named Father Martin Keveny had rescued an illegal Irish immigrant girl from County Kerry who was living under "slave-like conditions" as a

2. Jessika Auerbach contends that "the largest majority of nannies are employed by parents for whom the cost of full-time one-on-one child care represents a carefully budgeted, and sometimes much resented, expense" (2007, 138).

nanny and housekeeper for a New Jersey family. And on May 16, 2007, the *New York Times* reported that the federal government had charged a Long Island couple "with keeping two Indonesian domestic workers as virtual prisoners in their home for more than five years under conditions they called 'modern-day slavery.'" On December 18, 2007, the *Times* reported that the couple was convicted on twelve counts, including "involuntary servitude . . . [and] forced labor." If nothing else, domestic service in modern America certainly offers variety.

As long as middle- to upper-middle-class American women continue to work outside the home for wages and face the problem of reconciling long work hours with neverending housework, it is likely that they will continue to seek paid household help for at least the cleaning of their homes, whether they hire individuals or commercial cleaning services. Single men, too, the number of which is unknown, also will continue to hire people to clean their homes.[3] Middle- to upper-middle-class women employed outside the home who have children, as well as single fathers, are also likely to hire help in the form of babysitters or nannies for child care purposes. It is highly unlikely that middle-class Americans will ever again be able to hire live-in domestic servants on the same scale that they did in the nineteenth and early twentieth centuries. But some people, especially the very wealthy, will continue to hire live-in servants to take care of their personal needs, as well as to cook, clean, and provide child care for them. Barring the invention of robots that can independently and reliably perform household cleaning and child care tasks, the demand for household workers, especially cleaners, will continue. It is equally likely that immigrant women will continue to supply that demand. And since payment for much of this domestic work will continue to be under the table, obtaining valid statistics on the number of people working in domestic service will continue to be very difficult. Accordingly, the undesirable conditions associated with domestic service, including lack of benefits and potential exploiting of workers, will continue, at least for some domestic workers. The continued availability of domestic work in the United States, however, also means that women with few other options will at least have service work open to them, and the wages they earn in their work will benefit their families here and abroad, through the remittances they send home. It is even possible that service work will continue to provide an acculturating

3. One woman who cleaned for me told me that she had male as well as female clients.

experience for some young female domestic workers. Thus, the story of the Irish Bridget has relevance for contemporary employers of domestics, for the limited number of Irish immigrant girls now involved in domestic service, and for the large number of Latina immigrants and female immigrants from the Caribbean who now staff the occupation's ranks (Thistle 2006, 175; Momsen 1999, 13).

Study of the Irish Bridget cuts across many scholarly disciplines. By focusing on women, the story of the Irish Bridget broadens our knowledge of the history of the Irish in America. At the same time, it also expands our understanding of women's history, immigration history, ethnic history, and labor history in the United States.

The *New York Times* reported on December 10, 2000, that when the Lower East Side Tenement Museum and University Settlement jointly offered an English-language and life-skills class for new immigrants, they used letters, diaries, and oral histories from earlier generations to show how those immigrants dealt with the immigration experience in America. Thus, long after they acculturated to America, the story of the Irish Bridgets offers something of value to contemporary female immigrants who, like Chinese immigrant Siaoying Beng, ask, "How can a person who is homesick learn to live in the new country?"

Works Cited

Index

Works Cited

Adams, William Forbes. 1980. *Ireland and Irish Emigration to the New World from 1815 to the Famine.* Baltimore: Genealogical Publishing. (Orig. pub. 1932.)

Ahearn [Fitgzerald], Ella. 1989. Interview DP-02, by Andrew Phillips. Oral History Collection, Ellis Island Immigration Museum, Statue of Liberty National Monument, New York. Mar. 22.

Aisling Irish Community Center. 2006. *While Mem'ry Brings Us Back Again: A Collection of Memoirs.* Yonkers, N.Y.: Aisling Irish Community Center.

Akenson, Donald Harman. 1996. *The Irish Diaspora: A Primer.* Toronto: P. D. Meany.

Alba, Richard D. 1990. *Ethnic Identity: The Transformation of White America.* New Haven: Yale Univ. Press.

Almeida, Linda Dowling. 1992. "'And They Still Haven't Found What They're Looking For': A Survey of the New Irish in New York City." In *Patterns of Migration,* vol. 1 of *The Irish World Wide: History, Heritage, Identity,* edited by Patrick O'Sullivan, 196–221. London: Leicester Univ. Press.

———. 2001. *Irish Immigrants in New York City, 1945–1995.* Bloomington: Indiana Univ. Press.

Ames, Kenneth L. 1992. *Death in the Dining Room, and Other Tales of Victorian Culture.* Philadelphia: Temple Univ. Press.

Anthony, Katharine. 1914. *Mothers Who Must Earn.* Russell Sage Foundation, West Side Studies. New York: Survey Associates.

Appel, John J. 1971. "From Shanties to Lace Curtains: The Irish Image in *Puck,* 1876–1910." *Comparative Studies in Society and History* 13, no. 4 (Oct.): 365–75.

Arnold, Betty Fitzgerald. 1996. Interview by author. Tape recording. Albany, N.Y. Mar. 26.

Auerbach, Jessika. 2007. *And Nanny Makes Three.* New York: St. Martin's Press.

Bacon, Elizabeth Mickle. 1943. "The Growth of Household Conveniences in the United States from 1865 to 1900." Ph.D. diss., Radcliffe College.

Barker, C. Hélène. 1915. *"Wanted: A Young Woman to Do Housework": Business Principles Applied to Housework.* New York: Moffat, Yard.

Beckham, Polly. 2002. "A Little Cache of Green: The Savings Habits of Irish Immigrant Women in 1850 Philadelphia." *Pennsylvania History* 69, no. 2: 230–65.

Beecher, Catharine E., and Harriet Beecher Stowe. 1994. *The American Woman's Home*. Hartford, Conn.: Stowe-Day Foundation. (Orig. pub. 1869.)

Bolden, Dorothy. 1976. "Forty-two Years a Maid, Starting at Nine in Atlanta." In *Nobody Speaks for Me! Self-Portraits of American Working Class Women*, edited by Nancy Seifer, 138–77. New York: Simon and Schuster.

Bourke, Angela. 1988. "The Traditional Lament and the Grieving Process." *Women's Studies International Forum* 11, no. 4: 287–91.

Bourke, Austin. 1993. *"The Visitation of God"? The Potato and the Great Irish Famine*. Dublin: Lilliput Press.

Bourke, Joanna. 1993. *Husbandry to Housewifery: Women, Economic Change, and Housework in Ireland, 1890–1910*. Oxford: Clarendon Press.

Bowker, R. R. 1871. "In Re Bridget: The Defence." *Old and New* 4: 497–501.

Boyle [Kelly], Mary Catherine Theresa. 1995. Interview EI-613, by Paul E. Sigrist Jr. Oral History Collection, Ellis Island Immigration Museum, Statue of Liberty National Monument, New York. May 2.

Brady, Ellen [pseud.]. 1977. Interview MZ-30, by Joan Morrison and Charlotte Zabusky. Oral History Collection, Ellis Island Immigration Museum, Statue of Liberty National Monument, New York. Mar. 7.

Brady, Sarah. 1975. Interview MZ-9, by Charlotte Zabusky. Oral History Collection, Ellis Island Immigration Museum, Statue of Liberty National Monument, New York. Oct. 11.

Breathnach, Ciara. 2004. "The Role of Women in the Economy of the West of Ireland, 1891–1923." *New Hibernia Review* 8, no. 1: 80–92.

———. 2005. *The Congested Districts Board of Ireland, 1891–1923: Poverty and Development in the West of Ireland*. Dublin: Four Courts Press.

Bridget. 1871. *Harper's Bazaar*, Nov. 11, 706.

Browne, Carlotta Ophelia. 1852. Letter to the editor. *Boston Daily Evening Transcript*, Feb. 18.

Buckley, Alison. 2004. "'Let the Girls Come Forth': The Early Feminist Ideology of the Irish Women Workers' Union." In *Irish Women's History*, edited by Alan Hayes and Diane Urquhart, 103–14. Dublin: Irish Academic Press.

Bushman, Richard L. 1993. *The Refinement of America: Persons, Houses, Cities*. New York: Vintage Books. (Orig. pub. 1992.)

Byron, Reginald. 1999. *Irish America*. Oxford: Clarendon Press.

Campbell, Ake. 1937. "Notes on the Irish House." *Folkliv*, nos. 2–3: 207–34.

Campbell, Helen. 1889. *Prisoners of Poverty: Women Wage-Workers, Their Trades, and Their Lives*. Boston: Roberts Brothers. (Orig. pub. 1887.)

Carbery, Mary. 1973. *The Farm by Lough Gur: The Story of Mary Fogarty (Sissy O'Brien)*. Dublin: Mercier Press. (Orig. pub. 1937.)

Carleton, William. 1971. *Traits and Stories of the Irish Peasantry.* 4 vols. Freeport, N.Y.: Books for Libraries Press. (Orig. pub. 1853.)

Carpenter, Niles. 1969. *Immigrants and Their Children.* New York: Arno Press and the New York Times.

Casey, Cornelius T. 2006. Interview by author. Tape recording. Troy, N.Y. June 16.

Cassidy, Tanya. 1997. "Sober for the Sake of the Children: The Church, the State, and Alcohol Use Amongst Women in Ireland." In *Women and Irish Society: A Sociological Reader,* edited by Anne Byrne and Madeleine Leonard, 447–64. Belfast: Beyond the Pale Publications.

Chambers, Mary D. 1936. *Table Etiquette: Menus and Much Besides.* Boston: Boston Cooking-School Magazine. (Orig. pub. 1932.)

Chaplin, David. 1978. "Domestic Service and Industrialization." In *Comparative Studies in Sociology: An Annual Compilation of Research,* edited by Richard F. Tomasson, 1:97–127. Greenwich, Conn.: JAI Press.

Clark, Clifford E., Jr. 1987. "The Vision of the Dining Room: Plan Book Dreams and Middle-Class Realities." In *Dining in America, 1850–1900,* edited by Kathryn Grover, 142–72. Amherst: Univ. of Massachusetts Press.

Clark, Dennis. 1973. *The Irish in Philadelphia: Ten Generations of Urban Experience.* Philadelphia: Temple Univ. Press.

———. 1977. "The Irish Catholics: A Postponed Perspective." In *Immigrants and Religion in Urban America,* edited by Randall M. Miller and Thomas D. Marzik, 48–68. Philadelphia: Temple Univ. Press.

———. 1982. *The Irish Relations: Trials of an Immigrant Tradition.* East Brunswick, N.J.: Associated Univ. Presses.

Clark-Lewis, Elizabeth. 1987. "'This Work Had a End': African-American Domestic Workers in Washington, D.C., 1910–1940." In *"To Toil the Livelong Day": America's Women at Work, 1780–1980,* edited by Carol Groneman and Mary Beth Norton, 196–211. Ithaca: Cornell Univ. Press.

———. 1994. *Living in, Living Out: African-American Domestics in Washington, D.C., 1910–1940.* Washington, D.C.: Smithsonian Institution Press.

Clarkson, L. A., and E. Margaret Crawford. 1988. "Dietary Directions: A Topographical Survey of Irish Diet, 1836." In *Economy and Society in Scotland and Ireland, 1500–1939,* edited by Rosalind Mitchison and Peter Roebuck, 171–91. Edinburgh: John Donald Publishers.

———. 2001. *Feast and Famine: A History of Food and Nutrition in Ireland, 1500–1920.* Oxford: Oxford Univ. Press.

Clear, Caitriona. 1997. "No Feminine Mystique: Popular Advice to Women of the House in Ireland, 1922–1954." In *Women and Irish History,* edited by Maryann Gialanella Valiulis and Mary O'Dowd, 189–205. Dublin: Wolfhound Press.

———. 2000. *Women of the House: Women's Household Work in Ireland, 1926–1961.* Dublin: Irish Academic Press.

Coble, Alana Erickson. 2006. *Cleaning Up: The Transformation of Domestic Service in Twentieth Century New York City.* New York: Routledge.

Coburn, Carol K. 1991. "Learning to Serve: Education and Change in the Lives of Rural Domestics in the Twentieth Century." *Journal of Social History* 25, no. 1: 109–22.

Coker, Caleb, ed. 1992. *The News from Brownsville: Helen Chapman's Letters from the Texas Military Frontier, 1848–1852.* Published for the Barker Texas History Center by the Texas Historical Association in cooperation with the Center for Studies in Texas History at the Univ. of Texas at Austin.

Coleman, Mary. 1985. "Irish Lace and Irish Crochet." In *Irish Women: Image and Achievement; Women in Irish Culture from Earliest Times,* edited by Eiléan Ní Chuilleanáin, 85–94. Dublin: Arlen House.

Colen, Shellee. 1989. "'Just a Little Respect': West Indian Domestic Workers in New York City." In *Muchachas No More: Household Workers in Latin America and the Caribbean,* edited by Elsa M. Chaney and Mary Garcia Castro, 171–94. Philadelphia: Temple Univ. Press.

Colum, Padraic. 1937. *The Road Round Ireland.* New York: Macmillan. (Orig. pub. 1926.)

Connell, K. H. 1996. *Irish Peasant Society.* Portland, Ore.: Irish Academic Press. (Orig. pub. 1968.)

Convery [Horan], Margaret. 1991. Interview EI-39, by Paul E. Sigrist Jr. Oral History Collection, Ellis Island Immigration Museum, Statue of Liberty National Monument, New York. Apr. 24.

Conzen, Kathleen Neils. 1984. "Patterns of German-American History." In *Germans in America: Retrospect and Prospect,* edited by Randall M. Miller, 14–36. Philadelphia: German Society of Pennsylvania.

Cook, Clarence. 1995. *The House Beautiful: An Unabridged Reprint of the Classic Victorian Stylebook.* New York: Dover Publications. (Orig. pub. 1881.)

Cooper, Sheila McIsaac. 2004. "From Family Member to Employee: Aspects of Continuity and Discontinuity in English Domestic Service, 1600–2000." In *Domestic Service and the Formation of European Identity: Understanding the Globalization of Domestic Work, 16th–21st Centuries,* edited by Antoinette Fauve-Chamoux, 277–96. Bern: Peter Lang.

Corcoran, Mary P. 1996. "Emigrants, Eirepreneurs, and Opportunists." In *The New York Irish,* edited by Ronald H. Bayor and Timothy J. Meagher, 461–80. Baltimore: Johns Hopkins Univ. Press.

Costello [McGloin], Mary Marguerita. 1994. Interview EI-457, by Janet Levine. Oral History Collection, Ellis Island Immigration Museum, Statue of Liberty National Monument, New York. Apr. 12.

Cott, Nancy. 1977. *The Bonds of Womanhood: "Woman's Sphere" in New England, 1780–1835.* New Haven: Yale Univ. Press.

Cowan, Ruth Schwartz. 1983. *More Work for Mother: The Ironies of Household Technology from the Open Hearth to the Microwave.* New York: Basic Books.

Cox [Harney], Mary. 1991. Interview EI-107, by Paul E. Sigrist Jr. Oral History Collection, Ellis Island Immigration Museum, Statue of Liberty National Monument, New York. Oct. 11.

Crawford, E. Margaret. 1995. "Food and Famine." In *The Great Irish Famine,* edited by Cathal Póirtéir, 60–73. Dublin: Mercier Press.

Crowley, Tony. 2005. *War of Words: The Politics of Language in Ireland, 1537–2004.* Oxford: Oxford Univ. Press.

Cruea, Susan M. 2005. "Changing Ideals of Womanhood During the Nineteenth-Century Woman Movement." *American Transcendental Quarterly* 19, no. 3: 187–204.

Cullen, L. M. 1990. "Patrons, Teachers, and Literacy in Irish: 1700–1850." In *The Origins of Popular Literacy in Ireland: Language Change and Educational Development, 1700–1920,* edited by Mary Daly and David Dickson, 15–44. Dublin: Department of Modern History, Trinity College–Dublin, and Department of Modern Irish History, Univ. College–Dublin.

Cusack, Mary Frances [Sister Mary Francis Clare]. 1872. *Advice to Irish Girls in America, by the Nun of Kenmare.* New York: J. A. McGee.

Daly, Mary E. 1981. "Women in the Irish Workforce from Pre-industrial to Modern Times." *Saothar: Journal of the Irish Labour History Society* 7: 74–82.

———. 1990. "Literacy and Language Change in the Late Nineteenth and Early Twentieth Centuries." In *The Origins of Popular Literacy in Ireland: Language Change and Educational Development, 1700–1920,* edited by Mary Daly and David Dickson, 153–66. Dublin: Department of Modern History, Trinity College–Dublin, and Department of Modern Irish History, Univ. College–Dublin.

———. 1997a. "'Turn on the Tap': The State, Irish Women, and Running Water." In *Women and Irish History,* edited by Maryann Gialanella Valiulis and Mary O'Dowd, 206–19. Niwot, Colo.: Irish American Book Company.

———. 1997b. *Women and Work in Ireland.* Studies in Irish Economic and Social History no. 7. Dundalk: Economic and Social History Society of Ireland, Dundalgan Press.

———. 2006. *The Slow Failure: Population Decline and Independent Ireland, 1922–1973.* Madison: Univ. of Wisconsin Press.

Danaher, Kevin. 1964. *In Ireland Long Ago.* Dublin: Mercier Press.

Davidoff, Leonore, and Ruth Hawthorn. 1976. *A Day in the Life of a Victorian Domestic.* London: George Allen and Unwin.

DeBovet, Madame [Anne Marie]. 1891. *Three Months Tour in Ireland.* Translated and condensed by Mrs. Arthur Walter. London: Chapman and Hall.

DeForest, Virginia. 1855. "Biddy's Blunders." *Godey's Lady's Book and Magazine,* Apr., 329–30.

Delay, Cara. 2005. "Confidantes or Competitors? Women, Priests, and Conflict in Post-famine Ireland." *Eire-Ireland* 40, nos. 1–2 (Spring–Summer): 107–25.

Denvir, Gearóid. 1995. "One Hundred Years of Conradh Na Gaeilge." *Eire-Ireland* 30, no. 1: 105–29.

Deshon, Rev. George. 1978. *Guide for Catholic Young Women, Especially for Those Who Earn Their Own Living.* 31st ed. New York: Arno Press. (Orig. pub. 1897.)

Desmond, H. J. 1900. "A Century of Irish Immigration." *American Catholic Quarterly Review* 25: 518–30.

Devlin, William E. 1984. *We Crown Them All: An Illustrated History of Danbury.* Woodland Hills, Calif.: Windsor Publications.

Dickens, Charles. 1874. "Servants in America." *All the Year Round,* Oct. 3, 584–88.

Dickson, David. 1990. Preface to *The Origins of Popular Literacy in Ireland: Language Change and Educational Development, 1700–1920,* edited by Mary Daly and David Dickson. Dublin: Department of Modern History, Trinity College–Dublin, and Department of Modern Irish History, Univ. College–Dublin.

———. 1995. "The Other Great Irish Famine." In *The Great Irish Famine,* edited by Cathal Póirtéir, 50–59. Dublin: Mercier Press.

Dill, Bonnie Thornton. 1988. "'Making Your Job Good Yourself': Domestic Service and the Construction of Personal Dignity." In *Women and the Politics of Empowerment,* edited by Ann Bookman and Sandra Morgen, 33–52. Philadelphia: Temple Univ. Press.

Diner, Hasia R. 1983. *Erin's Daughters in America: Irish Immigrant Women in the Nineteenth Century.* Baltimore: Johns Hopkins Univ. Press.

———. 2007. "The Accidental Irish." In *Migration in History,* edited by Marc S. Rodriguez and Anthony T. Grafton, 118–58. Rochester: Univ. of Rochester Press.

"Dinner vs. Ruffles and Tucks." 1870. *Putnam's Magazine,* June, 708–11.

Doherty, Gillian M. 2004. *The Irish Ordnance Survey: History, Culture, and Memory.* Portland, Ore.: Four Courts Press.

Doran [Cavanaugh], Lillian. 1993. Interview EI-268, by Paul E. Sigrist Jr. Oral History Collection, Ellis Island Immigration Museum, Statue of Liberty National Monument, New York. Mar. 28.

Dorr, Rheta Childe. 1910. *What Eight Million Women Want.* Boston: Small, Maynard.

"A Dowager's Advice on How to Catch and Keep the Cook." 1934. *Arts and Decoration,* June, 24–25.

Downing, A. J. 1969. *The Architecture of Country Houses.* New York: Dover Publications. (Orig. pub. 1850.)

Doyle, David Noel. 1996. "The Remaking of Irish-America, 1845–80." In *Ireland under the Union: II, 1870–1921,* vol. 6 of *A New History of Ireland,* edited by W. E. Vaughan, 725–63. Oxford: Clarendon Press.

Dudden, Faye E. 1983. *Serving Women: Household Service in Nineteenth-Century America.* Middletown, Conn.: Wesleyan Univ. Press.

Dunlevy, Mairead. 1999. *Dress in Ireland: A History.* Doughcloyne, Wilton, Cork: Collins Press. (Orig. pub. 1989.)

Eaton, Isabel. 1973. "Special Report on Negro Domestic Service in the Seventh Ward Philadelphia." In *The Philadelphia Negro,* edited by W. E. B. Du Bois, 427–509. Millwood, N.J.: Kraus-Thomson Organization. (Orig. pub. 1899.)

Ehrenreich, Barbara. 2001. *Nickel and Dimed: On (Not) Getting by in America.* New York: Henry Holt.

Ellet, Mrs. Elizabeth. 1857. *The Practical Housekeeper: Containing 500 Receipts and Maxims.* Available online at http://digital.lib.msu.edu/projects/cooksbooks/books/practicalhousekeeper/prho.pdf.

Elliott, Bruce S., David A. Gerber, and Suzanne M. Sinke, eds. 2006. *Letters Across Borders: The Epistolary Practices of International Migrants.* New York: Palgrave MacMillan.

Ernst, Robert. 1994. *Immigrant Life in New York City, 1825–1863.* Syracuse: Syracuse Univ. Press. (Orig. pub. 1949.)

Evans, E. Estyn. 1977. *Irish Heritage.* Dundalk: Dundalgan Press. (Orig. pub. 1942.)

———. 1989. *Irish Folk Ways.* London: Routledge. (Orig. pub. 1957.)

"The Experiences of a 'Hired Girl.'" 1912. *Outlook,* Apr. 6, 778–80.

Fahey, Tony. 1987. "Nuns in the Catholic Church in Ireland in the Nineteenth Century." In *Girls Don't Do Honours: Irish Women in Education in the 19th and 20th Centuries,* edited by Mary Cullen, 7–30. Dublin: Women's Education Bureau.

Fallows, Marjorie R. 1979. *Irish Americans: Identity and Assimilation.* Englewood Cliffs, N.J.: Prentice-Hall.

Fanning, Charles, ed. 1997. *The Exiles of Erin: Nineteenth-Century Irish-American Fiction.* 2d ed. Chester Springs, Pa.: Dufour Editions.

Feely [Harren], Mary. 1996. Interview by author. Tape recording. Greenwich, N.Y. Aug. 4.

Fitzgerald, Maureen. 2006. *Habits of Compassion: Irish Catholic Nuns and the Origins of New York's Welfare System, 1830–1920.* Urbana: Univ. of Illinois Press.

Fitzpatrick, David. 1980. "Irish Emigration in the Later Nineteenth Century." *Irish Historical Studies* 22, no. 86 (Sept.): 126–43.

———. 1984. *Irish Emigration, 1801–1921.* Studies in Irish Economic and Social History. Dundalk: Dundalgan Press.

———. 1985. "Marriage in Post-Famine Ireland." In *Marriage in Ireland,* edited by Art Cosgrove, 116–31. Dublin: College Press.

———. 1987. "The Modernisation of the Irish Female." In *Rural Ireland, 1600–1900: Modernisation and Change,* edited by Patrick O'Flanagan, Paul Ferguson, and Kevin Whelan, 162–80. Cork: Cork Univ. Press.

———. 1989. "Emigration, 1801–70." In *Ireland under the Union: I, 1801–1870,* vol. 5 of *A New History of Ireland,* edited by W. E. Vaughan, 562–622. Oxford: Clarendon Press.

———. 1990. "'A Share of the Honeycomb': Education, Emigration, and Irishwomen." In *The Origins of Popular Literacy in Ireland: Language Change and Educational Development, 1700–1920,* edited by Mary Daly and David Dickson, 167–87. Dublin: Department of Modern History, Trinity College–Dublin, and Department of Modern Irish History, Univ. College–Dublin.

———. 1996. "Emigration, 1871–1921." In *Ireland under the Union: II, 1870–1921,* vol. 6 of *A New History of Ireland,* edited by W. E. Vaughan, 606–52. Oxford: Clarendon Press.

Flanagan [Zeilan], Cecelia. 1994. Interview EI-514, by Janet Levine. Oral History Collection, Ellis Island Immigration Museum, Statue of Liberty National Monument, New York. Aug. 2.

Flatley [Cleary], Helen. 1996a. Interview by author. Tape recording. July 31.

———. 1996b. Interview by author. Tape recording. Aug. 7.

Foley, Mark C., and Timothy W. Guinnane. 1999. "Did Irish Marriage Patterns Survive the Emigrant Voyage?" *Irish Economic and Social History* 26: 15–34.

Foster, R. F. 1989. *Modern Ireland, 1600–1972.* New York: Penguin Books. (Orig. pub. 1988.)

Frederick, Mrs. Christine. 1914. "Suppose Our Servants Didn't Live with Us." *Ladies' Home Journal,* Oct., 102.

Gailey, Alan. 1987. "Changes in Irish Rural Housing, 1600–1900." In *Rural Ireland, 1600–1900: Modernisation and Change,* edited by Patrick O'Flanagan, Paul Ferguson, and Kevin Whelan, 86–101. Cork: Cork Univ. Press.

Gavin [Duffy], Theresa. 1991. Interview EI-95, by Paul E. Sigrist Jr. Oral History Collection, Ellis Island Immigration Museum, Statue of Liberty National Monument, New York. Sept. 24.

A German House Servant. 1925. "Seeing America from the Kitchen." *Living Age,* Feb. 28, 465.

Glasco, Laurence A. 1975. "The Life Cycles and Household Structure of American Ethnic Groups: Irish, Germans, and Native-Born Whites in Buffalo, New York, 1855." *Journal of Urban History* 1, no. 3 (May): 339–64.

Gleeson, James T. 1993. Interview EI-277, by Janet Levine. Oral History Collection, Ellis Island Immigration Museum, Statue of Liberty National Monument, New York. Apr. 15.

Glenn, Evelyn Nakano. 1986. *Issei, Nisei, War Bride: Three Generations of Japanese American Women in Domestic Service.* Philadelphia: Temple Univ. Press.

———. 1990. "The Dialectics of Wage Work: Japanese-American Women and Domestic Service, 1905–1940." In *Unequal Sisters: A Multicultural Reader in*

U.S. Women's History, edited by Ellen Carol DuBois and Vicki L. Ruiz, 345–72. New York: Routledge.

———. 1992. "From Servitude to Service Work: Historical Continuities in the Racial Division of Paid Reproductive Labor." *Signs: Journal of Women in Culture and Society* 18, no. 1 (Autumn): 1–43.

Graham, Florence Vaughn. 2006. Interview by author. Tape recording. Glenmont, N.Y. Nov. 26.

Greaney, Aine. 1998. 'Young at Heart: Oldest Irish Woman Dies in Boston." *Irish Voice* (New York), July 29–Aug. 11, 36.

Greeley, Andrew M. 1988. "The Success and Assimilation of Irish Protestants and Irish Catholics in the United States." *Sociology and Social Research* 72: 229–37.

Green, E. R. R. 1994. "The Great Famine (1845–1850)." In *The Course of Irish History*, edited by T. W. Moody and F. X. Martin, 263–74. Boulder: Roberts Rinehart. (Orig. pub. 1967.)

Green, Harvey. 1983. *The Light of the Home: An Intimate View of the Lives of Women in Victorian America*. New York: Pantheon Books.

Grossman, Allyson Sherman. 1980. "Women in Domestic Work: Yesterday and Today." *Monthly Labor Review* (Aug.): 17–21.

Guinnane, Timothy W. 1997. *The Vanishing Irish: Households, Migration, and the Rural Economy in Ireland, 1850–1914*. Princeton: Princeton Univ. Press.

Hagedorn, Hermann, and Gary G. Roth. n.d. *Sagamore Hill: An Historical Guide*. Oyster Bay, N.Y.: Theodore Roosevelt Association.

Haley, Jacquetta. 1994. "Sunnyside's Other Residents: The Servants." *Westchester Historian: Quarterly of the Westchester County Historical Society* 70, no. 1 (Winter): 3–12.

Hall, Mr. and Mrs. S. C. 1860. *Ireland: Its Scenery, Character, Andc.* 3 vols. London: Virtue. (Orig. pub. 1841–43.)

Harrington, Kate. 1855. "Irish Blunders." *Godey's Lady's Book and Magazine*, Apr., 247.

Harris, Trudier. 1982. *From Mammies to Militants: Domestics in Black American Literature*. Philadelphia: Temple Univ. Press.

Hartley, Florence. 1993. *The Ladies' Book of Etiquette, Fashion, and Manual of Politeness*. Davenport, Iowa: Amazon Drygoods. (Orig. pub. 1860.)

Harzig, Christiane. 2007. "Domestics of the World (Unite?): Labor Migration Systems and Personal Trajectories of Household Workers in Historical and Global Perspective." In *Immigration, Incorporation, and Transnationalism*, edited by Elliot R. Barkan, 39–62. New Brunswick, N.J.: Transaction Publishers.

Haskell, Mrs. E. F. 1861. *The Housekeeper's Encyclopedia*. New York: D. Appleton. Edited by R. L. Shep as *Civil War Cooking: The Housekeeper's Encyclopedia*. Mendocino, Calif.: R. L. Shep, 1992.

Hassey, Catherine Foy. 1995a. Telephone conversation with author. Sept. 24.

———. 1995b. Interview by author. Tape recording. New Bedford, Mass. Nov. 12.

Hearn, Mona. 1993. *Below Stairs: Domestic Service Remembered in Dublin and Beyond, 1880–1922.* Dublin: Lilliput Press.

Henry, Rev. Michael J. 1900. "A Century of Irish Emigration: Its Causes and Results." In *Mission of Our Lady of the Rosary for the Protection of Irish Immigrant Girls,* 7–27. New York: n.p.

Herrick, Christine Terhune. 1904. *The Expert Maid-Servant.* New York: Harper and Brothers.

Hewitt, Nancy A. 2002. "Taking the True Woman Hostage." *Journal of Women's History* 14, no. 1 (Spring): 156–62.

Higham, John. 1994. *Strangers in the Land: Patterns of American Nativism, 1860–1925.* New Brunswick: Rutgers Univ. Press. (Orig. pub. 1955.)

Hill, Myrtle, and Vivienne Pollock. 1993. *Images and Experience: Photographs of Irishwomen, c. 1880–1920.* Belfast: Blackstaff Press.

Hochschild, Arlie Russell. 2002. "Love and Gold." In *Global Woman: Nannies, Maids, and Sex Workers in the New Economy,* edited by Barbara Ehrenreich and Arlie Russell Hochschild, 15–30. New York: Metropolitan.

Hodges, Graham. 1996. "'Desirable Companions and Lovers': Irish and African Americans in the Sixth Ward, 1830–1870." In *The New York Irish,* edited by Ronald H. Bayor and Timothy J. Meagher, 107–24. Baltimore: Johns Hopkins Univ. Press.

Holt, Hamilton, ed. 1906. "The Life Story of an Irish Cook." In *The Life Stories of Undistinguished Americans, as Told by Themselves,* 143–49. New York: Young People's Missionary Movement.

Hondagneu-Sotelo, Pierette. 1994. "Regulating the Unregulated? Domestic Workers' Social Networks." *Social Problems* 41, no. 1 (Feb.): 50–64.

———. 2001. *Doméstica: Immigrant Workers Cleaning and Caring in the Shadows of Affluence.* Berkeley and Los Angeles: Univ. of California Press.

Horgan, Ellen Somers. 1988. "The American Catholic Irish Family." In *Ethnic Families in America: Patterns and Variations,* edited by Charles H. Mindel, Robert W. Habenstein, and Roosevelt Wright Jr., 45–75. 3d ed. New York: Elsevier Science Publishing.

Horn, Pamela. 1975. *The Rise and Fall of the Victorian Servant.* New York: St. Martin's Press.

Hotten-Somers, Diane M. 2001. "Relinquishing and Reclaiming Independence: Irish Domestic Servants, American Middle-Class Mistresses, and Assimilation, 1850–1920." *Eire-Ireland* 36, nos. 1–2 (Spring–Summer): 185–201.

"Household Service." 1860. *Harper's New Monthly Magazine,* Feb., 405–10.

Hout, Michael, and Joshua R. Goldstein. 1994. "How 4.5 Million Immigrants Became 40 Million Irish Americans: Demographic and Subjective Aspects of the Ethnic Composition of White Americans." *American Sociological Review* 59 (Feb.): 64–82.

Howells, William Dean. 1986. *The Rise of Silas Lapham.* New York: Penguin Classics. (Orig. pub. 1885.)

Hoy, Suellen. 1995a. *Chasing Dirt: The American Pursuit of Cleanliness.* New York: Oxford Univ. Press.

———. 1995b. "The Journey Out: The Recruitment and Emigration of Irish Religious Women to the United States, 1812–1914." Special double issue. *Journal of Women's History* 6–7, nos. 4 and 1 (Winter–Spring): 64–98.

Hynes, Eugene. 1978. "The Great Hunger and Irish Catholicism." *Societas* 8, no. 1 (Spring): 137–56.

Ignatiev, Noel. 1995. *How the Irish Became White.* New York: Routledge.

Ikels, Charlotte. 1985. "Parental Perspectives on the Significance of Marriage." *Journal of Marriage and the Family* 47 (May): 253–64.

Jacobs, Margaret D. 2007. "Working on the Domestic Frontier: American Indian Domestic Servants in White Women's Households in the San Francisco Bay Area, 1920–1940." *Frontiers: A Journal of Women's Studies* 28, nos. 1–2: 165–99.

Jacobson, Matthew Frye. 2000. *Whiteness of a Different Color.* Cambridge: Harvard Univ. Press. (Orig. pub. 1998.)

Jenkins, Philip. 2003. *The New Anti-Catholicism: The Last Acceptable Prejudice.* Oxford: Oxford Univ. Press.

Jensen, Richard J. 2002. "'No Irish Need Apply'? A Myth of Victimization." *Journal of Social History* 35, no. 2: 405–39.

Kaplan, Elaine Bell. 1987. "'I Don't Do No Windows': Competition Between the Domestic Worker and the Housewife." In *Competition: A Feminist Taboo?* edited by Valerie Miner and Helen E. Longino, 92–105. New York: Feminist Press.

Kasson, John F. 1978. *Amusing the Million: Coney Island at the Turn of the Century.* New York: Hill and Wang.

———. 1987. "Rituals of Dining: Table Manners in Victorian America." In *Dining in America, 1850–1900,* edited by Kathryn Grover, 114–41. Amherst: Univ. of Massachusetts Press.

———. 1995. *Rudeness and Civility: Manners in Nineteenth-Century Urban America.* New York: Hill and Wang. (Orig. pub. 1990.)

"Katie Is Leaving—Again." 1941. *New York Times Magazine,* Aug. 31.

Katzman, David M. 1978. *Seven Days a Week: Women and Domestic Service in Industrializing America.* New York: Oxford Univ. Press.

Kaylin, Lucy. 2007. *The Perfect Stranger: The Truth about Mothers and Nannies.* New York: Bloomsbury.

Keenan [Materia], Josephine. 1994. Interview EI-482, by Janet Levine. Oral History Collection, Ellis Island Immigration Museum, Statue of Liberty National Monument, New York. June 22.

Kellor, Frances A. 1915. *Out of Work: A Study of Unemployment.* Rev. ed. New York: G. P. Putnam's Sons. (Orig. pub. 1904.)

Kelly [Craven], Ann. 1991. Interview EI-102, by Paul E. Sigrist Jr. Oral History Collection, Ellis Island Immigration Museum, Statue of Liberty National Monument, New York. Oct. 2.

Kelly, Mary C. 2005. *The Shamrock and the Lily: The New York Irish and the Creation of a Transatlantic Identity, 1845–1921.* New York: Peter Lang.

Kelly [Loughlin], Rose. 1995. Interview EI-607, by Janet Levine. Oral History Collection, Ellis Island Immigration Museum, Statue of Liberty National Monument, New York. Apr. 30.

Kennedy, Brian P. 1993. "The Traditional Irish Thatched House: Image and Reality, 1793–1993." In *Visualizing Ireland: National Identity and the Pictorial Tradition,* edited by Adele M. Dalsimer, 165–79. Boston: Faber and Faber.

Kennedy, Robert E., Jr. 1973. *The Irish: Emigration, Marriage, and Fertility.* Berkeley and Los Angeles: Univ. of California Press.

Kerber, Linda K. 1988. "Separate Spheres, Female Worlds, Woman's Place: The Rhetoric of Women's History." *Journal of American History* 75, no. 1 (June): 9–39.

Kiberd, Declan. 2001. "Confronting Famine: Carleton's Peasantry." Chap. 16 in *Irish Classics.* Cambridge: Harvard Univ. Press.

Kinealy, Christine. 1995. *This Great Calamity: The Irish Famine, 1845–52.* Boulder: Roberts Rinehart. (Orig. pub. 1994.)

Kinmonth, Claudia. 2006. *Irish Rural Interiors in Art.* New Haven: Yale Univ. Press.

Lacknee [Jones], Bridget. 1974. Interview NPS-78, by Margo Nash. Oral History Collection, Ellis Island Immigration Museum, Statue of Liberty National Monument, New York. Nov. 16.

Lane, Fintan. 2005. "Rural Labourers, Social Change, and Politics in Late Nineteenth-Century Ireland." In *Politics and the Irish Working Class, 1830–1945,* edited by Fintan Lane and Donal Ó Drisceoil, 113–39. Houndmills, Basingstoke, Hampshire: Palgrave Macmillan.

Larkin, Emmet. 1999. "The Devotional Revolution in Ireland, 1850–1875." In *The Historical Dimensions of Irish Catholicism.* Washington, D.C.: Catholic Univ. of America Press. (Orig. pub. 1976.)

Lasser, Carol. 2001. "Beyond Separate Spheres: The Power of Public Opinion." *Journal of the Early Republic* 21, no. 1 (Spring): 115–23.

Laughlin, Gail. 1901. *Domestic Service: A Report Prepared under the Direction of the Industrial Commission.* Washington, D.C.: General Printing Office.

Leavitt, Sarah A. 2002. *From Catharine Beecher to Martha Stewart: A Cultural History of Domestic Advice.* Chapel Hill: Univ. of North Carolina Press.

Levine, Edward. 1966. *The Irish and Irish Politicians: A Study of Cultural and Social Alienation.* Notre Dame: Univ. of Notre Dame Press.

Lintelman, Joy. 1989. "'America Is the Woman's Promised Land': Swedish Immigrant Women and American Domestic Service." *Journal of American Ethnic History* 8, no. 2 (Spring): 9–23.

———. 1991. "'Our Serving Sisters': Swedish-American Domestic Servants and Their Ethnic Community." *Social Science History* 15, no. 3 (Fall): 381–95.

Lucas, A. T. 1951. "The Hooded Cloak in Ireland in the Nineteenth Century." *Journal of the Cork Historical and Archaeological Society* 56: 104–19.

Luddy, Maria. 1995. *Women in Ireland, 1800–1918: A Documentary History.* Cork: Cork Univ. Press.

———. 2000. "Women and Work in Nineteenth- and Early Twentieth-Century Ireland: An Overview." In *Women and Paid Work in Ireland, 1500–1930,* edited by Bernadette Whelan, 44–56. Dublin: Four Courts Press.

———. 2005a. "Women's History." In *Nineteenth-Century Ireland: A Guide to Recent Research,* edited by Laurence M. Geary and Margaret Kelleher, 43–60. Dublin: Univ. College–Dublin Press.

———. 2005b. "Working Women, Trade Unionism, and Politics in Ireland, 1830–1945." In *Politics and the Irish Working Class, 1830–1945,* edited by Fintan Lane and Donal Ó Drisceoil, 44–61. Houndmills, Basingstoke, Hampshire: Palgrave Macmillan.

Lynch-Brennan, Margaret. 2007. "Ubiquitous Bridget: Irish Women in Domestic Service, 1840–1930." In *Making the Irish American: History and Heritage of the Irish in the United States,* edited by J. J. Lee and Marion R. Casey, 332–53. New York: New York Univ. Press. (Orig. pub. 2006.)

———. Collection of letters written by members of the Irish emigrant Malone-McHenry family donated to the author by her late cousin Anne Shalvoy Graham and one copy of a May 13, 1978, letter written by Hugh Augustus Shalvoy to his granddaughter Karen Shalvoy Elias; the original remains in the hand of Karen Shalvoy Elias.

Lynd, Robert. 1910. *Home Life in Ireland.* Chicago: A. C. McClurg. (Orig. pub. 1909.)

Lyons, Paddy. 2006. "Ireland, Britain, and Mass Literacy in Nineteenth-Century Europe." In *Ireland and Europe in the Nineteenth Century,* edited by Leon Litvack and Colin Graham, 89–100. Dublin: Four Courts Press.

Lysaght, Patricia. 1999. "Women in the Great Famine." In *The Great Famine and the Irish Diaspora in America,* edited by Arthur Gribben, 21–47. Amherst: Univ. of Massachusetts Press.

MacCurtain, Margaret. 1985. "The Historical Image." In *Irish Women: Image and Achievement; Women in Irish Culture from Earliest Times,* edited by Eiléan Ní Chuilleanáin, 37–49. Dublin: Arlen House.

Macdonald, Cameron L. 1998. "Manufacturing Motherhood: The Shadow Work of Nannies and Au Pairs." *Qualitative Sociology* 21, no. 1: 25–53.

Mackey [Gillespie], Sarah. 1979. Interview NPS-119, by Harvey Dixon. Oral History Collection, Ellis Island Immigration Museum, Statue of Liberty National Monument, New York. Oct. 16.

MacLysaght, Edward. 1999. *The Surnames of Ireland.* 6th ed. Dublin: Irish Academic Press. (Orig. pub. 1985.)

Magennis [Lamberti], Kathleen. 1994. Interview EI-439, by Paul E. Sigrist Jr. Oral History Collection, Ellis Island Immigration Museum, Statue of Liberty National Monument, New York. Feb. 25.

Maguire, John Francis. 1969. *The Irish in America.* New York: Arno Press and the New York Times. (Orig. pub. 1868.)

Mahon, Bríd. 1998. *Land of Milk and Honey: The Story of Traditional Irish Food and Drink.* Dublin: Mercier Press. (Orig. pub. 1991.)

———. 2000. *Rich and Rare: The Story of Irish Dress.* Dublin: Mercier Press.

Malcolm, Elizabeth. 1982. "The Catholic Church and the Irish Temperance Movement, 1838–1901." *Irish Historical Studies* 23, no. 89 (May): 1–16.

———. 1986. *"Ireland Sober, Ireland Free": Drink and Temperance in Nineteenth-Century Ireland.* Dublin: Gill and Macmillan.

———. 1999. "The Rise of the Pub: A Study in the Disciplining of Popular Culture." In *Irish Popular Culture, 1650–1850,* edited by J. S. Donnelly Jr. and Kerby A. Miller, 50–77. Portland, Ore.: Irish Academic Press.

Martin, Linda, and Kerry Segrave. 1985. *The Servant Problem: Domestic Workers in North America.* Jefferson, N.C.: McFarland.

Maschio, Geraldine. 1992. "Ethnic Humor and the Demise of the Russell Brothers." *Journal of Popular Culture* 26, no. 1 (Summer): 81–92.

Mattingly, Doreen J. 1999a. "Job Search, Social Networks, and Local Labor-Market Dynamics: The Case of Paid Household Work in San Diego, California." *Urban Geography* 20, no. 1: 46–74.

———. 1999b. "Making Maids: United States Immigration Policy and Immigrant Domestic Workers." In *Gender, Migration, and Domestic Service,* edited by Janet H. Momsen, 62–79. New York: Routledge.

———. 2001. "The Home and the World: Domestic Service and International Networks of Caring Labor." *Annals of the Association of American Geographers* 91, no. 2: 370–86.

Mayhew, Edgar de N., and Minor Myers Jr. 1980. *A Documentary History of American Interiors, from the Colonial Era to 1915.* New York: Charles Scribner's Sons.

McDannell, Colleen. 1986a. "Catholicism and the Irish-American Male." *American Studies* 27, no. 2: 19–36.

———. 1986b. *The Christian Home in Victorian America, 1840–1900.* Bloomington: Indiana Univ. Press.

———. 1996. "Going to the Ladies' Fair: Irish Catholics in New York City, 1870–1900." In *The New York Irish,* edited by Ronald H. Bayor and Timothy J. Meagher, 234–51. Baltimore: Johns Hopkins Univ. Press.

McDonagh, Maryellen. 2002. Interview by author. Tape recording. May 29.

McGeoghegan, Bridget [Bertha McGaffighan Devlin]. 1985. Interview AKRF-43, by Dana Gumb. Oral History Collection, Ellis Island Immigration Museum, Statue of Liberty National Monument, New York. Sept. 19.

———. 1987. Interview GPI-23, by Guggenheim Productions. Oral History Collection, Ellis Island Immigration Museum, Statue of Liberty National Monument, New York. Feb. 12.

McGowan, Sharon. 1992. "Irish Women Immigrants' Experience in Domestic Work in America: Past and Present." Senior project, Bard College.

McKinley, Blaine Edward. 1969. "'The Stranger in the Gates': Employer Reactions Toward Domestic Servants in America, 1825–1875." Ph.D. diss., Michigan State Univ.

McLaughlin, Emma, and Nicola Kraus. 2002. *The Nanny Diaries.* New York: St. Martin's Press.

McMahon, Richard. 2000. "The Regional Administration of Central Legal Policy." In *Ireland in the Nineteenth Century: Regional Identity,* edited by Leon Litvack and Glenn Hooper, 156–68. Dublin: Four Courts Press.

McMahon, Sean. 1997. *A Short History of Ireland.* Chester Springs, Pa.: Dufour Editions. (Orig. pub. 1996.)

McManus, Antonia. 2004. *The Irish Hedge School and Its Books, 1695–1831.* Dublin: Four Courts Press.

Mendez, Jennifer Bickham. 1998. "Of Mops and Maids: Contradictions and Continuities in Bureaucratized Domestic Work." *Social Problems* 45, no. 1 (Feb.): 114–34.

Miller, Annette Jaynes. 1905. "Why I Never Have Trouble with My Servants." *Ladies' Home Journal,* Mar., 4.

Miller, David W. 2005a. "Landscape and Religious Practice: A Study of Mass Attendance in Pre-Famine Ireland." *Eire-Ireland* 40, nos. 1–2 (Spring–Summer): 90–106.

———. 2005b. "Religious History." In *Nineteenth-Century Ireland: A Guide to Recent Research,* edited by Laurence M. Geary and Margaret Kelleher, 61–76. Dublin: Univ. College–Dublin Press.

Miller, Kerby A. 1985. *Emigrants and Exiles: Ireland and the Irish Exodus to North America.* New York: Oxford Univ. Press.

———. 1999. "'Revenge for Skibbereen': Irish Emigration and the Meaning of the Great Famine." In *The Great Famine and the Irish Diaspora in America,* edited by Arthur Gribben, 180–95. Amherst: Univ. of Massachusetts Press.

———. Collection of Irish emigrant letters. Columbia, Mo.

Miller, Kerby A., David N. Doyle, and Patricia Kelleher. 1995. "'For Love and Liberty': Irish Women, Migration, and Domesticity in Ireland and America, 1815–1920." In *Irish Women and Irish Migration,* vol. 4 of *The Irish World Wide: History, Heritage, Identity,* edited by Patrick O'Sullivan, 41–65. London: Leicester Univ. Press.

Miller, Kerby A., and Paul Wagner. 1994. *Out of Ireland: The Story of Irish Emigration to America.* Washington, D.C.: Elliott and Clark Publishing.

"Mistress and Maid." 1885. *Donahoe's Magazine,* May, 442–44.

Moloney, Deirdre M. 1999. "A Transatlantic Reform: Boston's Port Protection Program and Irish Women Immigrants." *Journal of American Ethnic History* 19, no. 1 (Fall): 50–66.

Momsen, Janet Henshall. 1999. "Maids on the Move: Victim or Victor." In *Gender, Migration, and Domestic Service,* edited by Janet H. Momsen, 1–20. New York: Routledge.

"The Morals and Manners of the Kitchen." 1873. *Nation,* Jan., 6–7.

More, Louise Bolard. 1971. *Wage-Earners' Budgets: A Study of Standards and Cost of Living in New York City.* New York: Arno Press and the New York Times. (Orig. pub. 1907.)

Morrill, Anna McGuffey. 1993. "Timeline Vignette: Cincinnati Memories." *Timeline, a Publication of the Ohio Historical Society* 10, no. 2 (Mar.–Apr.): 3–35.

Morrison, Joan, and Charlotte Fox Zabusky. 1980. *American Mosaic: The Immigrant Experience in the Words of Those Who Lived It.* New York: E. P. Dutton.

Murphy, Maureen. 1992. "Charlotte Grace O'Brien and the Mission of Our Lady of the Rosary for the Protection of Irish Immigrant Girls." *Mid-America: An Historical Review* 74, no. 3 (Oct.): 253–70.

———. 2000. "Bridget and Biddy: Images of the Irish Servant Girl in *Puck* Cartoons, 1880–1890." In *New Perspectives on the Irish Diaspora,* edited by Charles Fanning, 152–75. Carbondale: Southern Illinois Univ. Press.

———, ed. 2005. *Your Fondest Annie: Letters from Annie O'Donnell to James P. Phelan, 1901–1904.* Dublin: Univ. College–Dublin Press.

Murray, Aife. 1999. "Miss Margaret's Emily Dickinson." *Signs: Journal of Women in Culture and Society* 24, no. 3: 697–732.

Murray [Lynn], Eileen. 1994. Interview EI-509, by Janet Levine. Oral History Collection, Ellis Island Immigration Museum, Statue of Liberty National Monument, New York. July 31.

Nasaw, David. 1993. *Going Out: The Rise and Fall of Public Amusements.* New York: Basic Books.

Neal, Alice B. 1857a. "The Crisis." *Godey's Lady's Book and Magazine,* May, 519–24.

———. 1857b. "'Fetch' and Carry." *Godey's Lady's Book and Magazine,* Feb., 112–17.

Nelson, Bruce. 2007. "'Come Out of Such a Land, You Irishmen': Daniel O'Connell, American Slavery, and the Making of the 'Irish Race.'" *Eire-Ireland* 42, nos. 1–2 (Spring–Summer): 58–81.

Neville, Grace. 1992. "'She Never Then After That Forgot Him': Irishwomen and Emigration to the United States in Irish Folklore." *Mid-America: An Historical Review* 74, no. 3 (Oct.): 271–89.

———. 1995. "Dark Lady of the Archives: Towards an Analysis of Women and Emigration to North America in Irish Folklore." In *Chattel, Servant, or Citizen: Women's Status in Church, State, and Society,* edited by Mary O'Dowd and Sabine Wichert, 200–214. Belfast: Institute of Irish Studies, Queen's Univ. of Belfast.

New York State. Executive Department, State Board of Charities. Record of Inmates, Rensselaer County Poor House, under Act Chapter 140, Laws of 1875. A1978, Roll 171. New York State Archives, Albany.

Nicholson, Asenath. 1847. *Ireland's Welcome to the Stranger; or, An Excursion Through Ireland in 1844 and 1845 for the Purpose of Personally Investigating the Condition of the Poor.* New York: Baker and Scribner.

Ní Chuilleanáin, Eiléan. 1985. "Women as Writers: Danta Grá to Maria Edgeworth." In *Irish Women: Image and Achievement; Women in Irish Culture from Earliest Times,* edited by Eiléan Ní Chuilleanáin, 111–26. Dublin: Arlen House.

Nicolosi, Ann Marie. 2005. "Discursive Bodies in Nineteenth-Century America." *Reviews in American History* 33, no. 3: 372–78.

Ní Ghráda, Máiréad. n.d. *Progress in Irish.* N.p.: Educational Company.

Nilsen, Kenneth E. 1996. "The Irish Language in New York City, 1850–1900." In *The New York Irish,* edited by Ronald H. Bayor and Timothy J. Meagher, 252–74. Baltimore: Johns Hopkins Univ. Press.

———. 2004. "'The Language That the Strangers Do Not Know': The Galway Gaeltacht of Portland, Maine, in the Twentieth Century." In *They Change Their Sky: The Irish in Maine,* edited by Michael C. Connolly, 297–335. Orono: Univ. of Maine Press.

Nolan, Janet A. 1989. *Ourselves Alone: Women's Emigration from Ireland, 1885–1920.* Lexington: Univ. Press of Kentucky.

———. 1998. "Education and Women's Mobility in Ireland and Irish America, 1880–1920: A Preliminary Look." *New Hibernia Review* 2, no. 3 (Autumn): 78–88.

———. 2004. *Servants of the Poor: Teachers and Mobility in Ireland and Irish America.* Notre Dame: Univ. of Notre Dame Press.

Nolan, John. 1891. "Mission of Our Lady of the Rosary." *Irish Ecclesiastical Record* 12 (Sept.): 776–85.

O'Brien, Charlotte G. 1884. "The Emigrant in New York." *Nineteenth Century* 16, no. 92 (Oct.): 530–49.

O'Carroll, Ide. 1990. *Models for Movers: Irish Women's Emigration to America*. Dublin: Attic Press.

Ó Céirín, Kit, and Cyril Ó Céirín. 1996. *Women of Ireland: A Biographic Dictionary*. Minneapolis: Irish Books and Media.

Ó Cíosáin, Niall. 1990. "Printed Popular Literature in Irish, 1750–1850: Presence and Absence." In *The Origins of Popular Literacy in Ireland: Language Change and Educational Development, 1700–1920*, edited by Mary Daly and David Dickson, 45–57. Dublin: Department of Modern History, Trinity College–Dublin, and Department of Modern Irish History, Univ. College–Dublin.

———. 2005. "Gaelic Culture and Language Shift." In *Nineteenth-Century Ireland: A Guide to Recent Research*, edited by Laurence M. Geary and Margaret Kelleher, 136–52. Dublin: Univ. College–Dublin Press.

Ó Cléirigh, Nellie. 2003. *Hardship and High Living: Irish Women's Lives, 1808–1923*. Dublin: Portobello Press.

Ó Corráin, Donncha. 1979. "Women in Early Irish Society." In *Women in Irish Society: The Historical Dimension*, edited by Margaret MacCurtain and Donncha Ó Corráin, 1–13. Westport, Conn.: Greenwood Press.

Ó Danachair, Caoimhín. 1962. "Changes in the Irish Landscape." *Ulster Folklife* 8: 65–71.

———. 1972. "Traditional Forms of the Dwelling House in Ireland." *Journal of the Royal Society of Antiquaries of Ireland* 102: 77–96.

O'Dowd, Mary. 2005. *A History of Women in Ireland, 1500–1800*. Harlow, England: Pearson Education.

Ó Giolláin, Diarmuid. 1999. "The Pattern." In *Irish Popular Culture, 1650–1850*, edited by James S. Donnelly Jr. and Kerby A. Miller, 201–21. Dublin: Irish Academic Press.

Ó Gráda, Cormac. 1995. *Ireland: A New Economic History, 1780–1939*. Oxford: Clarendon Press. (Orig. pub. 1994.)

O'Hara, Patricia. 1998. *Partners in Production: Women, Farm, and Family in Ireland*. Oxford: Berghahn Books.

O'Malley, Patricia Trainor. 1997. Interview by author. Tape recording. Oct. 16.

———. Collection of letters written to her Irish immigrant relations. Boynton Beach, Fla., and Cape Cod, Mass.

O Muirithe, Diarmaid. 1972. *A Seat Behind the Coachman: Travellers in Ireland, 1800–1900*. Dublin: Roberts Wholesale Books.

O'Riordan, Tomás. 2001. "The Introduction of the Potato into Ireland." *History Ireland* 9, no. 1 (Spring): 27–31.

Orser, Charles E., Jr. 2005. "An Archaeology of a Famine-Era Eviction." *New Hibernia Review* 9, no. 1 (Spring): 45–58.

"Our Domestic Service." 1875. *Scribner's Monthly Illustrated Magazine,* Nov., 273–78.

Palmer, Phyllis. 1989. *Domesticity and Dirt: Housewives and Domestic Servants in the United States, 1920–1945.* Philadelphia: Temple Univ. Press.

Park-McCullough House Association Archives. Servant scrapbook. North Bennington, Vt.

Parreñas, Rhacel Salazar. 2001a. *Servants of Globalization: Women, Migration, and Domestic Work.* Stanford: Stanford Univ. Press.

———. 2001b. "Transgressing the Nation-State: The Partial Citizenship and 'Imagined (Global) Community' of Migrant Filipino Domestic Workers." *Signs: Journal of Women in Culture and Society* 26, no. 4 (Summer): 1129–54.

"The Passing of the Household Servant." 1922. *Literary Digest,* July 8, 19–20.

Pattison, Mary. 1918. *The Business of Home Management: The Principles of Domestic Engineering.* New York: Robert M. McBride.

Peiss, Kathy. 1986. *Cheap Amusements: Working Women and Leisure in Turn-of-the-Century New York.* Philadelphia: Temple Univ. Press.

Pendleton, Thomas J. 2002. E-mail message to the author. Jan. 27.

Pettengill, Lillian. 1903. *Toilers of the Home: The Record of a College Woman's Experience as a Domestic Servant.* New York: Doubleday, Page.

Pfeiffer, Walter, and Maura Shaffrey. 1990. *Irish Cottages.* London: Weidenfeld and Nicolson.

Pillsbury, Parker. 1869. "Domestic Service." *Revolution,* Aug. 12, 88–89.

Pisani, Michael J., and David W. Yoskowitz. 2002. "The Maid Trade: Cross-Border Work in South Texas." *Social Science Quarterly* 83, no. 2 (June): 568–79.

Potter, George. 1960. *To the Golden Door: The Story of the Irish in Ireland and America.* Boston: Little, Brown.

Rainwater, Dorothy. 1987. "Victorian Dining Silver." In *Dining in America, 1850–1900,* edited by Kathryn Grover, 173–204. Amherst: Univ. of Massachusetts Press.

Rhodes, Rita. 1992. *Women and Family in Post-Famine Ireland: Status and Opportunity in a Patriarchal Society.* New York: Garland Publishing.

Rich, Kevin J. 2000. *Irish Immigrants of the Emigrant Industrial Savings Bank, 1850–1853.* Vol. 1. New York: Broadway-Manhattan.

———. 2005. *Irish Immigrants of the Emigrant Industrial Savings Bank.* Vol. 2. New York: Kevin J. Rich.

Ridge, John T. 1996. "Irish County Societies in New York, 1880–1914." In *The New York Irish,* edited by Ronald H. Bayor and Timothy J. Meagher, 275–300. Baltimore: Johns Hopkins Univ. Press.

———. 2005. "Dance Halls of Irish New York." *New York Irish History: Annual Journal of the New York Irish History Roundtable* 19: 39–53.

———. 2006. "Irish Town and Local Societies in New York." *New York Irish History: Annual Journal of the New York Irish History Roundtable* 20: 39–53.

Roberts, Dorothy. 1997. "Spiritual and Menial Housework." *Yale Journal of Law and Feminism* 9: 51–62.

Roberts, Mary Louise. 2002. "True Womanhood Revisited." *Journal of Women's History* 14, no. 1 (Spring): 150–55.

Robinson, Mary V. 1924. *Domestic Workers and Their Employment Relations.* Bulletin of the Women's Bureau, no. 39. Washington, D.C.: U.S. Government Printing Office.

Roediger, David R. 2002. *The Wages of Whiteness.* Rev. ed. New York: Verso. (Orig. pub. 1991.)

———. 2005. *Working Toward Whiteness.* New York: Basic Books.

Rollins, Judith. 1985. *Between Women: Domestics and Their Employers.* Philadelphia: Temple Univ. Press.

Romero, Mary. 1992. *Maid in the U.S.A.* New York: Routledge.

Rorabaugh, W. J. 1987. "Beer, Lemonade, and Propriety in the Gilded Age." In *Dining in America, 1850–1900,* edited by Kathryn Grover, 24–46. Amherst: Univ. of Massachusetts Press.

Rosenzweig, Roy. 1983. *Eight Hours for What We Will: Workers and Leisure in an Industrial City, 1870–1920.* New York: Cambridge Univ. Press.

Rossiter, Ann. 1993. "Bringing the Margins into the Centre: A Review of Aspects of Irish Women's Emigration from a British Perspective." In *Irish Women's Studies Reader,* edited by Ailbhe Smyth, 177–202. Dublin: Attic Press.

Rowley, William E. 1971. "The Irish Aristocracy of Albany, 1798–1878." *New York History* 52, no. 3 (July): 275–304.

Rubinow, I. M. 1911. "Household Service as a Labor Problem." *Journal of Home Economics* 3 (April): 131–40.

Rubinow, I. M., and Daniel Durant. 1910. "The Depth and Breadth of the Servant Problem." *McClure's Magazine,* Mar., 576–88.

Rudd, Joy. 1988. "Invisible Exports: The Emigration of Irish Women in This Century." *Women's Studies International Forum* 11, no. 4: 307–11.

Ruiz, Vicki L. 1987. "By the Day or the Week: Mexicana Workers in El Paso." In *Women on the U.S.-Mexico Border: Responses to Change,* edited by Vicki L. Ruiz and Susan Tiano, 61–76. Boston: Allen and Unwin.

Russell-AE, G. W. 1978. *Selections from the Contributions to "The Irish Homestead" by G. W. Russell-AE.* Edited by Henry Summerfield. Vol. 1. Atlantic Highlands, N.J.: Humanities Press.

Ryan, Barbara. 2006. *Love, Wages, Slavery: The Literature of Servitude in the United States.* Urbana: Univ. of Illinois Press.

Ryan, Dennis P. 1983. *Beyond the Ballot Box: A Social History of the Boston Irish, 1845–1917.* East Brunswick, N.J.: Fairleigh Dickinson Univ. Press.

Sadlier, Mrs. J. [Mary Anne Madden Sadlier]. 1863. *Bessy Conway; or, The Irish Girl in America.* New York: D&J Sadlier. (Orig. pub. 1861.)

The St. Pius X Parish Family . . . 25th Anniversary Commemorative Booklet. 1976. N.p.

Salmon, Lucy Maynard. 1901. *Domestic Service.* 2d ed. New York: Macmillan. (Orig. pub. 1897.)

Salzinger, Leslie. 1991. "A Maid by Any Other Name: The Transformation of 'Dirty Work' by Central American Immigrants." In *Ethnography Unbound: Power and Resistance in the Modern Metropolis,* edited by Michael Burawoy et al., 139–60. Berkeley and Los Angeles: Univ. of California Press.

Sayers, Peig. 1962. *An Old Woman's Reflections: The Life of a Blasket Island Storyteller.* Translated by Séamus Ennis. Oxford: Oxford Univ. Press. (Orig. pub. 1939.)

———. 1974. *Peig: The Autobiography of Peig Sayers of the Great Blasket Island.* Translated by Bryan MacMahon. Syracuse: Syracuse Univ. Press. (Orig. pub. 1973.)

Schlereth, Thomas J. 1991. *Victorian America: Transformations in Everyday Life, 1876–1915.* New York: HarperCollins.

Schrier, Arnold. 1958. *Ireland and the American Emigration.* Minneapolis: Univ. of Minnesota Press.

———. Collection of Irish emigrant letters. Cincinnati.

"The Servant Question." 1865. *Nation,* Oct., 527–28.

Sexton [Walsh], Ann. 1986. Interview AKRF-200, by Nancy Dallette. Oral History Collection, Ellis Island Immigration Museum, Statue of Liberty National Monument, New York. June 26.

Simms, Katharine. 1979. "Women in Norman Ireland." In *Women in Irish Society: The Historical Dimension,* edited by Margaret MacCurtain and Donncha Ó Corráin, 14–25. Westport, Conn.: Greenwood Press.

Sklar, Kathryn Kish. 1973. *Catharine Beecher: A Study in American Domesticity.* New Haven: Yale Univ. Press.

———. 1991. "Catharine Beecher (1800–1878)." In *Portraits of American Women,* edited by G. J. Barker-Benfield and Catherine Clinton, 1:169–86. New York: St. Martin's Press.

Smith, David M. 1996. "'I Thought I Was Landed!': The Congested Districts Board and the Women of Western Ireland." *Eire-Ireland* 31, nos. 3–4 (Fall–Winter): 209–27.

Smith, Elizabeth. 1980. *The Irish Journals of Elizabeth Smith, 1840–1850.* Edited by David Thomson with Moyra McGusty. Oxford: Clarendon Press.

Smith, Mary Gove. 1906. "Immigration as a Source of Supply for Domestic Workers." *Bulletin of the Inter-municipal Research Committee* 2, no. 8 (May): 5–9.

Smith-Rosenberg, Carroll. 1985. "The Female World of Love and Ritual: Relations Between Women in Nineteenth-Century America." In *Disorderly Conduct: Visions of Gender in Victorian America,* 53–76. New York: Alfred A. Knopf.

"Social Conditions in Domestic Service." 1900. *Massachusetts Labor Bulletin* 13 (February): 1–17.

Spofford, Harriet Prescott. 1977. *The Servant Girl Question*. New York: Arno Press. (Orig. pub. 1881.)

Springsteed, Anne Frances. 1894. *The Expert Waitress: A Manual for the Pantry, Kitchen, and Dining-Room*. New York: Harper and Brothers.

Steinberg, Stephen. 1981. *The Ethnic Myth: Race, Ethnicity, and Class in America*. New York: Atheneum.

Stout, Matthew. 2005. "Historical Geography." In *Nineteenth-Century Ireland: A Guide to Recent Research*, edited by Laurence M. Geary and Margaret Kelleher, 77–103. Dublin: Univ. College–Dublin Press.

Stowe, Mrs. Harriet Beecher. 1879. "Ireland's Daughters in Their New Homes." *Donahoe's Magazine*, Jan., 53–55.

Strasser, Susan. 1982. *Never Done: A History of American Housework*. New York: Pantheon Books.

Sutherland, Daniel E. 1981. *Americans and Their Servants: Domestic Service in the United States from 1880 to 1920*. Baton Rouge: Louisiana State Univ. Press.

Sutherland, Kate. 1852. "Cooks." *Godey's Lady's Book and Magazine*, May, 392–95.

Synge, J. M. 1980. *In Wicklow, West Kerry, and Connemara*. Totowa, N.J.: Rowan and Littlefield. (Orig. pub. 1910.)

TeBrake, Janet K. 1992. "Irish Peasant Women in Revolt: The Land League Years." *Irish Historical Studies* 28, no. 109 (May): 63–80.

A Thankful Husband. 1909. "How My Wife Keeps Her Maids." *Harper's Bazaar*, Dec. 4, 1231.

Thistle, Susan. 2006. *From Marriage to the Market: The Transformation of Women's Lives and Work*. Berkeley and Los Angeles: Univ. of California Press.

Tocqueville, Alexis de. 1990. *Democracy in America*. Vol. 2. New York: Vintage Classics. (Orig. pub. 1840.)

Tomes, Robert. 1871. *The Bazar Book of Decorum: The Care of the Person, Manners, Etiquette, and Ceremonials*. New York: Harper and Brothers.

Travers, Pauric. 1995. "Emigration and Gender: The Case of Ireland, 1922–60." In *Chattel, Servant, or Citizen: Women's Status in Church, State, and Society*, edited by Mary O'Dowd and Sabine Wichert, 187–99. Belfast: Institute of Irish Studies, Queen's Univ. of Belfast.

Unger, Mary E. 2006. Interview by author. Tape recording. Loudonville, N.Y. Apr. 21.

U.S. Bureau of the Census. 1975. *Historical Statistics of the United States, Colonial Times to 1970*. Pt. 1. Washington, D.C.: U.S. Bureau of the Census.

Valiulis, Maryann. 1995. "Neither Feminist nor Flapper: The Ecclesiastical Construction of the Ideal Irish Woman." In *Chattel, Servant, or Citizen: Women's*

Status in Church, State, and Society, edited by Mary O'Dowd and Sabine Wichert, 168–78. Belfast: Institute of Irish Studies, Queen's Univ. of Belfast.

Van Raaphorst, Donna L. 1988. *Union Maids Not Wanted: Organizing Domestic Workers, 1870–1940.* New York: Praeger.

Varley, Maureen Maher. 2001. Conversation with author. Nov. 8.

Vecchio, Diane. 2006. "Ties of Affection: Family Narratives in the History of Italian Migration." *Journal of American Ethnic History* 25, nos. 2–3 (Winter–Spring): 117–33.

Vogue's Book of Etiquette: Present-Day Customs of Social Intercourse with the Rules for Their Correct Observance. 1925. New York: Conde Nast Publications. (Orig. pub. 1923.)

Wadhams, Caroline Reed. 1917. *Simple Directions for the Cook.* New York: Longmans, Green.

Wall, Maureen. 1995. "The Age of the Penal Laws (1691–1778)." In *The Course of Irish History,* edited by T. W. Moody and F. X. Martin, 217–31. Boulder: Roberts Rinehart. (Orig. pub. 1967.)

Walter, Bronwen. 2004. "Irish Domestic Servants and English National Identity." In *Domestic Service and the Formation of European Identity: Understanding the Globalization of Domestic Work, 16th–21st Centuries,* edited by Antoinette Fauve-Chamoux, 471–88. Bern: Peter Lang.

Watson, Amey E. 1932. *Household Employment in Philadelphia.* Bulletin of the Women's Bureau, no. 93. Washington, D.C.: U.S. Government Printing Office.

Wehner-Franco, Silke. 1994. *Deutsche Dienstmädchen in Amerika, 1850–1914.* New York: Waxmann.

Welter, Barbara. 1976. "The Cult of True Womanhood, 1800–1860." In *Dimity Convictions: The American Woman in the Nineteenth Century,* 21–41. Athens: Ohio Univ. Press.

West, Maureen. 2004. "The North Atlantic Motorway: Crossing and Recrossing from Ireland to America." Paper presented at the Thirteenth Irish-Australian Conference, Irish Spaces: Homeland, Asylum, Empire, Diaspora, Univ. of Melbourne, Sept. 28.

West, Patricia. 1992. "Irish Immigrant Workers in Antebellum New York: The Experience of Domestic Servants at Van Buren's Lindenwald." *Hudson Valley Regional Review* 9 (Sept.): 112–26.

"What Is Thought of Our Irish Girls Abroad." 1880. *Donahoe's Magazine,* May, 437.

Whelan, Kevin. 1995. "Pre- and Post-Famine Landscape Change." In *The Great Irish Famine,* edited by Cathal Póirtéir, 19–33. Dublin: Mercier Press.

White, Philip L. 1967. "An Irish Immigrant Housewife on the New York Frontier." *New York History* 48: 181–88.

White, Richard. 1998. *Remembering Ahanagran: Storytelling in a Family's Past.* New York: Hill and Wang.

Whitelock, W. W. 1906. "The Servant Question in Germany." *Harper's Bazaar,* May, 467.

Whyte, J. H. 1995. "The Age of Daniel O'Connell (1800–47)." In *The Course of Irish History,* edited by T. W. Moody and F. X. Martin, 248–62. Boulder: Roberts Rinehart. (Orig. pub. 1967.)

Williams, Susan R. 1987. Introduction to *Dining in America, 1850–1900,* edited by Kathryn Grover, 3–23. Amherst: Univ. of Massachusetts Press.

———. 1996. *Savory Suppers and Fashionable Feasts: Dining in Victorian America.* Knoxville: Univ. of Tennessee Press. (Orig. pub. 1985.)

Winsberg, Morton D. 1985. "Irish Settlement in the United States, 1850–1980." *Eire-Ireland* 20: 7–14.

Wittke, Carl. 1952. "The Immigrant Theme on the American Stage." *Mississippi Valley Historical Review* 39 (Sept.): 211–32.

———. 1956. *The Irish in America.* Baton Rouge: Louisiana State Univ. Press.

"Your Humble Servant." 1864. *Harper's New Monthly Magazine,* June, 53–59.

Index

Italic page number denotes illustration.

Selected titles from Irish Studies

Anglo-Irish Autobiography: Class, Gender, and the Forms of Narrative.
Elizabeth Grubgeld

The Gonne-Yeats Letters, 1893–1938.
Anna MacBride White and A. Norman Jeffares, eds.

An Irish Literature Reader: Poetry, Prose, Drama. 2d Edition.
Maureen O'Rourke Murphy and James MacKillop

Irish Orientalism: A Literary and Intellectual History.
Joseph Lennon

Irish Women Writers Speak Out: Voices from the Field.
Caitriona Moloney and Helen Thompson, eds.

John Redmond and Irish Unity, 1912–1918.
Joseph P. Finnan

Joyce and Reality: The Empirical Strikes Back.
John Gordon

Prodigal Father: The Life of John Butler Yeats (1839–1922).
William M. Murphy

Two Irelands: Literary Feminisms North and South.
Rebecca Pelan

Twentieth-Century Irish Drama: Mirror up to Nation.
Christopher Murray